EUROPEAN UNION LAW

IN A NUTSHELL

Fifth Edition

By

RALPH H. FOLSOM
Professor of Law
University of San Diego

The first edition of this book was titled
Folsom's "European Community Law in a Nutshell."

Mat #40361898

Nutshell Series, In a Nutshell, the Nutshell Logo and West Group are trademarks registered in the U.S. Patent and Trademark Office.

COPYRIGHT © 1992, 1995 WEST PUBLISHING CO.
© West, a Thomson business, 1999, 2004
© 2005 Thomson/West
  610 Opperman Drive
  P.O. Box 64526
  St. Paul, MN 55164–0526
  1–800–328–9352
Printed in the United States of America

ISBN 0–314–16039–6

TEXT IS PRINTED ON 10% POST CONSUMER RECYCLED PAPER

PREFACE TO THE FIFTH EDITION

It is impossible to capture in one small "nutshell" the vastness and excitement that accompanies European Union (EU) law. The accession of ten new members, the Charter of Fundamental Rights, the Treaty of Nice of 2003, and a proposed Constitution for Europe are indicative of momentous developments. In addition there is new coverage of product standards, consumer protection, company law, regional policy, intellectual property rights, mergers regulation, public enterprise competition, and E-commerce law in the European Union. Truly this is one of the great undertakings of modern times.

Once again I have tried to present not only the big picture, but also to analyze in more detail some of the most critical developments. This selectivity was undertaken primarily with North American and other audiences located outside Europe in mind. Thus there is special emphasis throughout the book on the external impact of European law, e.g., in its single market legislation, litigation procedures, trading rules and business competition law. It is important to bear in mind, however, that it is not just the externalities of the law that command attention. The internal operations of the Common Market are significant not only for Europeans, but also to the many foreign investors flocking to the world's largest and most lucrative market.

Inevitably, I have made judgments about what to emphasize, what to exclude and the like. I have also taken a few liberties in characterizing European law and procedure by using terminology that is familiar to Americans. It is my sincere hope that the final product will meet the needs of students, lawyers, faculty, government officials and people in business who seek an introduction to the European Union and its law.

Although the title to this book has become European Union Law, the European Community is very much alive. Indeed, the Maastricht Treaty on European Union of 1993 (TEU) is largely comprised of the Treaty Establishing the European Community *aka* the Treaty of Rome 1957 (as amended).

In this edition, I have eliminated almost all of the internal citations to the cases, legislation and the Treaty of Rome, along with the formerly appended treaties. The result is a text which is more consistent with the size and style established by the West Group for Nutshells, and a book that is simply easier to read and digest. Full citations and much more extensive coverage are available in Folsom's *Principles of European Union Law* (2005), which is part of the Thomson/West Concise Hornbook paperback series. *Principles* also reproduces the TEU and Rome Treaties previously appearing as appendices in this Nutshell.

RALPH H. FOLSOM

San Diego, California

ACKNOWLEDGMENTS

Many colleagues and students have contributed over the years to my learning and understanding of European Community (now Union) law. For me, it really all began in Britain from 1972–75 when I was an LL.M. student at the London School of Economics followed by two years as a Lecturer in Law at the University of Warwick. Those were formative times, not only for me, but also for Britain as it joined the Community in 1973. Since 1975 I have greatly benefited from teaching and professional contacts at the University of San Diego's summer legal studies program in Europe. These programs are organized each year through the USD Institute on International and Comparative Law.

Special thanks is due to Thomson/West for their support over many years. I have also benefited from utilization of the excellent coursebook by Professors Bermann, Goebel, Davey and Fox on *European Union Law* published by West.

*

A TIMELINE OF
EUROPEAN INTEGRATION

1948 — Benelux Customs Union Treaty

1949 — COMECON Treaty (Eastern Europe, Soviet Union) —Su answer to W Europe integration

1951 — European Coal and Steel Community ("Treaty of Paris")

1957 — European Economic Community (EEC)
EC Treaty ("Treaty of Rome"), European Atomic Energy Community Treaty (EURATOM)

1959 — European Free Trade Area Treaty (EFTA)
1967 – Merging treaty - all the councils, commissions, COS, Parliaments merged to form 1 of each single budget
1968 — EEC Customs Union fully operative

1973 — Britain and Denmark switch from EFTA to EEC; Ireland joins EEC; Norway rejects membership; remaining EFTA states sign industrial free trade treaties with EEC

1979 — Direct elections to European Parliament

1981 — Greece joins EEC

1983 — Greenland "withdraws" from EEC

1986 — Spain and Portugal join EEC, Portugal leaves EFTA

1987 — Single European Act amends Treaty of Rome to initiate campaign for a Community without internal frontiers by 1993
Internal market harmonization
more power to Parliament

VII

1989 - Court of 1st Instance

1990 — East Germany merged into Community via reunification process

1991 — COMECON defunct; trade relations with Central Europe develop rapidly

1993 — Maastricht Treaty on European Union (TEU) ratified and operational, EEC officially becomes EC *Superimposed over Treaty of Rome*

Amends ECSC EEC, Euratom ⟵✗

1994 — European Monetary Institute established

1995 — Austria, Finland, and Sweden join EU, Norway votes no again

1999 — Amsterdam Treaty ratified and operational

1999 — Common currency (EURO) managed by European Central Bank commences with 11 members

2003 — Treaty of Nice ratified and operational, draft Constitution for Europe released

2004 — Cyprus, Estonia, Slovenia, Poland, Hungary, the Czech Republic, Slovakia, Latvia, Lithuania, Malta join EU

2006 — Projected ratification of Constitution for Europe

2007 — Accession of Bulgaria, Romania expected

OUTLINE

OUTLINE

OUTLINE

TABLE OF CASES

References are to Pages

TABLE OF CASES

EUROPEAN UNION LAW

IN A NUTSHELL

Fifth Edition

*

CHAPTER 1

THE HISTORY AND GROWTH OF THE EUROPEAN UNION

War, twice in the Twentieth Century and for ages previously, has plagued the European continent. The desire for peace after World War II helps explain the beginnings of European integration. As Allied control of West Germany declined in the late 1940s, the return of Germany's basic war industries became a prominent issue. Coal and steel in particular were seen as essential to war-making potential on the continent. Many feared that if these basic industries were left in national hands, future wars between traditional enemies might emerge. Winston Churchill, in his famous Zurich speech of 1946, urged the establishment of a United States of Europe. He meant that there should be a partnership between France and Germany. The United Kingdom would simply act as a friend and sponsor of this partnership but would not participate. France was especially concerned about what it often called "the German problem." The solution that emerged in 1951 was the creation of the European Coal and Steel Community (ECSC).

TREATY OF PARIS (1951)

The Coal and Steel Community was the first of Western Europe's major treaties of integration. The basic theory behind this development was that war would be more difficult to pursue if European institutions empowered with substantial regulatory authority controlled the coal and steel industries. Known as the Schuman Plan after Robert Schuman, the Foreign Minister of France, the ECSC was opened for membership in 1950. Although addressed to much of Europe, only France, Germany, Italy and the three Benelux countries (Belgium, Luxembourg and The Netherlands) joined by signing the Treaty of Paris in April of 1951. West Germany and Italy, of course, were still politically weak from the aftermath of World War II. The Benelux countries, though often united in perspective, were not significantly influential to the development of the European Coal and Steel Community. Thus the Community essentially represented French ideas and these ideas permeated its founding treaty.

The Treaty of Paris is a complicated document. It is very detailed and legalistic, what the French call a "traité-loi." Its regulatory approaches to the coal and steel industries are diverse. On the one hand, there are provisions which permit substantial European control over prices, the level of subsidies, investment incentives, production levels, transportation rates, discriminatory and restrictive trade practices, employment and industrial structure. These controls represent a regime of French "dirigisme". At the same time, other provisions of the Treaty of Paris contemplate freer trade and more competitive coal and steel markets with only occasional governmental intervention. Over the years, regulation of the coal and steel industries in the ECSC went through different cycles but predominantly followed the French regime.

The Treaty of Paris remained the legal basis for European law governing these two industries until 2002. At that time the coal and steel industries were subsumed under the much broader and more economically significant Treaty of Rome of 1957 which established the European Economic Community (EEC) for an "unlimited period" of time.

Lasting Regional Institutions

The most critical features of the Treaty of Paris were those establishing regional institutions for the governance of coal and steel. Here the French perspective that new institutions were required, to which substantial power would be conveyed by national governments, prevailed. The willingness to transfer control over coal and steel to European institutions seems even more remarkable when the prevalence of government ownership of companies in those industries is taken into account. In contrast, the British at that time were of the view that governance of coal and steel in the pursuit in peace did not require the establishment of numerous powerful European institutions. Thus it is in the Treaty of Paris that the four fundamental European institutions of governance originate: The Council of Ministers, the Commission, the Court of Justice, and the Parliament.

These institutions are sometimes referred to as *supranational* in character although this term is no longer in fashion. They are neither national nor international (i.e., intergovernmental). Within the limits of the treaties empowering them, they exercise sovereignty. Each of the four major institutions will be reviewed subsequently. For now, it is worth noting that their origins strongly reflect the French view that only European institutions could solve "the German problem."

TREATY OF ROME (1957)

As the post-war economies of Europe revitalized, it became increasingly evident that France and Britain were vying for leadership of Western Europe. Each had its own vision of how to proceed beyond the limited European Coal and Steel Community with which Britain became loosely "associated" in the mid–1950s. The British maintained that a free trade area, as distinct from more advanced forms of integration such as a customs union, a common market, an economic community or an economic union, was all that was required for economic integration in Western Europe.

Competing Alternatives for European Integration

The major difference between a free trade area and a customs union is the presence of a common external tariff in the latter. Common market treaties additionally provide for the free movement of what economists call the "factors of production": capital, labor, enterprise and technology. Economic communities seek to coordinate or harmonize economic policies important to the functioning of the common market, e.g., transport, taxation, monetary matters and government subsidies. Economic unions embrace a more or less complete harmonization or coordination of national policies related to the economy of the union. The difference between a treaty establishing an economic community and one creating an economic union is in the number and importance of integrated national policies.

Britain continued to believe regional integration could be achieved with a minimum of European governance and a maximum of retention of national sovereignty. France, on the other hand, generally envisioned a broader economic community modeled and implemented on the basic design provided by the Treaty of Paris, although even it had begun to express reservations about the degree of power vested in the ECSC. France had the support and could point to the successful integration of the Benelux countries. Belgium, Luxembourg and The Netherlands had signed a Customs Union Treaty in January of 1948. By the middle of the 1950s, the Benelux nations were close to agreement on a comprehensive economic union. Benelux integration was already providing substantial economic growth to its member nations. Though not as heavily ladened with European institutions as the Coal and Steel Community, the Benelux union served as a pacesetter for wider European economic integration. To a limited degree this remains true. The Treaty of Rome expressly permits the existence and completion of the Benelux Union to the extent that its objectives are not attained through the European initiative.

In June of 1955 a conference of the foreign ministers of the European Coal and Steel Community, responding to a Benelux memorandum, authorized an intergovernmental committee to study and report on the prospects for a Western European common market and peaceful use of atomic energy. This committee, still heavily influenced by French perspectives but increasingly subject to a resurgent West Germany, laid the foundations for the Treaty of Rome establishing the European Economic Community in 1957. The Committee was led by a dynamic Belgian, Paul–Henri Spaak. Its report is sometimes referred to as the Spaak Plan and focuses on the fusion of markets. Adoption of the Committee's report and its embodiment in the Treaty of Rome was influenced by an equally dynamic Frenchman long an advocate of European integration. Jean Monnet organized a pressure group known as the Action Committee for the United States of Europe.

EURATOM , E EC, ECSC

At the same time, by separate treaty in 1957, a third European community was created. This is the European Atomic Energy Community (EURATOM). EURATOM is a very specialized community focused on joint research and peaceful development of atomic energy. Its Supply Agency owns all fissionable materials located within the member states not intended for defense requirements. About 35 percent of all electricity, and 14 percent of all EU energy needs, are now supplied by nuclear plants. EURATOM has joined the Treaty on the Non–Proliferation of Nuclear Weapons. In the Chernobyl aftermath, renewed attention has been paid to EURATOM safety standards and the Court of Justice has held that the Commission's advisory opinion must be obtained prior to approval of the final plans for radioactive effluent disposal. Nevertheless, EURATOM is the least significant of the three European communities.

The Treaty of Rome and the EURATOM Treaty follow the institutional pattern of the Treaty of Paris. Each of these treaties empowers a Council of Ministers, a Commission (called High Authority in the ECSC Treaty), an Assembly (Parliament) and a Court of Justice. This led to an unnecessary and confusing institutional structure which was remedied in part by merging the Court and Parliament in 1957 and later the Council and Commission by the so-called "Merger Treaty" of 1967. Since then, there has been one Council, one Commission, one

Parliament and one Court, all staffed by the same people. Each of these European Union institutions, however, derives its power and authority from the terms and conditions of whatever treaty it is acting under. In other words, the treaties were not merged, only their institutions. Thus when the Commission acts on coal and steel matters, the legality of its actions is measured by the Treaty of Paris. When the Council legislates on atomic energy, the EURATOM treaty controls, and so forth. Given the scope of the Treaty of Rome, the institutions of the Union most often operate under its terms and implementing protocols and legislation.

Treaty of Rome

The Treaty of Rome that established the European Economic Community in 1957 remains the penultimate source of European Union law. In November 1993, the Treaty of Rome was officially renamed the Treaty establishing the European Community. Dropping the word "Economic" from its title was symbolic of the expanded political, social and other non-economic roles of the Community in European affairs. At the same time, the Maastricht Treaty on European Union (TEU) was superimposed over the Treaty of Rome (thereby adding certain common provisions as well as coverage of foreign and security policy and justice and home affairs). The resulting document is titled the "Treaty on European Union together with the Treaty establishing the European Community."

Some have analogized the Treaty of Rome to a constitution. Certainly it is the founding document of the European Community. The European Court of Justice has referred to the Treaty of Rome as the "constitutional charter of a Community based on the rule of law." Under this charter, the member states have limited their sovereignty in ever widening fields of law. Unlike the Coal and Steel Treaty, the Treaty of Rome is open-ended in much of its language, a "traité-cadre" or "traité de procédure" in French terms. It provides the framework and process upon which to build the European Community. The Treaty as amended to date is divided into six parts and over 300 articles. When compared with the narrowness of the Treaty of Paris establishing the European Coal and Steel Community in 1951, the Treaty of Rome is breathtaking in scope.

The Treaty of Rome commences with some fundamental principles. These principles elaborate upon the goal of establishing a common market throughout the member states. The Treaty lists the activities to achieve its objectives. This listing is found in Article 3 and includes the elimination of customs duties and quotas on internal trade, the establishment of a common external tariff and trade policy towards third countries, the free movement of persons, services and capital, the adoption of common policies on agriculture and transportation, the institution of a "system" of nondistorted competition within the Common Market, and the approximation of member state laws.

Treaty on European Union

In 1993, the Treaty of Rome was amended substantially by the Treaty on European Union (TEU). Creation of an economic and monetary union with emphasis upon price stability became a primary goal. The listing of activities in pursuit of that goal was expanded to include environmental, social, research and development, trans-European network, health, education, development aid, consumer protection, energy, civil protection, internal market, visas and other policy endeavors of the European Union. Article 4 details the ambitious program of economic and monetary union launched by the TEU. Article 5 on the other hand, seeks to limit regional activities to those areas where the results are best achieved at the European (versus national) level. This is known as the "subsidiarity principle" and is the subject of intense controversy.

Though the Treaty of Rome as drafted in 1957 was much less dirigiste than the Coal and Steel Treaty, Britain once again abstained from membership because of the nature and extent of the European controls over the economy. Britain, too, was still preoccupied with its empire-based trade relations. Europe was important, but it had not yet become critical to British trading interests.

EFTA (1959) and COMECON

Early United States support for European integration came through the Marshall Plan which was distributed through the Organization for European

Economic Cooperation. This organization had no real political power, but successfully mediated some differences in national economic policies prevalent during the late 1940s. By 1957, the cold war between the United States and the Soviet Union was evident. This caused the United States to be generally supportive of the EEC initiative under the theory that a united Europe would present a stronger defense to Soviet aggression.

The Soviets, in turn, increasingly emphasized Eastern European integration through the Council for Mutual Economic Assistance (COMECON). This effort, commenced in 1949, was basically seen as a counterweight to the developments in Western European integration. Locked behind the Iron Curtain, the countries of Eastern Europe found themselves producing whatever the Soviet economic plans required. In exchange, they mostly received subsidized oil and other basic resources.

European Free Trade Area (EFTA)

The fragmentation of Europe's economy during the 1950s became even more accentuated by the emergence of another competing organization. Led by Britain, many of the fringe or traditionally neutral nations of Western Europe organized themselves into the European Free Trade Area (EFTA) in 1959. Austria, Denmark, Iceland, Norway, Portugal, Sweden and Switzerland joined this undertaking. With eight nations essentially surrounding the core six nations who created the EEC in 1957, Britain felt that it had contained French influence and ideas in the economic sphere. True to British philosophy, the EFTA Treaty was very limited in scope. It applied only to free trade in industrial goods, omitting coverage of agriculture, transport, labor, capital, technology and services to mention only a few areas fully incorporated into the Treaty of Rome. Moreover, the British view on the nature of the governmental institutions required to achieve industrial free trade prevailed. A single institution, the EFTA Council, was created. Since it normally followed a unanimous voting principle, each of the member states retained a veto over new policy developments within the EFTA group. The surrender of national sovereignties to EFTA was minimized.

Thus, by 1960, Europe was economically allied into three major trade groups. France and an increasingly powerful West Germany led Italy and the Benelux states in the European Coal and Steel and Economic Communities. Britain and its partners were loosely integrated through the European Free Trade Association. And the whole of Eastern Europe came under the sway of Soviet dominance through COMECON. In addition, Finland became associated with EFTA and Greece and Turkey were associated with the EEC. Only Spain under Franco remained an economic outcast. More than a decade passed before major shifts in these alliances occurred.

THE TREATY OF ROME AND THE GATT

The General Agreement on Tariffs and Trade (GATT), adopted in 1948 and much amended and interpreted since then, governs many features of the free world trading system. Over 100 nations, including those of the European Union, now adhere to the GATT and of a host of "Uruguay Round" agreements administered by the World Trade Organization. In 1957, when the Treaty of Rome was signed, the United States, Britain and other GATT members protested that the Treaty was not in accord with the terms of Article 24 of the GATT.

GATT Article 24

Article 24 permits contracting parties to enter into free trade area and customs union agreements of a fixed or evolutionary character. The premise here is that regional economic groups can be viewed as gradual steps (second-best alternatives) along the road to freer, less discriminatory *world* trade. At the same time, Article 24 attempts to manage the internal trade-creating and external trade-diverting effects of regional economic groups. These effects are known in economic literature as "the customs union dilemma."

Free trade area and custom union proposals must run the gauntlet of a formal GATT (now WTO) approval procedure during which "binding" recommendations are possible to bring the proposals into conformity with Article 24. Such recommendations might deal with Article 24 requirements for the elimination of internal tariffs and other restrictive regulations of commerce on "substantially all" products originating in a customs union or free trade area. Or they might deal with Article 24 requirements that common external tariffs not be "on the whole higher or more restrictive" in effect than the general incidence of prior existing national tariffs. The broad purpose of Article 24, acknowledged therein, is to facilitate trade among the GATT contracting parties and not to raise trade barriers.

Article 24 and European Integration

It is under these treaty terms and through this GATT approval mechanism that most regional economic treaties, including those of Western Europe, have passed *without* substantial modification. Only the EFTA Treaty seems to have come genuinely close to meeting the terms of Article 24. The GATT, not the regional economic treaties, most often has given way. With the European Coal and Steel Community only two products were involved. Clearly no case could be made for its compliance with the requirement of elimination of internal trade barriers on "substantially all" products. Hence, the GATT members, passing over Article 24's own waiver proviso for proposals leading to a customs union or a free trade area "in the sense of Article 24," reverted to Article 25. That article allows a two-thirds vote by the contracting parties to waive any GATT obligation.

During passage through the GATT of the Treaty of Rome, many "violations" of the letter and spirit of Article 24 were cited by nonmembers. The derivation of the common customs tariff by arithmetically averaging existing national tariffs was challenged as more restrictive of trade than previous arrangements. Such averaging on a given product fails to take account of differing national import volumes. If a product was faced originally with a lower than average national tariff and a larger than average national demand, the new average tariff is clearly more "restrictive" of imports than before. Averaging in high tariffs of countries of low demand quite plausibly created more restrictions on third-party trade. If so, the letter and spirit of Article 24 were breached.

The economic association of Overseas Territories (mainly former French, Dutch and Belgian colonies) with the EEC also raised considerable difficulty under Article 24. The Community argued that these "association" agreements were free trade areas in the long run, while the GATT officials viewed them as rather open efforts at purely preferential tariff status. Similar problems arose later in the GATT review of the multitude of "evolving" free trade area treaties with Mediterranean nations. Finally, in 1975, the openly preferential and discriminatory Lomé Convention negotiated between the European Community and African, Pacific and Caribbean nations (including many former colonies) challenged the evolutionary character of Community "free trade areas" with developing states. Once again it was the GATT and not the European Community that gave way. In fairness, since 2000, the Cotonou Agreement at lease pledges the EU and its partners to reciprocal free trade principles. See Chapter 6.

Despite these and other arguments, the Treaty of Rome passed through the GATT study and review committees without final resolution of its legal status under Article 24. Postponement of these issues became permanent. GATT attempts—through the lawyer-like conditions of Article 24 to maximize trade creation and minimize trade diversion—must be seen in the European context as generally inadequate. Treaty terms became negotiable demands that were not accepted.

EFTA AND THE EEC RECONCILED (1973)

During the 1960s, Britain began to come to grips with the loss of its empire. Although special trading relations were often preserved with former colonies through the Commonwealth network, it became increasingly apparent that Britain's economic future lay more in Europe than Africa, Asia or the Caribbean. Moreover, the EEC had helped to spur a phenomenal economic recovery on the Continent at a time when many were questioning the competitiveness of British industry. For these reasons, and others, Britain began to seek membership as early as 1961 (only two years after the formation of EFTA). France under the leadership of Charles De Gaulle would have none of it. Since the Treaty of Rome provided (as the Treaty on European Union does) that all new memberships require a unanimous Council vote, France was effectively able to veto the British application. It was not until the resignation of De Gaulle in 1969 that the British were able in due course to secure membership in the EEC.

New Members

Agreement on the terms of British accession (including withdrawal from EFTA and the elimination of trade preferences with major Commonwealth nations) was reached in 1971, with an effective date of January, 1973. The switch from EFTA to the EEC by Britain under Conservative Party leadership was undertaken with an ambivalence that continues to be evident. It was only with reluctance that the British accepted the surrenders of sovereignty inherent in the Treaty of Rome. From 1973 onwards, more and more of the economic life of the United Kingdom would be governed by the four institutions of the European Community. British reluctance to join the Common Market was replayed in a 1975 national referendum under a Labor Party government. Approximately 60 percent of the populace voted to remain a member of the Community.

Denmark also switched sides in 1973. Norway was scheduled to become a member of the EEC at that time, and the terms of its membership had been negotiated, but the people of Norway rejected the Community in a national referendum. The rejection had a lot to do with the requirements of the Common Fisheries Policy which would have unacceptably opened Norwegian waters to fishermen from the continent, Britain and Ireland (which followed the British lead into the Community in 1973). This Policy also regulates the type and number of fish that can be caught in European waters, significantly subsidizes the fishing industry and protects it from foreign competition.

In addition to the expansion of the EEC to nine members, 1973 brought an even greater degree of European economic integration. Although EFTA remained intact, each of the remaining EFTA nations signed bilateral trade treaties with the expanded Community. These treaties governed trade relations between EFTA nations and the Community until 1994. They essentially provided for industrial free trade. Thus the 1973 enlargement of the European Economic Community was the catalyst for the most wide-scale and comprehensive effort at Western European integration yet to take place, the reconciliation of the EFTA and EEC trading alliances. This was an historic watershed in European economic integration.

New Members (1980s)

During the 1980s there was a strong trend toward increased membership in and expansion of the European Community. The only exception to this trend was the "withdrawal" of Greenland in 1983. Greenland had been admitted with Denmark in 1973, but voted in a home rule referendum (essentially rejecting the Common Fisheries Policy) to withdraw. It is now associated with the EU as an overseas territory of Denmark. Greece joined in 1981 and Portugal and Spain became members in 1986. Portugal left the EFTA group, and Spain finally overcame the yoke of General Franco.

THE EUROPEAN ECONOMIC AREA

Expanded relations between the European Community and the seven remaining EFTA states (Iceland, Norway, Sweden, Finland, Switzerland, Austria and Lichtenstein) have been under negotiation since the mid–1980s. These negotiations first envisioned closer economic relations short of membership. Late in 1991, a linkage of the two groups in what is called a European Economic Area (EEA) was agreed. The EEA generally embraced Community law on free movement of goods, services, persons and capital. But integration on agricultural, fisheries and tax policy was excluded and the EFTA nations retained their own border controls, tariffs, currencies and external trade policies. Antidumping measures, countervailing duties and illicit commercial practices law will not be applied to EEA trade. Political and defense union was also excluded from the EEA agreement.

Swiss Rejection

The revised EEA agreement had to be ratified by the European Parliament as well as all European Community and EFTA nations. Perhaps not surprisingly, the Swiss rejected the EEA in a national referendum held in December 1992. This rejection continues to cast doubt upon the Swiss membership request, but it did not cause the EEA to falter. Subsequent negotiations in 1993 produced a still further revised agreement minus Switzerland. This version of the EEA then made the required rounds of ratification and came into force January 1, 1994. Today, it applies only to Iceland, Lichtenstein and Norway. A series of 1999 EU agreements with Switzerland cover free movement of persons, transport, agriculture, procurement, and mutual recognition. In 2004, additional EU–Swiss agreements were reached on taxation of savings, fighting fraud, Swiss participation in the Schegen Accord, trade in processed agricultural goods, environmental cooperation, media programs and avoidance of double taxation on pensioners.

New Members (1990s)

One reason for the Community's advancement of the EEA and reluctance to accept new members was its intensive internal focus on the campaign for a fully integrated common market. Other reasons involve the practical problems associated with governance of a regional organization with a large number of nations. With 12 member states, the Community found it difficult to arrive at a consensus and move forward towards further integration without substantially overriding national interests. A union with more members would be all that more difficult to govern. Nevertheless, membership for all EFTA states that want it is a foregone conclusion.

The Maastricht accords (December 1991) opened the door to membership negotiations with Austria, Sweden, Finland and Norway. Accession agreements for these countries were concluded early in 1994 and ratification by the European Parliament was obtained in May of that year. Each of these countries scheduled a national referendum on membership in the European Union. The Austrians voted in June 1994 by a 2 to 1 margin to join. The Swedes, Finns and Norwegians went to the polls late in 1994, affirming accession for Finland and Sweden but not Norway. These memberships took effect January 1, 1995.

GROWTH IN MEMBERSHIP

It has always been a rule, at times unwritten, that members and applicants must support democratic governments. This principle was applied to Greece during the coup by the colonels in the late 1960s and early 1970s. The Community suspended trade relations with Greece during this period and the coup certainly delayed admission of that country. The commitment of the Community (now Union) to governance by representative democracy, the rule of law, social justice and respect for human rights was formalized in 1977 under a Declaration on Democracy by the heads of all the member state governments. At the same time, the Council, Commission and Parliament issued a Joint Declaration on Fundamental Rights to much the same effect. More recently, applicants are said to have to embrace the ever expanding body of regional legislation and case law, the "acquis communautaire." Short of exceptions or postponements negotiated through "accession treaties," this is true.

With 15 member states, the European Union became a powerful and lucrative economic market. Its aggregate population and gross domestic product exceeded that of the United States, Mexico and Canada, which implemented a Free Trade Agreement in 1994. The emergence of the North American Free Trade Area was just one of the continuing repercussions of the need to compete with the European Union in the global marketplace. The Union, in turn, became more receptive to new members. In 1991, association agreements with Poland, Hungary, the Czech Republic and Slovakia (then still Czechoslovakia) were reached. These "Europe Agreements" contemplated membership in the Union after a minimum 10–year transitional period. Similar agreements were reached with Romania, Bulgaria, Slovenia, Estonia, Latvia and Lithuania.

Membership Criteria

At the Copenhagen Summit in June of 1993, the European Council set the following membership criteria for these countries:

(1) stable democracies based upon a rule of law, human rights and protection of minorities;

(2) market economies able to compete within the new Europe; and

(3) the ability to make full commitments to political, monetary and economic union ("acquis communautaire").

Turkey has been associated with the EU as a trade ally since 1963. Relations were suspended during the military takeover of Turkey from 1981 to 1986. Turkey formally applied for membership in 1987 but was kept under study for many years. Late in 2004, the EU finally agreed to open memberships negotiations with Turkey. Apart from concerns about the stability of democracy in Turkey, Greek membership in the Union would seem to make admission unlikely. Furthermore, membership is limited by the Treaty on European Union to "European states". Morocco's application was rejected because it is not a European nation. Turkey's application presents difficult questions about its status in Europe and the meaning of the Treaty. Does "European" only have geographic implications or is there an expectation that members must also be culturally or religiously European?

In addition, there has been an incorporation of what was East Germany into the Union through the reunification process. The accession of East Germany to the Union renewed concerns over the role of Germany in Europe. Instead of four large member states (France, West Germany, Italy and the United Kingdom) of roughly equal populations, united Germany has substantially more people and potentially much more economic clout than any other member of the Union. This caused anxieties about keeping that country well anchored by European institutions.

New Members (2004)

Starting in 1997, following the Commission's recommendations, the European Union commenced negotiations for membership with Cyprus, Estonia, Slovenia, Poland, Hungary, the Czech Republic, Malta, Romania, Bulgaria, Lithuania, Latvia and Slovakia. Long in the making, accession agreements for all but Bulgaria and Romania were finalized late in 2002 with entry for the ten new member states definitively scheduled for May 1, 2004. Particularly sensitive issues such as full participation in agricultural subsidies and free movement of workers were finessed with extended periods. Nine of the 2004 member states ratified accession in national referendums, with only Greek Cyprus not holding a plebiscite. Romania and Bulgaria, and possibly Croatia, are expected to join in 2007.

EUROPE WITHOUT INTERNAL FRONTIERS

The campaign for a European Community without internal frontiers by the end of 1992 was the product of Commission studies in the mid–1980s which concluded that a hardening of the trade arteries of Europe had occurred. The Community was perceived to be stagnating relative to the advancing economies of North America and East Asia. Various projections of the wealth that could be generated from a truly common market for Western Europe suggested the need to revitalize the EC. A "white paper" drafted under the leadership of Lord Cockfield of Britain and issued by the Commission in 1985 became the blueprint for the 1992 campaign.

The Commission's white paper identified three types of barriers to a Europe without internal frontiers—physical, technical and fiscal. Physical barriers occur at the borders and for goods included national trade quotas, health checks, agricultural monetary compensation amount charges, statistical collections and transport controls. For people, physical barriers involve clearing immigrations, security checks and customs. Technical barriers mostly concern national standards and rules for goods, services, capital and labor which operate to inhibit free movement among the member states. Medical and surgical equipment and pharmaceuticals provide traditional examples of markets restrained by technical trade barriers. Fiscal barriers identified in the Commission's 1985 white paper centered on different value-added and excise taxation levels and the corresponding need for tax collections at borders. There were for example, very wide VAT differences on auto sales within the Common Market.

The Commission estimated that removal of all of these barriers could save the Community upwards of 100 billion ECUs (European Currency Units) in direct costs. In addition, another roughly 100 billion ECUs could be gained as price reductions and increased efficiency and competition took hold. Overall, the Commission projected an increase in the

Community's gross domestic product of between 4.5 to 7 percent, a reduction in consumer prices of between 6 to 4.5 percent, 1.75 to 5 million new jobs, and enhanced public sector and external trade balances. These figures were thus said to represent "the costs of non-Europe."

Single European Act

Major amendments to the Treaty of Rome were undertaken in the Single European Act (SEA) which became effective in 1987. Amendments to the Treaty can occur by Commission or member state proposal to the Council which calls an intergovernmental conference to unanimously determine their content. The amendments are not effective until ratified by all the member states in accordance with their respective constitutional requirements. Proposals originating in the Commission's 1985 white paper on a Europe without internal frontiers were embodied in the Single European Act. The SEA amendments not only expanded the competence of the European institutions, but also sought to accelerate the speed of integration by relying more heavily on qualified majority (not unanimous) voting principles in Council decision-making.

The Single European Act envisioned the adoption of 282 new legislative measures designed to fully integrate the goods, services and capital markets by the end of 1992. Nearly all of these measures and many more were adopted by the Council. Implementation at the national level proceeded more slowly, especially regarding insurance, investment advisors, and procurement. In 1996, the Commission reported that the single market program had increased internal trade by 20–30%, added 1% in GDP growth annually, and generated over 900,000 jobs.

Realization of the goal of a Europe without internal frontiers *for people* has proved harder to achieve. Most states agreed to remove their internal frontier controls on people under the 1990 "Schengen Accord." This accord was the product of intergovernmental agreement, not regional legislation. Ireland and the United Kingdom do not participate, but non-members Norway and Iceland do. The Schengen Accord covers such sensitive issues as visas, asylum, immigration, gun controls, extradition and police rights of "hot pursuit." The main points of contention were cross-border traffic of immigrants and criminals, especially terrorists and drug dealers. These issues were resolved largely by promises of greater intergovernmental cooperation, notably through computer linkages. Much of the substance of the Schengen Accord was incorporated into the Treaty of Rome by the Amsterdam Treaty of 1999 (below).

THE MAASTRICHT TREATY ON EUROPEAN UNION (1993)

Well before the realization of a Europe without internal frontiers under the Single European Act, Community and national leaders were forging another momentous round of European integration. These efforts bore fruit in the December 1991 summit meeting of the European Council in Maastricht, The Netherlands, where the "Treaty on European Union" (TEU) was signed. The Maastricht agreement, like the Single European Act, significantly amended the Treaty of Rome. Furthermore, it added what amounted to side agreements ("separate pillars") on common foreign and security policy and cooperation regarding justice and home affairs. Like the Single European Act's provisions on foreign policy, these side agreements did not amend the Treaty of Rome and stood on their own as separate intergovernmental agreements. As such, they were and largely remain outside the judicial review of the Court of Justice.

The most important Maastricht amendments to the Treaty of Rome concerned the ambiguous principle of "subsidiarity" and economic and monetary integration, notably a detailed timetable for the convergence of national economies and creation of a common currency. Other significant amendments included the conveyance to Parliament of a limited legislative and international agreements' veto, a power to conduct inquiries into maladministration, and a right to reject Commission appointments and new member state applicants. The TEU also added new Articles on cooperation regarding education, health and culture, the development of European citizenship rights, a formal commitment to respect the rights protected by the European Human Rights Convention, expanded economic aid to the least developed members (the "cohesion fund"), authorization of the Court of Justice to sanction delinquent member state governments by fines and penalties, and a Social Protocol (Britain excepted). The TEU formally authorized legislation on consumer protection, industrial policy, energy, tourism, visas and coordinated police action, largely by qualified majority voting which was also extended to transportation and most environmental law.

Ratification and Opt–Out Rights

The ink was no sooner dry on the Treaty on European Union when Denmark's voters by a slim margin rejected ratification in June 1992. Ireland and France (by an equally slim margin) ratified the TEU in national referenda and by year's end the Maastricht agreement had been ratified in all but Denmark and the United Kingdom. After concessions to Denmark were made at the December 1992 Edinburgh summit of the European Council, a new referendum was scheduled for May 1993. Denmark obtained confirmation of its right to opt out of a common currency and new rights to opt out of the TEU provisions on common defense, European citizenship and home and justice affairs. Europe a la carte carried the day. The Danes ultimately approved Maastricht, and a bitter Parliamentary battle in Britain brought similar results in August of 1993. After a constitutional challenge to ratification failed in Germany, the Treaty on European Union became effective November 1, 1993.

The following chart presents the major "opt-out" rights after Maastricht of various member states:

United Kingdom — Social Protocol,
                  Single Currency,
                  Schengen Accord (Internal border
                    controls over people).
Ireland   — Schengen Accord.
Denmark   — Schengen Accord,
                  Single Currency,
                  Defense,
                  Justice and Home Affairs,
                  European Citizenship.

It should be noted that the United Kingdom under the Labour Party administration of Prime Minister Blair opted into the region's Social Policy and the Social Protocol has been repealed.

THE AMSTERDAM TREATY (1999)

The Maastricht Treaty on European Union of 1993 called for another round of intergovernmental negotiations to revise both the TEU and the Treaty of Rome. Late in 1997, these negotiations bore fruit in the Amsterdam Treaty, which then faced national referenda and court challenges during the ratification process.

The Amsterdam Treaty is in many respects best known for what it did *not* accomplish, namely major institutional and agricultural policy reforms in anticipation of European Union membership expansions. The Treaty did significantly extend Parliament's co-decision legislative powers, and institutionalized procedures to deal with "serious and persistent" member state violations of democracy, human rights and the rule of law. It authorized legislative action to secure "freedom, security and justice" (an effective transfer of much of the TEU justice and home affairs power), including asylum, extradition and the essentials of the Schengen Accord, all subject to Court of Justice review but also British, Danish and Irish opt outs. Additional legislative powers cover employment incentives, public health, fraud prevention, customs cooperation, transparency principles and social policy (formerly the Social Protocol).

A complex provision on "flexibility" seeks to allow, subject to detailed controls but generally not (after Nice, below) vetoes, a minimum of eight member states to establish "closer cooperation" than others. This provision appears to reflect the realities of less than comprehensive participation in existing policies and programs such as defense, the common currency, the Schengen Accord and the like. Lastly, the Amsterdam Treaty adds a special protocol on the principles of subsidiarity and proportionality, and attempts to secure greater support for common foreign and security policies. Lastly, the Treaty of Rome and the Treaty on European Union were entirely renumbered by the Amsterdam Treaty, and all treaty references in this book reflect that renumbering.

THE TREATY OF NICE (2003)

With the Amsterdam Treaty in place, and new memberships looming, yet another round of intergovernmental negotiations was swiftly commenced.

By 2001, the Treaty of Nice was signed and sent on its way for national ratifications. Like the Amsterdam Treaty and its predecessors, Nice amends the Treaty of Rome, notably extending qualified majority legislative voting in the Council, authorizing the creation of specialized "judicial panels" attached to the Court of First Instance, and increasing the possibility of closer cooperation ("flexibility") by less than the Union's full membership. More significantly, the Enlargement Protocol to the Treaty of Nice establishes the rules of governance once the ten (eventually twelve) new members accede to the European Union. These byzantine institutional changes for the European Council, Commission, Parliament and Courts are covered in Chapters Two and Three. Lastly, a Charter of Fundamental Rights was "proclaimed" at Nice, but not made binding as a matter of law, and therefore not subject to ratification. See Chapter Three.

Ratification of the Treaty of Nice and its Enlargement Protocol ran into unexpected opposition in Ireland. Often cited as a model of how the European Union can benefit small countries, Irish law mandates a national referendum on EU ratifications. In the first vote, admittedly a low turnout, the Irish people soundly rejected the Treaty of Nice. Fear of loss of regional benefits to the economically struggling new members may have been critical to this surprising result. A year later, in 2002, after a major persuasion campaign by the Irish government and no provision for "opt-outs," the people voted "yes" on Nice by a wide margin. Shortly thereafter,

the accession of the new member states to the
European Union was finalized.

CHAPTER 2

LAW–MAKING IN EUROPE

The Europeans have been creating law at dazzling though sometimes irregular speed. The focus in this chapter is on law-making institutions and procedures. Without an understanding of these areas, it is almost impossible to function as a lawyer on EU matters.

Primary and Secondary Law

The two remaining treaties of the European communities (the EC and EURATOM) and the Maastricht Treaty on European Union, as amended, are the "primary" sources of regional law. The treaties have had a common set of institutions since 1967. These are the Council, the Commission, the Parliament and the Court of Justice (to which the Court of First Instance was attached in 1989). These institutions, supplemented by national legislatures, courts and tribunals have been busy generating a remarkably vast and complex body of "secondary" law.

Regarding legislation, some law is adopted directly at the regional level, but much of it is enacted by national governments under regional "direction." Similarly, some (and the most important) of the case law is created by decisions in the European

Court of Justice or Court of First Instance, but much development also occurs in the national courts acting in many instances with "advisory rulings" from the Court of Justice. European secondary law also includes international obligations, sometimes undertaken through "mixed" regional and national negotiations and ratifications.

THE POWER TO LEGISLATE

The starting point for a basic understanding of European law-making is, as always, the founding treaties. The Treaty of Rome is premised upon the idea of a regional government of limited or derived powers (compétence d'attribution). That is to say, the Treaty does not convey a general power to create law. European law-making is either specifically authorized or dependent upon the terms of Article 308. That article permits action if "necessary to attain, in the course of the operation of the common market, one of the objectives of the Community and this Treaty has not provided the necessary powers."

Article 308 has been used rather extensively, and in ways which suggest that there are relatively few limits upon what the region can legislate, or negotiate by way of international agreements, once a political consensus has been reached to move forward. For example, Article 308 was widely used as the legal basis for environmental programs well prior to the Single European Act amendments that specifically authorize action in this field. However, the Court of Justice has been retreating from a doctrine of *implied* powers under the Treaty of Rome, most notably concerning external relations' powers.

THE PRINCIPLE OF SUBSIDIARITY

The Treaty on European Union (Maastricht 1993) and to a lesser extent the Single European Act (1987) formalized "subsidiarity" and "proportionality" principles. The Amsterdam Treaty of 1999 added a Protocol on the application of the principles of subsidiarity and proportionality. These much debated principles hold that the region can act in areas where it does not *exclusively* have power only if the member states cannot sufficiently achieve the objectives, i.e., "by reason of scale or effects [the] proposed action [can] be better achieved by the Community" (subsidiarity principle). In all cases, European action must not go beyond what is necessary to achieve the objectives of the Treaty of Rome (proportionality principle).

Subsidiarity is a kind of "states' rights" amendment intended to limit the growth of regional government in Europe. An inter-institutional agreement by the Council, Commission and European Parliament on the application of subsidiarity principles by all institutions was quickly negotiated. Subsidiarity guidelines were adopted by the European Council in 1992 and a Protocol implemented in 1999 with the Amsterdam Treaty. Moreover, the Commission regularly reviews proposed and existing legislation in light of the subsidiarity principle. This has caused a number of legislative proposals and acts to be withdrawn or amended. Under the Subsidiarity Protocol, moreover, if a third or more of the *national* Parliaments give reasoned opinions that a proposal breaches the subsidiarity principle, the Commission must reconsider.

The European Council takes the position that subsidiarity principles do not have direct effect in member state legal systems. If this is correct, subsidiarity issues cannot be raised in litigation before member state courts and tribunals. However, interpretation of these principles and review of compliance by European institutions are subject to judicial review before the Court of Justice through challenges initiated by a member state or another regional institution. It is the Court, therefore, that will ultimately determine whether and to what degree subsidiarity will limit regional governance. To date, its opinions relating to subsidiarity have been studiously opaque though generally deferential to EU legislative powers and recitals of need. Should subsidiarity preclude action, member states are still required to ensure fulfillment of their Treaty of Rome obligations and abstain from measures that could jeopardize the objectives of that treaty.

LEGISLATION—DIRECTIVES AND REGULATIONS

Although variations do occur from treaty to treaty, Europe's legislative, administrative and judicial processes are generally similar. Unless otherwise indicated, the analysis in this chapter is drawn from the Treaty of Rome establishing the European Community. A review of the diagram at the end of this chapter may assist the reader in understanding the text that follows, particularly the institutions involved.

There are two primary types of legislative acts, directives and regulations. These should be distinguished from declarations, resolutions, guidelines, notices, policy statements, guidelines, recommendations, opinions and individual decisions, all of which rarely involve legislative acts and are sometimes referred to as "soft law." The latter can, however, be used to interpret related national or regional law. Article 249 of the Treaty of Rome clarifies the powers of the Council and the Commission, in accordance with the Treaty, to make regulations and issue directives. EC regulations are similar in form to administrative regulations commonly found in North America. EC directives, on the other hand, have no obvious parallel. The Court of Justice has repeatedly affirmed that both regulations and directives must state the "reasons" on which they are based.

A directive establishes regional policy. It is then left to the member states to implement the directive in whatever way is appropriate to their national legal system. This may require a new statute, a Presidential decree, an administrative act or even a constitutional amendment. Sometimes it may require no action at all. As Article 249 indicates, a directive is "binding as to the result to be achieved" but "leave[s] to the national authorities the choice of form and methods." The vast majority of the legislative acts of the single market campaign were directives. All directives contain time limits for national implementation. The more controversial the policy, the longer the likely allotment of time.

The Commission's civil servants initiate the process of legislation by drafting proposals which the Council (comprised of ministers from the governments of the member states) has the power to adopt into law. Although the Council and Parliaments may request the Commission to submit legislative proposals, neither can force the Commission to do so except by way of litigation before the Court of Justice. Only the Commission can draft legislative proposals. This makes the Commission the focal point of lobbying activities.

The Commission's legislative proposals are always influenced by what it believes the Council will accept. The Council, however, has the right to amend legislative proposals by unanimous vote. Readers will immediately note that the European Parliament does not have the power to propose legislation, nor the power to enact it! Parliament's role has traditionally been consultative. Secondarily, it is the source of proposed amendments when the so-called "cooperation" procedure applies. These absences of Parliamentary power are so fundamental that many observers decry a "democratic deficit" in Europe. This deficit has been minimally remedied under the Maastricht Treaty on European Union and the Amsterdam and Nice Treaties which convey "co-decision" powers to Parliament. These powers amount to a Parliamentary right to veto selected legislative proposals.

The Council does not always act through directives and regulations. At times, especially when the heads of state and government meet in the European Council, it issues "declarations" or "resolutions." Council resolutions and declarations are used when a political but not necessarily a legislative consensus has been reached. For example, the 1981 Council resolution on the adoption of Community passports with uniform characteristics fits this mold. This symbolic resolution has been fully implemented, adding significantly to the consciousness of the European Community among its citizens. Plans are afoot to gradually convert to European Union passports. Another example is the Council's Declaration on Democracy (1977) which "codifies" the longstanding tradition that no European state can join or remain associated with the EU without a pluralistic democratic form of government. A third example is the formulation of foreign policy resolutions by the European Council (see Chapter 8).

THE PARLIAMENT

The European Parliament (first called the Assembly in the treaties) was originally composed of representatives appointed by member state governments. In other words, the people's representation was indirect, although the members of the European Parliament (MEPs) had to be serving in their national parliaments. Since 1979, universal suffrage is employed to directly elect representatives to the Parliament.

Under the Treaty of Nice Enlargement Protocol, there are 99 MEPs from united Germany, 72 from Britain, France and Italy, 50 from Poland and Spain, 25 from Holland, 22 from Belgium, Greece and Portugal, 20 from the Czech Republic and Hungary, 18 from Sweden, 17 from Austria and Bulgaria, 13 from Denmark and Finland, 12 from Lithuania and Ireland, 8 from Latvia, 7 from Slovenia, 6 from Luxembourg, Cyprus and Estonia and 5 MEPs from Malta. These numbers correspond roughly to the populations of each country. A cap of 732 MEPs has been established, with pro rata MEP allocations expected when Bulgaria and Romania join in 2007. MEPs serve 5–year terms, and are presently divided into transnational political groups.

The European Parliament is a kaleidoscope of European politics. For example, there are groupings of Socialists, the European People's Party, the Liberal Democratic and Reformist Group, the Greens, the European Democratic Alliance, the Technical Group of the European Right, the Left Unity Group, the Rainbow Group and non-affiliated MEPs. Even these groupings fail to capture the full picture of diversity as the Socialists often realize once they start talking to each other. Since it takes majority votes to pass a measure in Parliament, alliances are essential.

There are numerous standing Parliamentary Committees. Each is responsible for reviewing and reporting on legislative proposals within its expertise such as agriculture, external relations, etc. In addition, unofficially allied groups of MEPs with special interests in particular areas of Union development (e.g., the European Monetary System and the internal market) have been formed. These groups are quite influential in proposing legislative amendments.

The member states fulfilled their obligations under the Treaty of Rome for direct elections. They were supposed to rapidly enact "uniform procedures" for these elections, but did not do so until 1998. Multi-member constituencies are now used with proportional representation. European Union MEPs may not be representatives in their national parliaments. Some commentators have suggested that this leads to an estrangement between European and national politicians.

A chronic issue in connection with the Parliament is to locate its seat. Parliament's plenary sessions are held in Strasbourg, its committee meetings in Brussels and its secretariat is in Luxembourg. Each nation has vied for a permanent assignment of Parliament to it. And the member states have sued to protect their existing allocations. One suspects that this litigation reflects the economic more than the political value associated with Parliament and its expense account spending members.

CONSULTATION, COOPERATION AND CO–DECISION

With direct elections, the impetus toward greater Parliamentary input into the legislative process has magnified. Traditionally, the Parliament has a right to be consulted and to give an "opinion" as part of the legislative process, and this continues to be the case on agricultural and commercial policy matters. That opinion is not binding upon the Commission or Council, but it can prove increasingly awkward if it is disregarded. For example, in 1980 the Court of Justice held that the Council acts illegally if it legislates without waiting for the Parliament's opin- *must wait for ? opinion* ion. Left unanswered is how long Parliament may delay giving an opinion, a tactic it has frequently used to extract concessions from the Commission on agriculture. If the Council amends the Commission's legislative proposal substantively, the Parliament has the right to be consulted and issue a second opinion. Since 1977, a "conciliation procedure" may be used whenever the Council departs from an opinion of the Parliament on proposed legislation of importance to income or expenses. This procedure was instituted by a Joint Declaration of the Parliament, Council and Commission.

An important step forward towards democratic governance was taken in the Single European Act of 1987. Article 252 (formerly Article 189c) of the

Treaty of Rome created a "cooperation procedure" which gave the Parliament more of a voice on selected legislation. Basically, when the Treaty required adherence to this procedure, the Parliament could reject or seek to amend the Council's "common position" on a legislative proposal from the Commission. One early study indicated that Parliament introduced nearly 1,000 amendments after the cooperation procedure was adopted in 1987. Of these, 72 percent were accepted by the Commission and 42 percent ultimately adopted by the Council.

The "cooperation procedure" applied selectively. Most significantly, it applied to nearly all internal market measures following the Single European Act of 1987. With the development of the cooperation procedure, and success in persuading the Commission and Council to adopt its amendments, Parliament became a second center of legislative lobbying.

The European Parliament also acquired significant powers under the Maastricht Treaty on European Union. On legislation, under what is called the "co-decision" procedure of Article 251, it has what amounts to a legislative veto over selected matters if conciliation through direct negotiations with the Council cannot be achieved. Co-decision after Maastricht applied to single market, education, culture, health, consumer protection, environmental, transportation and research affairs. Parliament in fact first exercised its veto rights over a biotechnology directive, out of concern about potential human cloning and, in 2001, against a corporate takeover directive which did not allow for "poison pill" defenses. Thus, three distinct European legislative processes resulted in 1993, each defined in terms of the role Parliament plays: consultative, cooperative and co-decisional.

The Amsterdam Treaty of 1999 and the Nice Treaty of 2003 mandated co-decision in many additional legislative areas. Only European Monetary Union matters remain subject to the cooperation procedure. Parliament still cannot draft or initiate legislation, but its veto power ensures influence and a sparingly used negative power over legislative outcomes. Most conciliation committees formed under the co-decision procedure have reached legislative compromises satisfactory to the Council and Parliament. Such compromises reduce the power of the Commission in Europe's law-making process. Even so, the European Parliament as a legislative institution is still waiting to come of age.

OTHER PARLIAMENTARY POWERS

Other powers of the European Parliament should be noted. First, it can put written and oral questions to the Council and the Commission on virtually any matter, legislative or otherwise. This prerogative mostly has nuisance and information gathering value. Absent forceful persuasion, it is not terribly influential. Second, Article 201 of the Treaty of Rome gives the Parliament the power to "censure" the Commission by a two-thirds vote. A motion of censure would require all Commissioners to resign, but the member states acting in common accord (not the Parliament) get to choose the new Commissioners, although Parliament may veto the nominees and the selection of the President of the Commission. These could conceivably be the very persons just censured. Parliament cannot selectively censure one Commissioner, nor can it censure the Council at all. A motion of censure has at times been threatened by Parliament, but never adopted. In 1999, Parliament came very close to censuring the commission for its inadequacies on corruption and mismanagement in regional programs. After an embarassing report by a committee of experts, the Commission resigned en masse in March of 1999 rather than face formal censure.

Third, the Parliament can initiate a lawsuit against the Council or Commission under Article 232 of the Treaty of Rome for failure to act. Parliament did exactly this when it sued the Council over the failure to implement a Common Transport Policy as required by the Treaty. The Court of Justice ruled that the Council had failed to act, but denied the Parliament a remedy given the imprecise nature of the Council's obligation to act. Nevertheless, the Council has since undertaken a number of reforms in the transport sector. See Chapter 4. The Parliament has selected other litigation alternatives. It can intervene as an interested party in cases pending before the Court, which in one instance it did quite successfully when challenging a regulation enacted by the Council without its consultation and opinion. But it does not appear to have a right to file briefs in Article 234 litigation (see Chapter 3). Since the Nice Treaty (2003), it can litigate the legality of acts of the Commission or Council under Article 230, even if its own prerogatives are not at stake.

Parliament's powers were expanded in 1993 by the Maastricht Treaty on European Union. If an international agreement of the touches upon a co-decisional area, or has institutional or budgetary implications, Parliament must approve. The Parliament also has a veto over nomination of the Commissioners and their President (which it threatened to exercise in 2004, resulting in different nominations), and may create committees to inquiry into alleged "contraventions or maladministration" of regional law. One-fourth of the members of the Parliament must request the creation of such a committee. Issues of this kind may come to Parliament's attention from citizens through a petitioning procedure to the Parliament or to its Ombudsman. Since the Parliament must assent to new member states, yet another veto power was established by the Treaty on European Union.

BUDGETARY LEGISLATION

The European Economic Community was originally financed by contributions from the member states. This created a fiscally dependent relationship. Since 1971, the Community (now Union) is funded through its "own resources," but still dependent upon the member states for their collection and transfer. The income is now principally derived from the common external tariff, agricultural levies on imports, a small but growing portion of the value-added tax (VAT) collected in every state, and an assessment based upon the gross domestic product (GDP) of the member states.

Some countries (like Germany) are habitually net payors to the regional budget. Others (like Portugal) are always net payees receiving funds under various common policies. Britain, initially a large net payor, negotiated a special agricultural rebate agreement in 1984 which now annually returns substantial sums to it.

Article 268 of the Treaty of Rome requires a balanced budget. This requirement has been met by increasing the level of regional revenues and occasionally reducing (agricultural) expenditures. Revenue-raising decisions are undertaken by the heads of state and government meeting in the European Council. In other words, Parliament lacks the power to tax. Control over the spending of these resources, however, is another area where the Parliament has sought to acquire power.

The budgetary process is outlined in Article 272 of the Treaty of Rome. The Commission creates a preliminary draft budget which it forwards to the Council. The Council revises it and then sends a draft budget to the Parliament. The Parliament can reject the draft budget in its entirety, something it did in 1979 and 1984. Article 272 gives the Parliament the power to propose changes in the budget regarding matters "necessarily resulting from this Treaty or from acts adopted in accordance therewith." This has increased Parliamentary influence over "compulsory expenditures" (mostly agricultural subsidies), but the Council has the final word.

Since 1975, Parliament has had ultimate control by way of amendment over "non-compulsory" EU expenditures, about 25 percent of the budget. As a practical matter, this gives the Parliament influence over expenditures in many of the new and important policy areas. However, Parliamentary amendments to the Council's draft budget cannot exceed the maximum rate of increase allowed under Article 272(9). This maximum involves a complex calculation by the Commission of inflation and gross domestic product (GDP) rates as well as national budget variations. Parliament, at the end of a laborious process with multiple communications to the Council, adopts the final budget.

Parliament and the Council often quarrel over creation of the budget, with Parliament prevailing more and more. Parliament and the Council review how the Commission has implemented the budget. The Court of Justice has indicated that the Commission's power to implement the budget does not include making decisions which are legislative in character. Upon Council recommendation, Parliament gives the Commission a "discharge" of its budgetary duties. The European Court of Auditors assists the Parliament and Council in these tasks, which are reasonably routine. In 1982, however,

Parliament refused to discharge the Commission, resulting in tighter controls thereafter. Parliament's power over the purse is increasing and its President reportedly remarked: "As long as Parliament does not have more power in other fields, there will be conflicts on the budget."

WHICH COUNCIL?

EU Council

The foregoing analysis of legislative process illustrates the dominant role given by the Treaty of Rome to "the Council" in regional affairs. The Council, officially known since 1993 as the Council of the European Union (EU Council), is a bit of a moving target. The EU Council consists of representatives of the governments of the member states. Thus there are presently 25 (27 in 2007 with the accession of Bulgaria and Romania) EU Council members. However, the people who comprise the Council change according to the topic at hand. The national ministers of foreign affairs, agriculture, economy and finance (ecofin), social affairs, environment, etc. are sent to Brussels to confer and vote on matters within their competence. Some refer to the Ecofin Council, the Environment Council, the Agriculture Council and so forth in order to differentiate the various EU Councils. Several different Council meetings can take place at once. The Presidency of these Councils rotates among the member states every six months and a certain amount of competition has emerged to see who can achieve the most under their Presidency. It is from all these meetings that the European legislation of the pours forth.

The EU Council is greatly assisted in their work by a Committee of Permanent Representatives known as COREPER. The Committee is comprised of high-ranking national civil servant and based in Brussels. COREPER in turn consults extensively with a large number of "working groups" composed of other national civil servant experts. Thus, by the time a legislative proposal from the Commission reaches the Council for a vote, the proposal has been thoroughly reviewed by COREPER and the appropriate working groups. If there is no controversy, the proposal is scheduled as an "A point" on the Council's agenda and virtually certain to be adopted. If no agreement is reached within CORE-PER, the proposal becomes a "B point" on the agenda which means that the EU Council of ministers will discuss and debate its merits. All formal votes of the Council are made public. Moreover, by unanimous vote, the Council may decide to televise or openly debate legislative initiatives. These changes are part of a broader program aimed at greater institutional "transparency" and less bureaucratic secrecy.

European Council

Then there is the "European Council." With growth, legislative and other decisions have inevitably become more political and thus more difficult. A new institution emerged to keep Europe moving, mostly forward but arguably (at times) backward. The "European Council" consists of the heads of the state or government of the member nations, a kind of ultimate EU Council of ministers. The heads of state have met twice a year since 1974 to formulate broad policy guidelines or initiatives for the Union. For example, the European Council has shown leadership on direct elections to Parliament, the European Monetary System, new memberships and innovative legislative agendas. Its meetings are sometimes called "summits," and Article 2 of the Single European Act of 1987 formally recognized their existence.

European Council summits (though sometimes fractious) have generally proved to be quite successful. They have greatly facilitated the development of common foreign and security policy positions. Although these meetings are undertaken in close consultation with the Commission and Parliament, they are not subject to the procedural rules of the Treaty of Rome. For example, whereas the EU Council of ministers must seek the opinion, cooperate or co-decide with the Parliament on legislative acts, the European Council need not do so. Whether the European Council can be subjected to judicial review by the Court of Justice is most unclear. This is the case despite the fact that European Council pronouncements (e.g., the Social Charter in 1989) may have important legal implications for the Union. Some fear that the European Council's ability to operate outside the Treaty of Rome may exacerbate the "democratic deficit."

VOTING PROCEDURES OF
THE EU COUNCIL

The voting procedures of the EU Council of ministers are critical to an understanding of law-making. The Treaty of Rome provides for simple majority voting unless otherwise specified. However, nearly all the voting rules of the Treaty do specify otherwise. The exceptions thus become the rule. The point of contention is always whether unanimous or "qualified majority" voting is required. Unanimous voting has the practical effect of giving each member state a veto over legislation and policy developments. If a consensus cannot be reached, the minority always seeks shelter under the Treaty of Rome for unanimous voting. The Treaty, however, has only a limited number of such mandates. This is especially true since the Single European Act of 1987, the Maastricht Treaty on European Union of 1993, the Amsterdam Treaty of 1999 and the Treaty of Nice of 2003. A partial list of unanimous voting requirements is provided below, notably including tax and social security matters.

Qualified Majority Voting Rules

Much of the voting in the EU Council now takes place on a "qualified majority" basis. The rules that define this procedure are given in Article 205. Under the Nice Treaty Enlargement Protocol for 27 member states there will be a total of 345 votes, with Germany, France, Italy and Britain having 29 qualified majority votes each. Spain and Poland will have 27 votes, Romania 14 votes, the Netherlands 13 votes, and Belgium, Greece, Portugal, the Czech Republic and Hungary 12 votes. Austria, Sweden and Bulgaria will have 10 votes, Denmark, Ireland, Finland, Slovakia and Lithuania 7 votes, Luxembourg, Latvia, Slovenia, Estonia and Cyprus 4 votes, and Malta has 3 qualified majority votes.

To adopt legislation by qualified majority, 258 votes starting in 2005 (255 after 2007) must be cast in favor by a majority of the member states (for measures requiring a proposal from the Commission) *or* two-thirds of the members (for all other measures). In addition, the qualified majority must when challenged by a member state constitute 62 percent of the total EU population. In the interim between 25 member states (2004) and 27 member states (2007, adding Romania and Bulgaria), proportionate adjustments to these voting rules will be made. Thus, compared with the law prior to the Treaty of Nice Enlargement Protocol, two demanding rules have been added: (1) The majority or two-thirds member state requirement; and (2) the percentage of population challenge requirement. The third requirement, the qualified majority vote count, has been tightened by slightly raising the percentage of votes needed to pass legislation. Byzantine hardly seems adequate to describe the new "triple majority" rules on qualified majority voting.

Note that under these rules, the "Big Six" cannot prevail without some support from smaller nations.

Put conversely, if the little nations stick together, they can block anything. Over the years, as the Community grew from 6 to 9 to 10 to 12 to 15 to 25 to 27 members, these political dynamics have always been preserved in the qualified majority voting rules. Other "blocking minorities" can emerge on North–South and East–West lines.

Demise of the Luxembourg Accord

Treaty of Rome terms notwithstanding, a special agreement known as the "Luxembourg accord" in the past favored unanimous voting. In 1965, France under General De Gaulle walked out of a Council meeting in a dispute over revenue and budgetary policy. Many believe that the real reason for the dispute was the fact that qualified majority voting was due to come into force in 1966. This was the major crisis of the early years of the Community of six. A compromise agreement was reached which when "very important interests" are at stake committed the Council to reaching solutions by consensus if at all possible. This "Luxembourg accord" then proceeds to express disagreement over what is to be done if a consensus cannot be reached. The French delegation took the view that discussions must continue until unanimity is achieved. The five other delegations took the position that the Treaty rules apply and a decision by qualified majority vote must follow.

For many years the Luxembourg accord was followed under the French perspective. Qualified majority voting was almost non-existent. Surprisingly, there was no challenge by the Commission before the Court of Justice to this breach of the Treaty's terms. Arguably, the Council was not acting in accordance with an essential procedural requirement of the Treaty. If so, the Commission could have brought suit under Article 230. As the Community grew to 12 member states, it became more and more difficult for the Council to arrive at a consensus. New legislation and new policy initiatives floundered as institutional and trade arteries hardened.

The Commission, recognizing the economic costs involved (especially vis-a-vis Europe's competitive position with North America and Japan), proposed in its "white paper" of 1985 a return and indeed expansion of qualified majority voting. These proposals bore fruit in the Single European Act of 1987. This Act amended the Treaty of Rome extensively. It was the authority for all of the legislation associated with the campaign to achieve a Europe without internal frontiers by the end of 1992, and much of that legislation was adopted by qualified majority vote under Article 95. Moreover, the Act amended the Treaty in a few instances to change unanimous voting requirements to a qualified majority. The Maastricht Treaty on European Union of 1993, the Amsterdam Treaty of 1999, and the Nice Treaty of 2003 made similar changes. The net result, operationally speaking, has been the demise of the French perspective to the Luxembourg accord. Unanimity is still sought, sometimes at great lengths, but qualified majority voting prevails. A partial list of provisions specifying qualified majority voting follows.

UNANIMOUS VOTING REQUIREMENTS

The Treaty of Rome and Treaty on European Union indicate that the EU Council needs a unanimous vote to act on following matters. All references are to the Articles as renumbered by the Amsterdam Treaty.

Article 23(1) (TEU)	— common foreign and security policy
Article 24 (TEU)	— id; international agreements
Article 34 (TEU)	— police and judicial cooperation in criminal matters
Article 42 (TEU)	— id; shift of matters to Treaty of Rome, Title IV
Article 49 (TEU)	— new members
Article 13	— discrimination based on sex,
(begin Treaty of Rome)	racial or ethnic origin, religion or belief disability, age or sexual orientation
Article 18	— right of residence
Article 19	— voting and candidate rights
Article 22	— new citizenship rights
Article 67	—— most visa, asylum and immigration matters
Article 88(2)	— state subsidy exceptions
Article 93	— taxation
Article 94	— harmonization of national laws
Article 95	— internal market tax, free movement of persons and employment legislation
Article 159	— economic and social cohesion
Article 175s(2)	— environmental taxes, land use planning, water resources, energy supplies

The significance of unanimous voting requirements was driven home in 1997 by British "non-
cooperation" in regional affairs as a protest against

blockage of its beef and cattle exports in the wake of the outbreak of "Mad Cow disease." British non-cooperation lasted about a month before a gradual removal of the ban on British beef was agreed. During that month, regional matters requiring a unanimous vote were held in suspended animation pending resolution of the dispute.

QUALIFIED MAJORITY VOTING

The Treaty of Rome and Treaty on European Union authorize qualified majority voting within the EU Council regarding the following areas. All references are to Articles as renumbered by the Amsterdam Treaty.

Article 7(TEU)	— sanctions for serious and persistent breach of Treaty obligations
Article 23(2) (TEU)	— foreign and security policy joint actions, common positions and their implementation
Article 34(2)(c) (TEU)	— implementation of police and judicial cooperation decisions
Article 40 (TEU)	— authorization of cooperation by selected member states on police and judicial matters (flexibility)
Article 11 (begin Treaty of Rome)	— authorization of cooperation by selected member states in most Treaty of Rome areas (flexibility)
Article 12	— nondiscrimination on grounds of nationality
Article 14	— implementation of community-wide collective bargaining agreements
Article 26	— creation of common external tariff
Article 37	— agriculture

Articles 40, 42	— free movement of workers, social security
Articles 44–46	— right of establishment
Article 47	— mutual recognition of diplomas
Articles 49, 52	— freedom to provide services
Articles 57, 59, 60	— free movement of capital
Articles 66, 67	— selected visa, asylum and immigration matters
Articles 71, 79	— road, rail and waterway transport
Article 80	— sea and air transport
Article 83	— competition law
Article 89	— state subsidies
Article 95	— internal market legislation except taxation, free movement of persons and employment
Article 96	— distortions of competition
Article 99	— broad economic guidelines, surveillance and recommendations to member states
Article 100	— emergency economic conditions
Articles 102, 103	— public finance prohibitions
Article 104	— excessive deficit sanctions
Article 106	— harmonization of coinage
Article 107	— ESCB statute and affairs
Article 111	— ECU exchange rates
Article 114	— Economic and Financial Committee
Articles 119, 120	— balance of payments crises
Articles 121, 122	— meeting of conditions for common currency and derogations
Articles 128, 129	— employment recommendations and incentives
Articles 132–133	— common external commercial policy
Article 135	— customs cooperation
Article 137(2)	— occupational health and safety
Article 141	— equal pay, opportunities and treatment
Article 148	— European Social Fund
Article 149	— education
Article 150	— vocational training

Article 151	— cultural affairs
Article 152	— public health
Article 153	— consumer protection
Article 156	— trans-European energy, transport and telecommunications networks
Article 157	— industrial competitiveness
Article 161	— coordination of structural funds
Article 162	— Regional Development Fund
Articles 166, 172	— research and development
Article 175	— environment
Article 181a	— cooperation with third countries
Article 179	— assistance to developing nations
Article 195	— Ombudsman regulations
Article 210	— salaries
Article 251	— co-decision legislative procedure
Article 252	— cooperative legislative procedure
Article 273	— budget proposals, emergency budgets
Article 276	— discharge of Commission budget duties
Article 280	— prevention of fraud
Article 283	— staff regulations
Article 285	— statistical studies
Article 286	— personal data privacy
Article 300	— international agreements
Article 301	— trade embargoes
Article 309	— suspensions of treaty rights

WHICH VOTING PROCEDURE?— THE LEGAL BASIS FOR LEGISLATION

With the revival of qualified majority voting in the Council, one critical question is the source of authority ("legal basis") under the Treaty of Rome for legislative action. For example, when nontariff trade barriers (NTBs) are removed via the traditional harmonization process, Article 94 mandates a unanimous vote. But if an NTB can be dealt with as part of the campaign for an internal market without frontiers, Article 95 stipulates a qualified majority vote in most cases. Naturally, the Council (composed of government representatives) and the member states favor interpretations that result in unanimous voting and greater retention of national sovereignty. Naturally, the Parliament favors interpretations that require use of the co-decision legislative procedures. Most of these areas correspond with qualified majority Council voting rules. Naturally, countries with "opt outs" favor interpretations which preserve those rights.

The Commission, as the independent "guardian of the treaties," favors interpretations that promote integration and particularly the internal market campaign. It thus tends to side with Parliament in disputes over the source of power for legislative enactments. But it did not do this when proposing post–Chernobyl safety legislation under EURATOM instead of Article 95 of the Treaty of Rome. This had the effect of avoiding Parliamentary cooperation procedures. The Parliament subsequently sued the Council before the European Court, which ruled its challenge to the EURATOM safety legislation admissible under Article 230, but denied relief on the merits.

Legal basis issues frequently reach the Court of Justice. Legislative authority issues came to a head in a Commission prosecution against the Council initiated on the very day that the Single European

Act was signed. The Court of Justice ruled that the Council violated Article 253 by failing to clearly state the legal basis for regulations implementing the generalized system of tariff preferences (GSP) for goods originating in the developing world. More importantly, the Court held that the Council enacted the regulations on the wrong legal basis. Both of these violations, which were longstanding Council practices, amounted to unlawful failures to act in accordance with the Treaty of Rome.

Article 308, "Necessary" Legislative Powers

The Commission had proposed adoption of the GSP regulations under the common external commercial policy provisions, specifically Article 133 which employs qualified majority voting. The Council replaced this proposal with vague language simply referring to "the Treaty" as the legal basis for its acts. In court, the Council explained that this reference was really to Article 133 *and* Article 308. Article 308 authorizes legislation necessary to achieve objectives for which specific enabling powers are otherwise not found in the Treaty of Rome. Article 308 had been previously used by the Council as the legal basis for a number of innovative programs and laws, including the Monetary Cooperation Fund, the Center for Development of Vocational Training, the Foundation for the Improvement of Living and Working Conditions, and environmental, research and development and energy legislation. It had also been used in areas where the Treaty contains other provisions, including agriculture, the customs union, services, the right of establishment and (as in the GSP case) external commercial policy.

Article 308 legislation must be enacted by a unanimous Council vote and does not require cooperation or co-decision with Parliament. By ruling that Article 133 alone was the proper legal basis for GSP regulations, the Court nullified the Council's unanimous decision and reaffirmed its power to subject Council actions to judicial review. The Commission now has more leeway when proposing legislation for which the Treaty stipulates qualified majority voting under what has become known as the "center of gravity" test. And the Council is clearly limited in its use of Article 308 to situations where no other authority to act is found in the Treaty of Rome as amended by the Single European Act, the Maastricht Treaty on European Union, the Amsterdam Treaty, and the Treaty of Nice.

THE COMMISSION AS AN INSTITUTION AND LAW–MAKER

The pivotal role of the European Commission in the law-making process should be evident. It alone drafts legislative proposals. As the GSP litigation makes clear, the Commission can also prosecute when proper legislative procedures are not followed. Furthermore, in certain areas (notably agricultural and competition law) the Commission has been delegated by the Council the authority to issue implementing regulations and decisions that establish law. These acts detail administrative rules rather than create new or broad policies. Thus the Council establishes the "target prices" for agriculture, but the Commission issues thousands of regulations aimed at actually realizing these goals. The Commission has also promulgated an important series of "group exemption" regulations for business competition law. See Chapter 7. These cover franchising, technology transfers, distribution and a variety of other business agreements. Lastly, the Commission is authorized by Article 86 of the Treaty of Rome to issue (on its own initiative) *directives* addressed to member states regarding public enterprises. This authority avoids the usual legislative process.

When exercising law-making powers conferred upon it by the Council, the Commission must first consult various committees. These requirements are known as the "comitology" rules of the Council. These rules, in essence, allow the Council to actively monitor the Commission as a law-maker. In most cases, they vest a power of reversal or modification in the Council.

The Commissioners and Their Tasks

Who and what is the European Commission? Under the Nice Treaty Enlargement Protocol, there will initially be 25 then 27 Commissioners, one from each member state. Germany, France, Italy, Britain and Spain will give up their second Commissioners. Moreover, after the accession of Romania and Bulgaria in 2007, it has been agreed that the EU

Council, acting unanimously, will reduce the number of Commissioners and establish a rotation system to "reflect satisfactorily the demographic and geographical range" of the member states. Commissioners are appointed by a qualified majority o the EU Council subject to Parliament's approval for five-year renewable terms. The President of the Commission is similarly appointed by the European Council and Parliament. Great pains are taken to ensure the independence of Commissioners from their home governments. Article 213 stipulates that Commissioners must be chosen on the basis of competence and their independence must be "beyond doubt." Any breach of this trust by Commissioners could lead to compulsory retirement, or since the Nice Treaty, dismissal by the President of the Commission.

Unlike the ministers of the EU Council, Commissioners are not supposed to function as representatives of their nations. Over the years, in large measure, this has been true. Indeed, Prime Minister Thatcher once failed to renew a British Commissioner's appointment because he had "gone native." Sent over to Brussels in a stormy period when the Prime Minister was quite hostile to developments, this Commissioner proceeded to act independently, too independently as it turned out. His non-renewal, however, broke with a longstanding tradition of regular reappointments for competent Commissioners. Renewal decisions have thus become more politicized in recent years and Commissioners no doubt look over their shoulders towards home as their five-year terms begin to expire.

The Treaty of Rome also establishes voting rules for the European Commission. Simple majority votes prevail. As a matter of custom, considerable deference is usually given to the Commissioner in charge of a DG when legislative or other proposals are being reviewed by the Commission as a whole. This is sometimes achieved by circulating files with proposed actions which are implemented unless objections are shortly received. Individual Commissioners can be delegated authority to act for the body on routine matters. For example, when the Commissioner on Agriculture adopts new regulations, these are likely to involve such delegation.

The Commission performs a number of functions in addition to those concerning law-making. The most important of these include its prosecutorial powers against individuals and enterprises for breach of selected laws, and against member states for failure to adhere to their treaty obligations. See Chapters 3 and 7. The Commission negotiates international trade and other agreements. See Chapter 6. It also administers the EU budget and publishes a general and a series of specific annual reports (e.g., on competition policy), all of which are a good way to survey regional affairs.

THE COMMISSION'S DEPARTMENTS

Each Commissioner supervises one or more "Directorate–Generals" or departments of the Commission. These "portfolios" are determined by the President of the Commission. Each Directorate–General (DG) has a Director–General of a nationality different than that of its supervising Commissioner. Each DG has a specific allocation of administrative, legislative drafting and law enforcement duties. Each DG has a staff of highly paid Eurocrats selected in part to ensure national diversity. The staff regulations officially refer to a "geographical distribution" (quotas) of employees based upon the populations of the various member states. Acts performed by Commissioners and their staff in an official capacity are immune from legal proceedings in national courts. Employees are also exempt from national income taxation, although they pay a nominal tax to the Community.

The DGs correspond roughly to the main divisions of the treaties. Many consider this to be an excessive and inefficient number of governmental departments. And some DGs, like environment and external relations, are seriously understaffed while others (especially personnel and information) seem grossly overstaffed.

The number of Directorates–General changes periodically as do their assignments. Ordinarily, these include Directorates for:

External Relations

Economic and Financial Affairs

Industry

Competition

Employment, Industrial Relations and Social Affairs

Agriculture

Transport

Development

Personnel and Administration

Information, Communication, Culture, Audiovisual

Environment, Nuclear Safety and Civil Protection

Science, Research and Development

Telecommunications, Information Market and Exploitation of Research

Fisheries

Internal Market and Financial Services

Regional Policies and Cohesion

Energy

Credit and Investment

Budgets

Financial Control

Customs Union and Indirect Taxation

Education Training and Youth

Enterprise Policy, Distributive Trades, Tourism and Cooperatives

Consumer Policy and Consumer Health

Each Commissioner also supervises a personal staff, known as a cabinet. Critics maintain that there has been excessive growth in the size and power of cabinets. These staff members have been known to override the advice of the various Directors–General and generally isolate their Commissioners from professional civil servant input. Defenders of these trends maintain that some of the DGs have been less than competent, and that the Commissioners need another, less bureaucratic perspective. The truth no doubt lies somewhere in between. Just as there are energetic and effective Commissioners, Directors–General and cabinets, none of these offices is immune from the deadwood syndrome.

THE COURT OF JUSTICE
AS A LAW–MAKER

United States students of law and attorneys are familiar (if not always comfortable) with the law-making role of U.S. courts. This perspective is a product of the common-law tradition inherited from England made explicit by the teachings of American realists. Such awareness is less present in European legal communities for a variety of reasons. One important factor is the predominance of the civil law tradition on the Continent. This tradition, with its heavy reliance upon abstract inductive (not deductive) reasoning, tends to obscure rather than illuminate the way in which judges on the Continent do in fact make law. Like their common-law counterparts, European judges must often fill in legislative gaps and arrive at conclusions based upon broadly worded legal language. Anyone who has ever read a "Code" knows that it invites, indeed often requires, law-making by judges. Nevertheless, the mystique that judges can only apply the law, not create it, weighs heavily in the minds of many Europeans.

It is against this background that the law-making achievements of the European Court of Justice take on a truly remarkable significance. There are presently 25 (27 in 2007) justices on the Court, one from each member nation. Thus only two or perhaps three are trained in the common law. All are prominent jurists who serve six-year terms by appointment of the member states acting in common accord. The Court was created by the Treaty of Paris in 1951 establishing the Coal and Steel Community. At that time neither Britain nor Ireland was a member. Its procedures and methods (but not its mentality) remain solidly based upon civil law, especially French law, traditions. See Chapter 3.

The Court of Justice emerged in the earliest years as a powerful law-maker. In part, this role was thrust upon it by the open-ended, constitutional language of the Treaty of Rome. In part, also, the Court simply embraced the role, drawing power and influence to it while constantly pushing Europe forward through its "integrationist jurisprudence." The supremacy doctrine and the "doctrine of direct effect" (see Chapter 3) have been called the twin pillars of this jurisprudence. No less potentially significant are the general principles of law articulated by the Court.

GENERAL PRINCIPLES OF LAW—FUNDAMENTAL RIGHTS, CHARTER OF FUNDAMENTAL RIGHTS

The law-making role of the Court of Justice is evident when it recognizes general principles of law, a kind of common law of the Common Market. This is similar to what occurs when the Court finds the general principles of tort liability common to the member states as required by Article 288. See Chapter 3. However, there is no other express Treaty authorization for the development by the Court of general principles of law. Article 220 does oblige the ECJ and, since 2003 the Court of First Instance, to ensure that "the law" is observed when interpreting and applying the Treaty of Rome.

In different contexts, as part of "the law," the Court of Justice has recognized a right of legitimate expectation, a right to be heard, the duty to respect fundamental human rights, a right to equality of treatment, and a duty to employ means that are proportional (not excessive) to the end sought. It is important to note that the Court can and has declared regional legislation invalid if it fails to adhere to general principles of law. Thus these principles, as articulated by the Court of Justice, are a *higher* source of law capable of overriding legal acts of the Community.

Other general principles of law recognized by the Court of Justice include contractual certainty, legal certainty, and the right to engage in trade union activities. A limited attorney-client privilege of confidentiality has been recognized by the Court of Justice as a general principle of law applicable to regional proceedings. This right, however, only applies to member state-licensed counsel. It does not apply to in-house counsel. See Chapter 7. A limited doctor-patient right of confidentiality has also been acknowledged by the Court.

Legal Certainty

A good example of the way in which ECJ-recognized general principles of law can permeate regional affairs is presented by the principle of legal certainty. This principle means that legal acts must be clear, precise and predictable to those subject to them. Legal certainty has been invoked in connection with regional competition, agricultural, customs, and social security law so as to protect individuals and their rights. For example, social security notices to workers in other member states must be in a language the worker can understand. In general, legal certainty bars the adoption of retroactive legislation. And the vast majority of the Court's decisions, in the name of legal certainty, apply prospectively. ECJ decisions otherwise are taken to represent what was always the correct law and thus retroactively date back to the creation of the law under consideration.

*Fundamental Rights Doctrine–European Convention
   on Human Rights*

In one decision, the Court recognized the relevance and drew upon the European Convention for the Protection of Human Rights and Fundamental Freedoms (1950). In other decisions, the Court of Justice drew upon Article 10 of the European Convention as support for freedom of expression within broadcasting law, and Article 6 for the right to a fair hearing. This Convention has been ratified by every member state. The Commission once proposed that the European Union accede to the Human Rights Convention. This would mean that the Union itself would be bound by the catalogue of human rights enumerated in it. These include property, privacy, fair trial, equal treatment, religious, associational and trade or professional rights. Article 6 of the Maastricht Treaty on European Union requires the Union to respect fundamental rights as guaranteed by the Human Rights convention, but stops short of actual accession to it. Article 6 also affirms that the Union is founded on principles of liberty, democracy, respect for human rights and fundamental freedoms, and the rule of law.

If the Union acceded to the Convention's "right of individual petition," citizens would be able to file complaints with the European Commission on Human Rights in Strasbourg, France against acts of regional institutions. The European Court of Human Rights in Strasbourg ultimately decides upon such complaints. Neither the Commission nor the Court of Human Rights are Union institutions.

They operate in a broader European sphere. Americans should particularly note that the Human Rights Court has ruled that extradition of criminals who face a possible death sentence and the "death row phenomenon" in the United States amounts to torture or an inhuman or degrading treatment or punishment in breach of the Convention.

The Court of Justice's decisions in the field of fundamental rights also draw upon the different constitutional traditions of the member states. The Court, in this respect, does not see itself as merely replicating human rights found in common at the national level. It is instead "inspired" by these traditions to create of its own accord a new body of European law of fundamental human rights and freedoms. Such human rights are not absolute and public interest exceptions not disturbing "the substance" of those rights may be allowed. One interesting and sensitive issue is the possible supremacy of regional law on fundamental rights over national rights.

Finally, the Treaty of Rome is not completely devoid of human rights protections. Article 12, for example, establishes the fundamental principle of nondiscrimination on grounds of nationality, including corporate nationality. This principle has been frequently invoked in litigation, very often to set aside national rules embodying such discrimination. Discrimination on grounds of nationality by private parties acting within the scope of the Treaty of Rome is also prohibited. Furthermore, Article 12 applies to the Community and its institutions. The principle of nondiscrimination on grounds of nationality applies to covert activities. Speaking generally, the Court of Justice has ruled that Article 12 requires comparable situations not to be treated differently and different situations not to be treated in the same way, unless such treatment is objectively justified (permissible differentiation).

Other provisions of the Treaty of Rome also touch upon fundamental human rights. These include the right to challenge Council or Commission action taken in breach of essential procedural requirements (see Chapter 3) and equal pay for equal work (see Chapter 5). In addition, Article 295 provides that the Treaty shall not prejudice the rules of the member states governing property ownership. However, this has not stopped the Commission and Council from extensively regulating agricultural land. See Chapter 5. And the Court of Justice has significantly limited the exercise of intellectual property rights when they inhibit internal trade. See Chapter 4.

EU Charter of Fundamental Rights

In 2000, a Charter of Fundamental Rights was "proclaimed" (but not made legally binding) by the European Council. The Charter focuses on dignity, freedoms, equality, solidarity, citizens rights and justice as its fundamental values. Its scope is far ranging: the death penalty is forbidden, as is "the reproductive cloning of human beings." Privacy rights, freedom of expression, the rights to work, health care and education, broad antidiscrimination rights (including against sexual orientation), the rights of children and the elderly, and the right to "cultural diversity" are recognized. Access to documents, petitioning rights, a fair trial and criminal procedure rights, and a general ban against "abuse of rights," are also enshrined. The Charter's relationship to the European Human Rights Convention is intended to be consistent, allowing for the possibility of higher levels of protection. Many critics have cited the inability of the ECJ and CFI to enforce the Charter as its principle flaw.

SUPREMACY DOCTRINE

None of the European treaties address the question of what to do when national and regional law are in conflict. There is no supremacy clause analogous to that found in the United States constitution. The issue is absolutely critical to the success or failure of European law in all its manifestations; the founding treaties, directives, regulations, ECJ and CFI decisions, international obligations, general principles of law, etc. Its omission from the treaties was perhaps necessary to secure their passage through various national parliaments. But the issue did not disappear, it was merely left to the European Court to resolve.

In a very famous 1964 decision, the Court of Justice ruled that it simply had to be the case that Community law is supreme. The Court reasoned that the whole of the Common Market edifice would be at risk if national laws at variance with regional law could be retained or enacted:

"The transfer by the states from their domestic legal systems to the Community legal system of the rights and obligations arising under the Treaty carries with it a permanent limitation of their sovereign rights, against which a subsequent unilateral act incompatible with the concept of the Community cannot prevail." *Costa v. ENEL* (1964) Eur.Comm.Rep. 585.

Invalidity of National Laws

Under its supremacy doctrine, the European Court of Justice has (effectively speaking) invalidated countless national laws as in conflict with regional law. Supremacy notwithstanding, member states may maintain or introduce more stringent law on working conditions, social policy, consumer protection and the environment, provided those laws are compatible with the Treaty of Rome.

Repeal or amendment of conflicting national law is a duty of the member states that can be reviewed by the Court of Justice in further legal proceedings. An alternative growing in use and encouraged by the European Court is creative judicial interpretation by national courts so as to incorporate regional law requirements and avoid conflicts. For quite some time after *Costa v. ENEL,* and even somewhat today, national courts, legislatures and executives have resented the supremacy doctrine. They adhere, in the end, to this judge-made law because of their mutual interest in the success of the enterprise and their respect for the rule of law by its prestigious Court.

National Constitutional Rights and Supremacy

One especially sensitive point has been the conflict of national constitutional rights and regional law. Unlike Britain, many Continental states have written constitutions and some have specialized courts or tribunals vested with exclusive powers of constitutional interpretation. Both Germany and Italy, for example, have such "constitutional courts." The Court of Justice has explicitly ruled that *every* national court or tribunal must apply regional law in its entirety so as to set aside *any* conflicting provision of national law. This duty arises out of European Community law.

In France, implementation of this duty by its highest courts has been mixed. The Conseil d'Etat (but not the Cour de Cassation) did not consistently invalidate French law because it (under French law) is not empowered to review the constitutionality of administrative acts. The Conseil d'Etat was slow to acknowledge regional law as a source of review power and duty. But there are signs in its most recent decisions that the Conseil d'Etat has come in from the cold on supremacy.

The German and Italian constitutional courts also initially refused to strike down inconsistent national law. Indeed, the Bundesverfassungsgericht went so far as to review and find European law deficient as against German constitutional protections for human rights. Both courts have retreated from their initial positions. By and large, they have accepted the supremacy doctrine of the European Court and their duty to set aside contrary national law. In the human rights area, however, neither has fully given up its review powers as the controversial German Constitutional Court rulings regarding the Maastricht Treaty on European Union and Europe's regulation of trade in bananas (yes, bananas) make all too clear. In a case where Irish constitutional restraints on the advertising of the availability of abortion services in Britain were challenged as incompatible with the Treaty of Rome, there were also signs within the Irish Supreme Court that supremacy might not prevail. And in Denmark any use of implied powers under Article 308 as the legal basis for regional acts is constitutionally suspect.

The collision and reconciliation of the European Court's supremacy doctrine with national constitutions illustrates an essential feature of the regional legal system. The efficacy of the system depends heavily upon the willingness of national judges to acknowledge and adhere to regional law, in particular to adhere to the European Court's interpretation of that law. This dependency has meant that the outer limits of the Court's authority and credibility are really to be found among the national judiciaries. On supremacy, the European Court has largely prevailed. Indeed, even in Britain where issues of supremacy are hypersensitive, the House of Lords has acknowledged that there is nothing novel in according supremacy to European law. In other areas, notably the question of giving "direct effect" to regional directives (see Chapter 3), the process of education and persuasion continues.

CONSULTATION – ASSENT PROCEDURE

Chart 1

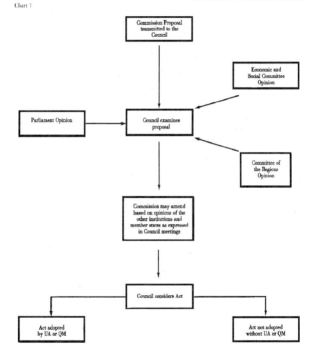

Economic and Social Committee and Committee of the Regions opinions are not required in all cases and not in the assent procedure.

COOPERATION PROCEDURE

Chart 2

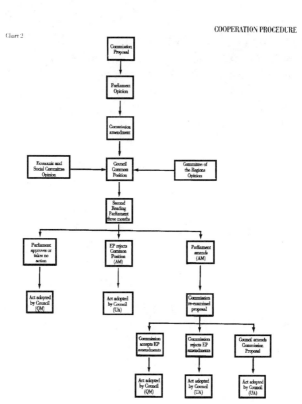

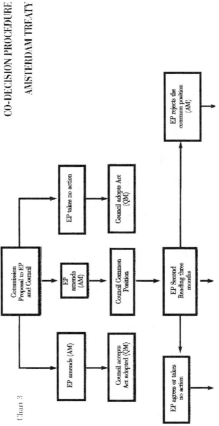

CO-DECISION PROCEDURE
AMSTERDAM TREATY

Chart 3

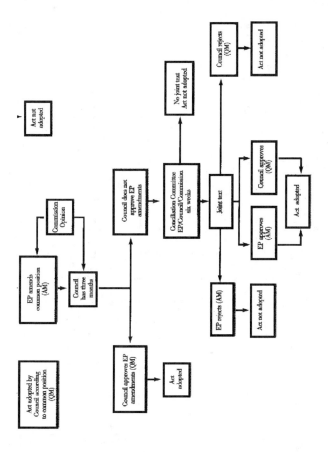

CHAPTER 3

LITIGATING EUROPEAN LAW

There has been an explosive growth in litigation of European law. The bulk of this growth has taken place in national courts and tribunals. These bodies are vested with wide (but not final) authority to resolve European legal issues. For example, contracts disputes can raise a host of legal questions. Is an exclusive dealing distribution contract enforceable as a matter of competition law? Can goods to which a sales contract applies be freely traded in the Common Market? Is payment for sales across borders protected by regional law? Does an employment contract fail to provide equal pay for equal work? Can employees be terminated because of their nationality? May patent licensing agreements contain grant-back clauses? Can franchisees be limited to certain geographic markets? What joint ventures can be established for research and development purposes?

Administrative decisions present another fertile field of European law litigation. When can customs officers seize goods in transit between member states? When can they collect money in such situations? When can immigration authorities keep workers from other member states out? When can they deport them? When can professional licensing boards deny the applications of citizens of the European Union? Can national authorities deny EU nationals the right to establish a restaurant? Can they require residency or work permits? What about the families of all these persons? What about pensions, social security, health insurance and other job-related benefits for resident workers? These listings only scratch the surface of European law litigation in national courts and tribunals.

The explosion in litigation must be qualified. Not all areas of law fall within the jurisdiction of the European Court of Justice (ECJ) and its judicial doctrine. For example, to the extent that the nations involved rely upon intergovernmental conventions to reach their goals, these agreements do not follow the typical litigation patterns described below. Such conventions will have their own dispute settlement mechanisms unless they specifically convey jurisdiction to the ECJ. For example, the "Brussels Convention" on jurisdiction and enforcement of civil and commercial judgments makes such a conveyance. Moreover, commencing with the 1987 Single European Act amendments to the Treaty of Rome, certain areas of European Union activity are undertaken outside normal legislative and litigative frameworks. More such exclusions, where intergovernmental procedures predominate, were added by the 1993 Maastricht Treaty on European Union and the Amsterdam Treaty of 1999, although the latter treaty and the Treaty of Nice of 2003 also removed certain exclusions. At this point, some EU foreign and security policy matters and some EU police and judicial cooperation in criminal matters do not fall within the litigation system analyzed in this chapter.

DIRECT EFFECTS DOCTRINE

The right to commence litigation in national forums must be given to the plaintiff by national law. In other words, European law has not (as yet) been interpreted to create national causes of action. What it does do, according to the "direct effects doctrine," is give litigants the right to raise many issues ("Euro-defenses" and "Euro-offenses") in national courts and tribunals. In doing so, individuals often function as guardians of the Treaty of Rome (like the Commission). Americans might analogize this role to that of "private attorneys general," a law enforcement technique adopted in a number of United States statutes. The Court of Justice has noted that the vigilance of private litigants enforcing their rights is an important element in the European legal system.

The direct effects doctrine is, to a very large degree, a product of the jurisprudence of the European Court of Justice. It can apply to treaties, directives, regulations, decisions and international agreements. When any of these measures are of direct effect, this impact generally commences from the date of its entry into force. But the direct effects doctrine is not automatically applied. For example, although the General Agreement on Tariffs and Trade (GATT) and the WTO Agreements are binding upon the Community and its member states, they have been construed by the Court not to have direct legal effects. Both the EU Council of ministers and the European Council tend to issue resolutions or declarations when there is a political consensus but no desire to adopt legislation. For the most part, the Court of Justice has held such acts incapable of creating direct legal effects in the member states.

Regulations

The legal effects of regulations are the easiest to understand. Article 249 of the Treaty of Rome provides that regulations are "directly applicable in all member states." In other words, regulations have immediate unconditional legal effect without any need for national implementation. They are law in the member states from the moment of issuance, binding upon all individuals, business organizations and governments. For litigants, when regulations are applicable, they control the outcome. This is true under the supremacy doctrine even in the face of contrary national law. See Chapter 2.

Directives

Directives are more difficult to understand. Article 249 does *not* specify that they shall have "direct applicability." In part, their design prohibits this. Directives are addressed to member states, instructing them to implement (in whatever way is required) certain regional policies within a fixed timetable. These policies do not become law in the member states until implemented or, if timely implementation does not follow, until the European Court rules that the directive is of "direct effect." Some national courts, notably in France, have opposed this judge-made doctrine.

Not all directives have direct effect. The Court of Justice has selectively ruled that only those directives that establish clear and unconditional legal norms and do not leave normative discretion to the member states are of direct effect. Most "framework" directives will not meet these criteria. Once the ECJ has decided that a European directive has direct effect, litigants can rely on it to the full extent of its application to member states, public service entities and local governments. Litigants can challenge contrary national law, including defective implementing measures if required.

Interpretative Duties

Unlike regulations, directives cannot be used to challenge private activities. Thus it is said that directives are incapable of "horizontal" direct effects. Even so, the Court of Justice has held that in applying national law the national courts and tribunals are required by Article 10 of the Treaty of Rome to interpret their law in light of the wording and purposes of all directives. National law must be interpreted in the light of regional directives even if the directive has not yet been implemented. Some commentators have characterized these duties, derived from the *Marleasing* case, as involving the "indirect effect" of directives.

The obligation to interpret national law in view of directives is limited by general principles of law and in particular the principles of legal certainty and non-retroactivity. Even so, in considerable private litigation before the tribunals and courts of member states, European directives will be given effect through judicial interpretations of national law. This is likely to have the same practical impact as would adoption of a "horizontal" direct effects doctrine at the regional level. Moreover, it has been argued that Article 10 mandates that *all* provisions of national law (not just those touched by directives) must be interpreted in conformity with *all* European law (not just directives). If this argument becomes binding law, the doctrine of direct effects will reach a zenith which few would have ever dreamed.

DIRECTLY EFFECTIVE TREATY PROVISIONS

The third major category of directly effective law originates in the treaties establishing the EURATOM and EC communities. The Court of Justice has ruled that parts of these treaties are capable of having immediate, binding legal effect in the member states. Here again the Court has been selective, sorting out which treaty provisions establish clear, unconditional and nondiscretionary legal norms. Those many articles of the treaties that are largely aspirational, procedural or written as guidelines for the exercise of member state discretion are unlikely to have direct effect.

The Court of Justice has consistently refused to view the treaties as merely creating obligations among the contracting states. Citing Article 234, the Court finds acknowledgment that the Treaty of Rome was intended to have effect in national legal regimes.

> "The conclusion to be drawn ... is that the Community constitutes a new legal order of international law for the benefit of which the States have limited their sovereign rights, albeit within limited fields, and the subjects of which comprise not only Member States but also their nationals. Independently of the legislation of Member States, Community law therefore not only imposes obligations on individuals but is also intended to confer upon them rights which become part of their legal heritage. These rights arise not only where they are expressly granted by the Treaty, but also by reason of obligations which the Treaty imposes in a clearly defined way upon individuals as well as upon the Member States and the institutions of the Community." *Van Gend en Loos v. Nederlandse Administratie der Belastingen* (1963) Eur.Comm.Rep. 1.

Once the Court has held a Treaty term directly effective in the member states, litigants before national courts and tribunals can rely fully upon it. They can, under the supremacy doctrine, use it to set aside contradictory national law. Like regulations, directly effective Treaty of Rome provisions apply horizontally to private parties. This follows, in the court's view, because national courts are an arm of the states that signed the Treaty and therefore bound to apply its law in all cases.

Directly Effective Treaty Provisions

The following is a partial list of the articles of the Treaty of Rome that have been held directly effective by the European Court of Justice. Many of these decisions are qualified.

Article 12	— no discrimination on grounds of nationality
Article 18	— right of free movement and residence
Articles 23–24	— customs union free trade rules
Article 25	— no internal customs duties or measures of equivalent effect
Article 28	— no internal trade quotas or measures of equivalent effect
Article 30	— no disguised restraints on internal trade
Article 31	— state trading monopolies cannot discriminate between nationals
Article 39	— free movement and employment of workers without nationality discriminations
Article 43	— right of establishment for self-employed
Article 49(1)	— freedom to provide services across borders
Article 50(3)	— national treatment of cross-border service providers
Articles 56, 57, 58	— current payments and capital transfers
Articles 72, 75, 76	— transport discriminations prohibited
Articles 81, 82, 86	— competition law prohibitions
Articles 87(1), 88(3)	— state subsidies cannot distort competition without Commission approval

Article 90	— national treatment on taxation of goods
Article 91	— no excessive tax rebates upon exports
Article 141	— equal pay for equal work, equal treatment
Article 294	— no discrimination on capital participation in companies

The following Treaty of Rome provisions have generally been held *not* to have direct legal effect. Again, many of these ECJ decisions are qualified.

Articles 2, 3	— general tasks and objectives
Article 10	— member state obligations to facilitate and not jeopardize Treaty of Rome
Article14	— completion of Europe without internal frontiers by 1992
Article 88	— state subsidies
Article 97	— harmonization of laws
Article 108	— balance of payments
Article 293	— negotiation of certain conventions

NATIONAL LEGAL REMEDIES FOR DIRECTLY EFFECTIVE LAW

Directly effective European law conveys at the national level immediate legal rights and obligations. What remedies can be secured in national courts and tribunals when regional law has these effects? The Treaty of Rome does not provide a ready answer. In general, the Court of Justice has held that directly effective rights must be enforceable in the national courts by means of remedies that are real, effective and nondiscriminatory. Interim or preliminary judicial and administrative remedies may be required to protect directly effective rights when national *or* regional law is challenged. The precise determination of remedies is a matter for the national courts to decide, subject to review by reference to the European Court. For example, one British court issued a notable interim order requiring public authorities to promise to pay damages if that country's Sunday trading bans ultimately were found invalid as the "price" for interlocutory injunctions sought by the authorities against Sunday traders. In another British case, the House of Lords referred equal treatment remedial issues concerning a ceiling on recovery of damages and denial of interest to the Court of Justice. The Court ruled against both limitations as inadequate to restore equality of treatment.

Member State Liability for Damages

In a major decision, *Francovich*, the Court of Justice has ruled that member state liability for damages to individuals caused by the state's infringement of European law is inherent in the scheme of the Treaty of Rome. This obligation follows from member state duties under Article 10 to ensure fulfillment of European law. The case involved an Italian failure to implement a directive on employee benefits in the event of insolvency. Whether or not the unimplemented directive is of direct effect does not matter, and faulty implementation or retention of contrary domestic law also gives rise to state liability whenever three conditions are met: (1) the law infringed is intended to confer individual rights; (2) the infringement is sufficiently serious; and (3) there is a direct causal link between the breach and damages sustained. Member state liability generally tracks Community tort liability under Article 288 and also extends to administrative acts and omissions. In a second major decision, *Kobler*, the Court of Justice has held that member states can be liable to individuals for damages when their *national courts* exceptionally breach EU law.

In the absence of precise regional rules on remedies for directly effective legal rights, the results vary from country to country and context to context. Many cases involve the question of repayment of custom duties, customs charges and taxes paid to governments under national laws that are invalidated by European law. Others concern national laws implementing regional law which is subsequently invalidated by the Court of Justice. The Court has reiterated in these decisions that the means of recovery for monies unlawfully paid to governments are controlled by national law. Thus, statutes of limitations, the forum, interest on the amounts paid and related issues are national legal questions. The Court has also reiterated that procedural hurdles which discriminate against recoveries based upon European rights when measured against procedures for similar domestic recoveries do not satisfy the requirements of the Treaty of Rome. And, in general, national rules on recovery of unlawful payments to governments cannot have the practical result of making it impossible to recover such sums.

ARTICLE 234—REFERRALS BY NATIONAL COURTS AND PRELIMINARY RULINGS

The European Court of Justice derived its doctrine of directly effective European law partly from Article 234 (formerly 177) of the Treaty of Rome. This article is the linchpin that joins the national legal systems of the member states to the European Court.

Article 234 vests jurisdiction in the European Court to give "preliminary rulings" (sometimes called "advisory rulings") on the interpretation of the Treaty, the validity and interpretation of acts by regional institutions, and other matters. These rulings occur when national courts or tribunals faced with an issue of European law request them. Professional bodies may or may not constitute "tribunals of a member state" for these purposes. Since the Treaty of Nice (2003), the ECJ has the power to allow some Article 234 cases to go to the Court of First Instance (below).

Discretionary References

Article 234 requests or "references" are discretionary with the judges of the lower-level courts and tribunals of the member states. They cannot be initiated as a matter of right by litigants, nor by arbitrators designated by contract to resolve a dispute when those arbitrators are not functioning as a court or tribunal of a member state. This is particularly notable because ever increasing numbers of business disputes are being taken to binding arbitration. The only recourse for review of an arbitrator's interpretation of European law is through ancillary or enforcement proceedings in the national courts.

Whenever a national court considers a reference necessary to enable judgment, it may seek the advice of the European Court by posing questions to it. It may do so even when the European Court or a higher national court has already ruled on the question of law at hand. In other words, the common law doctrine of binding precedent does not remove the discretion of lower courts to invoke Article 234. Similarly, the fact that appeals are mandatory under national law does not block utilization of Article 234 references to the ECJ if the lower court believes such a reference is necessary to enable it to give judgment.

In practice, lower courts refer European law issues to the ECJ quite regularly. However, these referral decisions may be subject to an interlocutory appeal within the national legal system. Such an appeal will not ordinarily require the ECJ to suspend its review of and decision on the reference. But if the appeal of the referral has the effect under national law of suspending the referral decision, then the Court of Justice will suspend its Article 234 proceeding. Thus, in most cases, the national interlocutory appeal of the referral decision and the ECJ's Article 234 proceeding will move forward simultaneously. Should the decision to refer be reversed on appeal, the Court of Justice will terminate its proceeding and not rule under Article 234.

Assuming the request comes from a proper national court or tribunal, the European Court of Justice cannot refuse the reference, even when it has already ruled on the legal issue. Once underway, the Commission almost always files a written brief expressing its opinion in Article 234 proceedings. The government of the member state whose court or tribunal is the source of the reference typically does so as well. After a preliminary ruling of the European Court is secured, the national court is obliged to implement that ruling in its final judgment. The ruling is also binding on appeal of that judgment, and (at a minimum) persuasive in courts of other nations.

Validity of EU and National Laws

The discretion of national courts to refer European law questions to the Court of Justice is largely removed whenever the question is one of the *invalidity* (not interpretation) of regional law. The Court of Justice has ruled that national courts cannot determine the invalidity of a European legal measure. The Court reasoned that divergent invalidity determinations could place the unity of the European legal order in jeopardy and detract from the general principle of legal certainty. However, national courts can declare regional legislation valid and proceed accordingly.

There is a dispute as to whether the European Court can pronounce without request upon the effects of an invalid measure, e.g., whether monies paid previously can be recovered. The Court asserts the power to spell out the consequences of its invalidity rulings under Article 234. It draws upon the analogy to Article 231 of the Treaty of Rome which conveys to the ECJ the power to determine the effects of decisions made in the context of Article 230 challenges to Council, Commission, Parliamentary or other action. The highest French courts are split as to the duty to follow the Court's Article 234 rulings on the consequences of invalid regional law. The Cour de Cassation adheres, while the Conseil d'Etat rejects. The Conseil d'Etat limits adherence to ECJ rulings to the scope of the questions posed by the national courts. The Court's rulings on repayment have been treated as gratuitous and uncontrolling since not requested. This dispute illustrates, more generally, the distinct tendency on the part of the European Court not to see itself confined by the limits of the questions posed by national forums under Article 234. Rarely, however, has such a hostile national response been received upon delivery of the ruling.

On questions of the validity of *national* laws under the European legal regime, the lower courts retain complete discretion to use the Article 234 reference procedures, or to immediately set aside national laws under the supremacy doctrine. See Chapter 2. Genuine disputes as to the compatibility of the national law of another member state may be referred to the European Court under Article 234. The Court will provide criteria for interpreting regional law so as to enable the referring court to solve the legal problem it faces. For example, in one decision on reference from a German court, by implication the European Court suggested that an Italian law conflicted with Directive 76/768 on cosmetics. Nevertheless, the Court's preliminary ruling jurisdiction cannot be invoked through "sham litigation" where there is no genuine dispute before the national court, only a desire to challenge the validity of national law. Purely hypothetical questions, and questions the ECJ believes are not connected to the underlying dispute, will not be answered by Court when responding under Article 234. The Court of Justice has also begun to reject Article 234 references that fail to provide adequate factual and legal information to enable it to respond.

In the early years, lower courts and tribunals in the member states hesitated to invoke the preliminary ruling procedure of Article 234. In some cases, this was a matter of ignorance, in others a matter of national pride. Over the years, Article 234 references of legal issues have risen dramatically. Today, they amount to about half of the Court of Justice's caseload, although this may decline once the CFI begins hearing preliminary rulings as authorized by the Treaty of Nice (2003). Article 234 references are undertaken not only out of need for advice, but also a growing sense of judicial cooperation. Absent such cooperation, there is great risk that different interpretations of European law would proliferate among member state forums.

Mandatory References

For the lower courts, Article 234 references are discretionary. For courts of last resort (no appeal as a matter of right), Article 234 *requires* a reference to the European Court except in interlocutory proceedings. This requirement insures that the European Court will have the last and supreme word. Thus, if a litigant is willing to exhaust his or her national judicial remedies, access to the European Court is supposed to be guaranteed. In most instances, this is exactly what happens. In others, the doctrine of "acte clair" has been invoked so as to avoid mandatory Article 234 references.

ACTE CLAIR

"Acte clair" originates in the French law. It posits that appeals need not be taken whenever the law and result in the case at hand are clear. Appeals in such circumstances are wasteful of judicial and litigant time and energy. The problem in the European context, of course, is that differences of opinion as to the clarity of regional law will often exist. If abused by national courts of last resort, acte clair could break rather than occasionally remove the linchpin of Article 234.

Entreprises Garoche Case

The *Entreprises Garoche* case provides a good example of French invocation of acte clair so as to totally avoid an Article 234 reference. A Dutch boat builder entered into a three-year exclusive dealing agreement with a French agent concerning France, Belgium, Switzerland, Monaco and Corsica. The Dutch builder undertook to refrain from selling in these territories directly or indirectly through agents. Shortly thereafter he sold two boats through an Italian dealer to two customers domiciled in Monaco. The French agent sued for breach of the exclusive dealing contract. The Tribunal de Commerce de Paris awarded him damages.

The Cour d'Appel de Paris and then the Cour de Cassation held that the contract was void under Articles 81 of the Treaty of Rome and not subject (for lack of notification to the Commission) to individual exemption under Article 81(3). Furthermore, the contract was outside the protection afforded by group exemption Regulation 67/67 because the isolation of national markets from other distributors resulted in high prices being charged by the French agent and hence did not allow consumers "a fair share of the resulting benefit". Thus the principle of the illegality under Article 81(1) of absolute territorial protection clauses prevailed. See Chapter 7. Moreover, the direct effect of European competition law in the French courts was not in doubt. The Dutch builder could rely on it as a matter of right.

None of these three French courts found it necessary to refer any of the issues in *Entreprises Garoche* to the European Court of Justice. Both the

Tribunal de Commerce and the Cour d'Appel invoked the acte clair doctrine while noting that their decisions were subject to appeal and hence not mandatorily referable. The Cour de Cassation, from which no appeal lies under the French legal system, agreed that the dispute was fundamentally centered on an interpretation of Article 3 of Regulation 67/67. That Regulation was clear to the highest French court in light of a 1971 Court of Justice opinion dealing with it. Consequently a "fresh interpretation" by way of reference in 1973 to the European Court was not required. Although it is difficult to criticize the actual results of the *Garoche* case in the French courts, their application of acte clair illustrates how dependent European law is on national courts and national legal principles.

CILFIT Case

Despite an initial annoyance at French invocations of acte clair, courts in other member states soon became converts. By 1982, when the European Court ruled definitively on the validity of this practice, it was faced with widespread but not particularly abusive utilization of acte clair. In *CILFIT,* the Italian Corte Suprema di Cassazione made a mandatory referral of the acte clair issue to the European Court. That is to say, the question it posed to the Court of Justice was whether it was absolutely obliged to refer all issues of interpretation of European law to the Court. The Court deferentially incorporated acte clair into European law as a gloss on the otherwise straightforward language of Article 234. In doing so, however, it was able to spell out the terms and conditions for its invocation:

"The correct application of Community law may be so obvious as to leave no scope for any reasonable doubt as to the manner in which the question raised is to be resolved. Before it comes to the conclusion that such is the case, the national court or tribunal must be convinced that the matter is equally obvious to the courts of the other Member States and to the Court of Justice. Only if those conditions are satisfied may the national court or tribunal refrain from submitting the question to the Court of Justice and take upon itself the responsibility for resolving it. . . .

It must be borne in mind that Community legislation is drafted in several languages and that the different language versions are all equally authentic. An interpretation of a provision of Community law thus involves a comparison of the different language versions. . . . Even where the different language versions are entirely in accord with one another, Community law uses terminology which is peculiar to it. Furthermore, it must be emphasized that legal concepts do not necessarily have the same meaning in Community law and in the law of the various Member States." *CILFIT v. Ministro della Santa* (1982) Eur. Comm.Rep. 3415.

MULTIPLE OFFICIAL LANGUAGES

In *CILFIT,* the Court of Justice issued a reminder of the problems of language in interpreting European law. The Coal and Steel Treaty sought to avoid these problems by making French the only official language of that treaty. Once fully enlarged, there will be over twenty working languages within the Common Market. Each working language can be consulted on questions of interpretation. However, with Treaty of Rome terms (such as Article 234) it is important to remember that English was *not* an official language prior to 1973 when the British joined. Thus, with reference to older legal documents *and* the Treaty of Rome, the French, German, Dutch or Italian versions are arguably more authoritative. The French version is considered the most authoritative of all because the Treaty of Rome was originally drafted in French. At a minimum, reference to different versions will promote greater understanding of the law. Attorneys practicing European law routinely consult different language versions of regulations, directives, decisions and treaties.

The European Court of Justice, when confronted with linguistic difficulties, has stressed the need to reconcile different official texts without giving preference to any one language. Difficulties of this kind are minimized in the foreign policy arena by using only English and French in the European Council. To the same effect, in Court of Justice or Court of

First Instance proceedings, the plaintiff generally gets to choose the official language of the case unless the defendant is from or is a member state (in which case the language of that member state prevails). When Article 234 proceedings are involved, the language of the nation whose court or tribunal is making the reference is official. The official language of the case is used in the pleadings, documents and oral hearings.

The Court's decision will be published in all working languages but only the language of the case is authentic. By custom, French is the internal working language of the Court of Justice. This means that judgments are debated and drafted in French. All other versions are translations, even when French is not the language of the case. Parliament, the Commission and the Court in public session, on the other hand, are a veritable babble of languages with simultaneous translations occurring. There are over 200 different possible pairs of official languages.

ARTICLES 230 AND 232—CHALLENGING REGIONAL INSTITUTIONS

In *CILFIT*, the Court of Justice also warned against the transferability of legal concepts. Article 230 of the Treaty of Rome provides a good example of these kinds of problems.

Article 230 gives the Court the power to review the legality of acts of the EU Council of ministers (but not the European Council), the European Commission, European Central Bank, acts jointly undertaken by the Parliament and EU Council, and acts of Parliament intended to produce legal effects on third parties. In unusual circumstances, individual acts of Parliament may also be challenged. Acts which are merely preparatory, such as the commencement of a competition law investigation by the Commission, cannot be challenged. To be challengeable, the "legal interests" of those under investigation must have been affected. Member states, the Commission or EU Council, and directly concerned individuals may challenge regulations, directives or enforcement decisions on specified grounds. Prior to the Maastricht Treaty on European Union, Parliament had no express authority to challenge Council or Commission action under Article 230. Now it and the European Central Bank may make such challenges for the purpose of protecting their prerogatives. No challenges may be brought against Council or Commission recommendations or opinions, but "soft" legal instruments (communications, instructions) that impose legal burdens or obligations can be challenged.

Challenging Acts

There are four grounds for challenging (often called "appealing") acts of European institutions. These are specified in Article 230 and originate in French administrative law governing "actions en recours pour excès de pouvoir." These grounds do not apply to challenges under Article 232, which concern failures to act as required by the Treaty of Rome ("actions en carence"). The four grounds are:

(1) lack of competence (i.e., *ultra vires,* or lack of jurisdiction or authority to act);

(2) infringement of an essential procedure ("administrative due process");

(3) infringement of the Treaty of Rome or any related rule of law (including general principles of law and international law); and

(4) misuse of powers.

Each of these grounds for challenging acts or failures to act has been extensively and uniquely developed in the jurisprudence of the European Court. For example, the term "misuse of powers" in Article 230 originated in the French administrative law concept of *détournement de pouvoir.*

Research on and an understanding of French administrative law thus becomes important to Article 230. Misuse of powers is a term of art in British administrative law which is narrower than the U.S. concept of abuse of administrative discretion. The original French concept is generally limited to situations in which public institutions or personnel use their powers for personal benefit, such as to favor a relative or for financial gain. Thus the concept of détournement de pouvoir does not transfer easily from French into British or United States law and language. Moreover, as *CILFIT* suggests, the Court of Justice is entirely free to develop its own doctrine in this area independent of its French origins.

Article 230 litigation must be brought within two months of the publication of the act that is being challenged or its notification to the appellant (in the absence of notice, two months from the day when that person had knowledge of it). Article 231 authorizes the Court to declare acts of institutions null and void if the appeal is well founded. This explains why Article 230 litigation is sometimes referred to as "actions for annulment." Regulations may be partially or fully annulled, or retain validity until replaced, at the Court's discretion. Article 230 cannot be used to challenge the validity of national legislation.

Challenging Failures to Act

Challenges for failure to act under Article 232 can only be brought if the relevant European institution has first been called upon to act, and only if it fails to "define its position" within two months thereafter. This definition is not necessarily an act that can itself be challenged under Article 230. The challenge for failure to act may then be brought in two additional months provided the institution's duty to act was owed to the plaintiff. If an Article 232 challenge is well founded, Article 233 in essence authorizes the Court to order action by the institution. In both Article 230 and 232 litigation, Article 231 imposes a duty on the regional institution to "take the necessary measures to comply with the judgment of the Court of Justice."

STANDING TO CHALLENGE REGIONAL INSTITUTIONS, PLEAS OF ILLEGALITY

Standing Issues

One limitation on Article 230 actions before the Court concerns the appeal rights of natural and legal persons. Such persons may only challenge decisions addressed to them, or regulations or decisions addressed to others which are of "direct and individual concern" to them. The Court has narrowly construed the concept of "directly concerned individuals" so as to effectively limit the number of private challenges capable of being raised under Article 230. However, in the competition law area where private interests are at stake when individual exemptions are issued by the Commission (see Chapter 7), the Court has been more liberal in its allowance of challenges by concerned third parties. Jurisdiction to hear challenges by private parties to Commission actions in the competition field has been transferred since 1989 to the Court of First Instance. The selectively liberal approach to Article 230 standing has also been followed regarding Commission decisions on antidumping duties, internal state aids, countervailable subsidies, and illicit commercial practices of non-member nations. See Chapter 6.

Article 232 governs the failure of a European institution to undertake actions required by the Treaty of Rome or other regional law. Actions by individuals and enterprises under Article 232 challenge the failure to address an act to the appellant. They cannot be used to compel discretionary Commission acts, such as Article 226 prosecutions of member states or competition law prosecutions of anticompetitive practices.

Pleas of Illegality

The expiration of the two months period for challenges to acts under Article 230 is not a firm statute of limitations. Article 241 allows any party to a proceeding where a regulation is in issue to plead the grounds for challenge specified in Article 230 in order to claim its inapplicability before the Court of Justice. This means, as a practical matter, that regulations can be challenged at any time by what is called a "plea of illegality." Moreover, the European Court has extended this plea to directives, decisions and other acts of European institutions. Private parties may thus wait until the implementation of regional law is of immediate concern to them without losing an ability to test the legality of that law. Pleas of illegality are frequently made in torts and contracts litigation, and can be made before national courts and tribunals which must refer such issues to the Court of Justice. Pleas of illegality are not allowed if the complainant had standing to challenge the act under Article 230 but failed to do so in a timely manner. Under this approach, it is unclear whether member states can plea illegality since they always have Article 230 standing.

International Litigation

Articles 230 and 232 have spawned an interesting series of European institutional litigations. In these cases, the Council, Commission and Parliament end up suing each other before the European Court of Justice. These suits reflect the struggle for power and influence among these institutions. One major limitation upon them was the absence until 2003 of a general authority for Parliamentary suits under Article 230 against Council or Commission acts.

The Parliament is authorized by the Treaty of Rome to file Article 232 suits when the Council or Commission has failed to act. The Parliament successfully sued the Council over its failure to act in accordance with Treaty obligations to implement a Common Transport Policy. The Council in turn has successfully sued the Parliament for excessive budgetary allocations. The Commission has challenged the Council frequently before the European Court. Some of its most important victories concern the proper "legal basis" for legislation and international agreements. See Chapter 2.

Articles 230 and 232 also provide the member states with the means to challenge the Commission. This is the reverse of the type of litigation that flows from Article 226 prosecutions of member states by the Commission. The Council can likewise be challenged by the member states under Articles 230 and 232. Member state challenges of legislative acts by the Council seem likely to rise as more qualified majority voting occurs and the minority seeks legal redress. See Chapter 2.

ARTICLE 226—PROSECUTIONS OF MEMBER STATES

Article 226 authorizes the Commission (alone) to bring an action before the Court of Justice against member states that have failed to fulfill their obligations under the Treaty of Rome. This authority is reinforced by some basic normative rules of the Treaty. In Article 10, the member states undertake to adopt "all appropriate measures" to ensure the fulfillment of obligations arising out of the Treaty of Rome or resulting from action taken by regional institutions. They "shall facilitate" achievement of its tasks and "shall abstain" from jeopardizing its objectives. These fundamental principles have frequently been the subject of litigation as the Commission seeks to enforce member state duties under European law. Although it has not yet done so, it appears that the Commission could even prosecute a member state *court* for failure to fulfill its Treaty obligations (e.g., mandatory Article 234 references). Government passivity in the face of private conduct (angry French farmer blockades) creating obstacles to internal trade has been successfully prosecuted. Informal promises to comply with EU rules are insufficient to avoid prosecution.

The Commission's prosecutorial powers under Article 226 must be distinguished from its ability in selected other circumstances to "directly" file actions against member states before the Court of Justice. Such direct actions do not involve the lengthy procedures described below in connection with Article 226 prosecutions. The Commission is authorized to sue the member states "directly" when they infringe regional rules on government subsidies to enterprises (see Chapter 5). This can also be done when the member states "improperly" invoke Article 30 exceptions to single market legislation adopted by qualified majority voting in the Council of Ministers (see Chapter 4).

Procedures and Penalties

Prior to commencing any Article 226 prosecutions before the Court of Justice, the Commission first delivers notice and the member state may submit a reply. Hundreds of such infringement notices are issued annually. The next stage involves issuance by the Commission of a reasoned opinion setting time limits for compliance. These time limits must be reasonable. The member state can submit a reply if it wishes. When a member state claims to have conformed to the opinion within the stipulated time limits, the burden of proof shifts to the Commission to prove otherwise. Negotiations may ensue at any time, and settlements frequently result. Almost 80 percent of all formal proceedings under Article 226 are settled.

If no settlement is reached, the Commission commences suit before the Court of Justice. Compliance after this point does not moot or remove the suit. The most common type of Article 226 enforcement action actually filed with the Court of Justice concerns member state failures to implement directives. Constitutional, political or legal problems are unacceptable excuses for such failures. Nor is the failure of other member states to implement the directive. All Article 226 prosecutions are discretionary with the Commission and cannot be forced by individual complaints.

Article 228 specifically requires member states to take the measures necessary to remedy failures identified by the Court in Article 226 proceedings. Prior to 1993, there were no obvious means by which the Court could enforce its judgments under Article 226 against member states. This contrasted with the power of the Court and the Commission in some areas of law to levy fines and penalties against individuals and corporations. Such fines and penalties can be collected in judgments enforced in the national courts. To compel a member state to follow European law, the Commission had little alternative but to bring yet another enforcement proceeding for determination before the Court. It actually did this on occasion. However, the Maastricht Treaty on European Union authorized the ECJ to levy fines and penalties against member states that do not take the measures necessary to remedy their Treaty of Rome failures, and this has occurred. Private litigants may also remedy member state failures, functioning in effect as attorneys general of regional law.

The unwillingness of member states to carry out Court rulings under Article 226 is a problem. It could test the very fabric of the Rome Treaty. In 2002, for example, the Commission commenced 1604 infringement proceedings against member states. An additional enforcement option would be to allow the Court to authorize the withholding of European subsidies and benefits from non-conforming states. Sanctions of this kind were possible under the Coal and Steel Treaty by joint Commission and Council action.

Article 239 allows member states to submit (by special agreement) disputes concerning the Treaty of Rome to the European Court. In Article 292, the member states have agreed not to submit such disputes to any method of settlement other than those of the Treaty. Article 227 authorizes member states to prosecute each other before the European Court for failure to fulfill Treaty obligations. For diplomatic and institutional reasons, these options are almost never pursued. The preferred approach is to persuasively complain to the Commission and then allow it to commence an Article 226 prosecution. Article 227 supports this approach by mandating a cooling off period of three months during which the Commission considers the arguments of both member states and issues a reasoned opinion.

CONTRACT AND TORT LITIGATION— COURT OF FIRST INSTANCE

Article 281 of the Treaty of Rome provides that the European Community is a legal person. As such, it can sue and be sued like most corporations or governments. These disputes can involve employees of the Community, parties with whom it has contracted and those who are victims of its negligence or other tortious behavior.

The Treaty of Rome conveys exclusive jurisdiction to the Court of Justice over employment and non-contractual liability (torts) disputes. It also can function as an arbitrator pursuant to dispute settlement clauses of contracts. Contract disputes involving the Community may otherwise be entertained in the national courts. Its contractual liability is governed by the law applicable to the contract in question.

Court of First Instance

Much of the work of the Court of Justice in employment and non-contractual liability litigation is now handled by the European Court of First Instance (CFI). This court was authorized by 1987 Single European Act amendments to the Treaty of Rome found in Article 225. The CFI has historically been "attached" to the European Court of Justice. Its general jurisdiction now extends to most EU litigation, including since the Treaty of Nice, preliminary rulings. However, the Court of First Instance does not hear Article 226 prosecutions of member states by the Commission, nor Article 230 or 232 challenges to EU institutional acts or failures to act when these are initiated by member states or regional institutions. It can hear such challenges and related "pleas of illegality" when they are privately initiated, for example in the business competition law area (see Chapter 7).

The CFI has additionally been granted jurisdiction over antidumping and countervailing duty trade law matters, and Community trademark disputes arising out of the Office for Harmonization in the Internal Market (OHIM). For example, Wrigley was denied registration of its Doublemint trademark because it described one of the product's common characteristics, a ruling upheld by the court. It is widely perceived that the CFI is now overloaded, and the Nice Treaty anticipates an offloading of staff and perhaps other areas to specialized "judicial panels," for which the CFI would function as an appeals court.

The purpose, in general, behind creation of the Court of First Instance (CFI) was to relieve the Court of Justice of some of its caseload. It commenced doing this in November of 1989. However, there is a right of appeal on points of law from the CFI to the Court of Justice. Article 51 of the Council Decision establishing the CFI indicates that such appeals lie on the grounds of lack of competence, procedural failures that adversely affect the appellants' interests, and infringement of European law by the CFI. Any failure by the CFI to follow prior ECJ decisions could amount to such an infringement. In addition, the Treaty of Nice amendments to Article 225 specify that CFI preliminary rulings posing a serious risk to the unity or consistency of Community law may be reviewed by the ECJ. To distinguish between the judgments of these courts, some law reporters now prefix Court of Justice case numbers with a "C" (Case C–213/89) (Court) and Court of First Instance cases with a "T" (Case T–81/90) (Tribunal). In the official European Court Reports, ECJ judgment page numbers are preceded by "I-," while CFI judgment are preceded by "II-."

Non-Contractual Liability

The Court of First Instance is partially heir to an interesting body of law on non-contractual (torts) liability created by the Court of Justice. In this area, the Court's role as a lawmaker was fully anticipated by the Treaty of Rome. Article 288 provides that the non-contractual liability of the Community is governed by the "general principles common to the laws of the member states." Under these principles, the Community is obliged to "make good any damage caused by its institutions or servants in the performance of their duties." For example, the negligent disclosure by the Commission of the identity of an informant who was a former employee of a company subject to competition law sanctions was an actionable tort. In this case, a Swiss informant was arrested, held in solitary confinement, interrogated and convicted under Swiss law for economic espionage. While in prison, his wife was interrogated by Swiss police officers and then committed suicide.

The European Court of Justice, and now the Court of First Instance when damages are sought in litigation properly before it, has had to determine

just what general principles of non-contractual liability are common to the laws of the member states.
At first, of course, there were only six civil law
states to consider. Now there are fifteen, including
two common law jurisdictions. The Court of Justice
has ruled that Article 288 does not require adherence to the highest common denominator of liability
law in the member states. Rather, the Court's duty
is to track down in the national laws the elements
or measures necessary to create liability principles
which are fair and viable. Such principles can include no-fault under the EC and EURATOM treaties.

It is now generally recognized that the Community is liable in non-contractual cases whenever its
tortious conduct causes actual damages. Such conduct includes faults of its officers and agents committed within the scope of their duties, including
negligence, bad faith and intentional misconduct.
Drawing from French administrative law, the Court
has also recognized torts resembling "faute de service." These liabilities occur when the Community
fails to function in the reasonably efficient manner
expected of a well run government even if such a
fault cannot be traced to negligence or misconduct
by specific officials.

Tortious conduct giving rise to liability includes
unlawful legal measures, e.g. directives or regulations, and unlawful failures to adopt such measures.
The "plea of illegality" is used to challenge such
activities. At first, the Court of Justice held that

damages actions on these bases could only be pursued if successful challenges had been previously undertaken under Article 230 or 232. In a good demonstration of its willingness to reverse itself, the Court has since held the opposite. Similarly, private parties need not challenge the validity of regional acts in national litigation prior to seeking damages relief before the Court. Here again the Court of Justice reversed its initial ruling to the contrary in the interest of the "proper administration of justice . . . and procedural efficiency."

Nevertheless, the chances of obtaining individual damages relief for European legislative acts are not great. The Court has limited this possibility to manifest and grave disregard by regional institutions of the limits of their powers in breach of superior rules of law protecting individuals. This is known as the *"Schöppenstedt* formula." And when European directives are implemented at the national level in ways which cause damages, national remedies (if available and effective) must first be pursued. But directives that partly harmonize an area of law intended for total harmonization are not actionable even if discriminatory.

JUDICIAL PRACTICE AND PROCEDURE

The structure and procedures of the European Court of Justice (ECJ) and the Court of First Instance (CFI) are quite similar. Each presently has, for example, 25 (27 in 2007) judges who serve six-year renewable terms upon appointment by the member states acting in common accord. There is one judge from each member state. The Court of First Instance does not, however, have Advocates–General appointed to it, although members of the Court may serve in that role. Moreover, the CFI only sits in chambers of one to three to five judges. The Court of Justice is also divided into chambers, but may sit en banc or as a "grand chamber" of 11 judges when cases are brought before it by member states or regional institutions, and in many Article 234 preliminary rulings. Some case reporters now identify the Court's opinions by chamber number.

To an American, the Court's most distinguishing features are its emphasis on written (versus oral) procedures, the dominance of the Court (not the parties) over development of the evidence, and the absence of dissenting opinions.

Proceedings

The Protocol on the Statute of the Court of Justice annexed to the Treaty of Rome and the Court's Rules of Procedure (approved by the Council) establish a two-part proceeding. The written part commences with an application to the Court's registrar and designation of an agent or legal representative. This designation must occur. In other words, litigants may not represent themselves before the Court. Any lawyer entitled to practice before a national court of a member state may act before the Court of Justice or Court of First Instance. The application serves as a "complaint" for notice purposes and thereby limits (in most cases) the issues and evidence that can be raised in the proceeding. Its filing also triggers the assignment of a reporting judge and an Advocate–General to the case. The fact of the application and a summary of the issues presented is published in the Official Journal.

The application is also sent to the respondent who has one month to file a written "defense." Plaintiff may then reply, to which the defendant may submit a rejoinder. All of these written submissions to the court resemble full evidentiary and legal briefs more than pleadings. When the Article 234 preliminary ruling procedure is being used, the parties, member states, the Commission and (where appropriate) the Council may submit written briefs to the Court. The Parliament does not appear to have this right of submission. In general, the member states and the regional institutions (including Parliament) always have a right to intervene in cases before the Court. Individuals and enterprises with an interest in the litigation have the same right. Trade and professional associations, consumer groups and unions have been particularly active as intervenors.

At the discretion of the Court, a preliminary inquiry may be held. The Court (typically acting through the reporting judge) can pose questions to the litigants. The role of a court in posing questions is part of the civil law tradition which predominates on the Court. It is a procedure that most common law students familiar with a more adversarial system will find a bit unusual. The Court also has the power to examine witnesses, call experts and generally develop the evidence before it. Limited rights of cross-examination are allowed to counsel when this occurs.

The second part of the proceeding before the Court is oral. The Court first hears the views of the reporting judge in charge of the case and then counsel for both sides. At the end of the oral procedure, the Court of Justice hears the Advocate–General, a special lawyer employed to analyze and evaluate all cases before the Court and give public opinions on the proper result under European law. Americans are typically unfamiliar with the role of an Advocate–General since there is no parallel in United States procedure. The closest parallel is the French Commissaire du Gouvernement at the Conseil d'Etat. The Advocate–General does not represent anyone and is a kind of permanent *amicus curiae* on behalf of justice.

There are presently eight Advocates–General (AG) appointed for six-year terms to the Court of Justice by the member states acting in common accord. Four of the AG come from the largest member states, and the others "represent" the remaining states. Their opinions are often much more informative than those of the Court in any given case. Whereas the Advocate–General is willing to spin out various hypotheticals and consider the broader ramifications of the legal principles at issue, the Court tends to write its opinions in a terse and summary fashion. It should be stressed that lawyers working with European law commonly use the opinions of the Advocate–General in their practice to forecast future developments and to better understand the judgments issued by the Court. Some of the most controversial cases in European law have involved instances where the Court has declined to agree with the opinions of the Advocate–General.

Judgments

The Court's judgment is drafted in French by the reporting judge. This draft is then discussed by the full court or chamber. The Court's decision is rendered *without dissent* in the language of the case. The absence of dissenting opinions shelters the judges from nationalistic pressures and critics. But it also makes analysis of opinions and projection of trends in the case law more difficult.

Costs are normally born by the losing party. Costs, for these purposes, generally include the Court's expenses, witnesses and experts, travel and subsistence of the parties to the Court's proceedings and reasonable legal fees. The Court's assessment powers on costs are wide and substantial litigation over costs has ensued. However, most litigation results in a settlement agreement as between the parties on payment of costs. The loser must also pay the costs of intervenors who have supported the successful litigant. The Court may make cash legal aid awards in appropriate cases and in the absence of national legal aid.

Litigation brought before the Court of Justice does not automatically suspend the act being challenged. It continues to operate pending the Court's decision. The Court (i.e., the President of the Court) may order suspension when it considers this necessary, along with any "interim measures." This is done only in exceptional circumstances of harm to the applicant. Pecuniary judgments against persons (not member states) are enforceable under the terms of Article 256. Once authenticated, the Court's judgment is enforced according to the ordinary judgment-creditor procedures of the member state where it is executed.

The Rules of Procedure for the Court of Justice permit revisions of judgments. No revision can occur more than ten years after judgment, and requests for revisions must be submitted within three months of the knowledge of new facts of decisive importance justifying revision. Such facts must have originally been unknown to both the Court and the litigant. Moreover, if the information could have been easily obtained during litigation, no revision of judgment will be allowed.

The Rules of Procedure also permit requests for interpretation of judgments when there are "difficulties" as to its meaning or scope. Such requests can be made by the parties or any Union institution with an interest in the judgment. They are granted when the effect of the judgment on the parties is uncertain, not when its consequences for others is at issue. Finally, third parties may seek reconsideration of judgments which will cause them damage. Requests for reconsideration must be made within two months of judgment, and the applicant must demonstrate no prior notice of the litigation.

JURISDICTION AND ENFORCEMENT OF CIVIL AND COMMERCIAL JUDGMENTS

The 1968 Jurisdiction and Enforcement of Judgments Convention (Brussels Convention) regulates jurisdiction among the member states and facilitates enforcement of civil and commercial judgments of the courts of the member states in each others' courts. In other words, the Brussels Convention introduced "full faith and credit" principles to the Europe. Much of its substance is reproduced in the Lugano Convention on Jurisdiction and Enforcement of Judgments in Civil and Commercial Matters (1988). The Lugano Convention extends these principles to all ratifying EFTA countries, such as Switzerland.

The Brussels Convention was converted for all but Denmark from an international agreement into legislation by Council Regulation 44/2001. A number of amendments were made at that time. In addition, Regulation 1348/2000 establishes speedy and reliable means for service of civil or commercial process. Regulation 1206/2001 facilitates the cross-border taking of evidence in civil and commercial matters. These regulations take the 1965 and 1970 Hague Conventions as their inspirations.

Jurisdiction

It is important to remember that the Brussels Convention and Regulation 44/2001 govern jurisdiction as well as enforcement of national court judgments. This means, as a practical matter, that it applies from the outset of the litigation once a jurisdictional challenge is raised and not just after judgment has been reached. Interpreting the Brussels Convention and the Regulation thus initially is the task of national trial courts. One elementary issue is the scope of applicability of the Convention to "civil and commercial matters." The Convention does not define these terms, except by exclusion. Most revenue, customs and administrative litigation along with legal status, capacity, matrimonial property, wills, succession, bankruptcy, social security and arbitration matters are not covered by the Brussels Convention. However, in 1998 a separate EU Convention on Jurisdiction, Recognition and Enforcement of Judgments in Matrimonial Matters was concluded. In 2000, Regulation 1346/2000 established jurisdictional, procedural and recognition rules for insolvency proceedings.

The ECJ has adopted an independent approach to the meaning of civil and commercial matters drawn from the Convention's purposes and the general principles of relevant law found in the member states. Special attention has been given to the original six civil law jurisdictions and their distinction between public and private law. Thus, most exercises of public authority by administrative bodies do not fall within the Convention. Marital dissolution property settlements are not covered by the Convention, but suits against estates by third parties over title to realty are. Employment contracts fall within its scope. The Convention's rules of jurisdiction thus mandate classification of the litigation in terms of the exclusions to civil and commercial matters.

The Brussels Convention and Regulation 44/2001 apply to all persons who are domiciled in a member state even if they are not citizens thereof. Thus, a United States-owned subsidiary incorporated in a European state benefits from the Convention whereas its parent would not. This coverage is important regarding the application of so-called "exorbitant jurisdiction" (below) and enforcement of judgments derived therefrom which will *not* apply to the subsidiary but will apply to the parent. Furthermore, generally speaking, defendants are to be sued where they are domiciled. The concept of "domicile" is thus critical. As the Convention does not define it, this is left to national law. National courts must be satisfied that jurisdiction is taken in accordance with the Convention. Co-defendants may be sued in nondomiciliary jurisdictions so closely connected that expediency requires suit to avoid the risk of irreconcilable judgment.

Persons may be sued in forums outside their state of domicile only if the Convention/Regulation so provides. It is unclear whether this approach effectively negates the British tradition of *forum non conveniens*. The Convention indicates that contract disputes are ordinarily to be litigated where the "place" of performance of the obligation occurs as determined by the law controlling the contract. This includes disputes as to the existence of contracts. Regulation 44/2001 replacing the Brussels Convention renders the place of performance of the obligation as that agreed or in the case of sale of goods, the place of delivery of goods, or in the case of provision of services, the place of provision. Special new rules govern employment contracts and favor employees. Torts are litigated at the place where the event or damage occurred. This has been construed to mean either the place where the defendant acted (e.g., manufactured a product) or where the injury was suffered.

The contract rules of the Brussels Convention do not apply to damages' actions between manufacturers and purchasers of their products with whom they have no privity of contract, even when the chain of sale is through wholly-owned subsidiaries. Such actions are ordinarily governed by the rules applicable to noncontractual (tortious) liability. If there are several contractual obligations in question, the national court must distinguish between principal and secondary obligations. In one case, a German architect sued a Dutch client over fees for plans for construction of buildings located in Germany. The principal obligation at issue was payment, not the plans or construction, which could be pursued in the courts of the Netherlands where the fees were to be paid. However, employment and consumer contracts come under special provisions designed to protect the weaker party. For example, the focus may be upon the place of work and not the place of the payment obligation when that would favor employees.

Civil damages or restitution flowing from criminal acts are to be litigated in the forum of the crime. Cases involving branches, agencies or other establishments may be pursued where located or in the domicile of the parent. The mere appointment of a commercial agent does not appear to trigger this rule. Suits for recovery of family and other support obligations ("maintenance") may be brought where the creditor is domiciled or "habitually resident," another undefined term. Additional Convention rules for jurisdiction which operate as alternatives to the general rule of suit where the defendant is domiciled have been created for trusts, admiralty, insurance (policy-holder's domicile option) and consumer contracts (consumer domicile). The rules on jurisdiction favor only ordinary consumers, not business consumers. Consumers, for these purposes, are economically weaker and less experienced private persons not engaged in commercial or professional activities. A German company trading currency futures could not, for example, benefit from the consumer domicile option of the Brussels Convention in its suit against a New York broker.

In a few areas, the Brussels Convention and Regulation 44/2001 convey exclusive jurisdiction to specified courts regardless of domicile or party agreement on choice of forum. These concern real property, company validity, public register, intellectual property validity, and enforcement of judgment litigations. As exceptions to the general rule, they have been narrowly construed. For example, although disputes between landlords and tenants (including unpaid rent) are treated as subject to exclusive jurisdictional rules under the Convention, disputes between tenants and subtenants are not.

The Convention/Regulation denies enforcement by European domiciliaries against European domiciliaries of certain judgments deemed to be based on "exorbitant jurisdiction" (e.g., jurisdiction based solely on citizenship or asset-based *in personam* jurisdiction). But, in a discriminatory measure of importance, it permits European domiciliaries to enforce judgments based upon exorbitant jurisdiction against non-European domiciliaries. Thus, a North American trader with assets somewhere in Europe could find itself at the wrong end of such discrimination. Other grounds for denial of enforcement of a judgment that is subject to the Brussels Convention include public policy, violation of defendant's procedural rights (service, notice), and the existence of an irreconcilable judgment of the enforcement court or another court (even one of a nation not party to the Brussels Convention).

Article 21 of the Brussels Convention provides that when the same cause of action is being litigated before the courts of two member states, the second court to be seised with litigation must stay or dismiss the proceeding pending resolution of the jurisdiction of the first court seised. This is the case even if the defendant is not domiciled in a member state, for example when the defendant is a U.S. corporation. Likewise, even courts designated as the parties chosen forum, must await the resolution of the first court's jurisdiction. It is in this sense that the doctrine of *forum non conveniens* is said to be precluded by the Brussels Convention.

Party Autonomy

Article 17 of the Brussels Convention affirms party autonomy to choose in writing a dispute settlement forum. This freedom does not apply regarding the insurance, consumer contract and exclusive jurisdiction areas. The Convention's affirmation of party autonomy will override national rules contrary to such autonomy, even in the employment area. Article 17 has been construed rather narrowly and party awareness and appreciation of the significance of choice of forum clauses must be proved. There must be, in other words, informed written consent. Company statute clauses adopted by shareholders designating jurisdiction can meet these criteria. However, when international trade contracts are involved, compliance with custom and practice is sufficient to enforce the choice of forum. The parties may avoid the stringency of Article 17 by designating determinative issues (e.g., place of performance of contracts) in their contract. The chosen place of performance will have jurisdiction. Such choices notwithstanding, if a party appears in another forum other than to contest jurisdiction, acquiescence to that forum will allow the litigation to proceed.

Article 17 permits parties from outside Europe to join in the selection of a member state court without fear of an exercise of jurisdiction elsewhere (e.g., the place of performance) in Europe. Article 17 also provides that if any judicial forum selection was concluded for the benefit of only one party, *that* party may sue elsewhere. The idea of permitting the sole beneficiary of what some might see as an adhesion clause to escape from its forum selection obligations has not been found compelling.

Recognition and Enforcement of Judgments

The regulatory regime governing jurisdiction established in the Convention/Regulation makes recognition and enforcement of subsequent civil and commercial judgments in Europe nearly automatic. This is true for money and non-money judgments, settlements and authentications. Moreover, recognition and enforcement of national court judgments falling within the jurisdictional scope of the Convention occurs regardless of the nationality or domicile of the parties. To facilitate use of the Convention, *full* legal aid in the enforcing state must be given to anyone who obtained full *or* partial legal aid in the source state. Recognition (but not enforcement) of the judgment is possible as soon as it is enforceable in its state of origin, even if appeals or further review are pending or available.

The *ex parte* enforcement procedures of the Convention/Regulation are exclusive and must be undertaken "without delay." This means that no collateral attack by the parties to the judgment may occur in another state and that the successful plaintiff must adhere to Convention procedures even if there are alternative means at less cost of obtaining enforcement. National courts are prohibited from charging a sliding scale of fees.

To obtain enforcement, the applicant need only provide supporting documentation on the original judgment and its enforceability under the law of the state of origin and, if required, translations. At this stage, the defendant is not summoned to appear. The decision on grant or denial of recognition and enforcement must be notified to the defendant and can be appealed by the losing party. The defendant may also appeal on points of law. But there is a presumption of recognition for judgments falling within the Convention which can only be rebutted on the grounds set out in Articles 27 and 28. The enforcing court may issue whatever interim protective relief measures it deems necessary to secure assets while appeals are pending even if such protection is not generally available under national law.

There are five grounds under Articles 27 and 28 (as modified by Regulation 44/2001) for refusing full or partial recognition and enforcement of judgments under the Brussels Convention. These are reviewed *ex parte* by the enforcing court, subject to appeal, and include:

- Public policy (but not as applied to Convention's jurisdictional rules).

- Protection of defendants' rights (e.g., service, opportunity to be heard and adequate time to prepare a defense).

- Irreconcilable conflict with an existing judgment in the enforcing state.

- Conflict with an earlier judgment in a state not party to the Convention.

- An agreement with a third party nation not to enforce judgments based upon exorbitant jurisdiction.

Since recognition and enforcement will be granted absent an *existing* judgment to the contrary in the enforcing state, the Convention essentially gives *res judicata* effect to civil and commercial judgments throughout Europe. But this does not mean that third party creditors interested in the enforcement because it might affect their own claims may not seek independent legal redress rescinding execution of an enforcement order under the Convention. Proper service of process under the law of the country of the defendant is a prerequisite to enforcement of a default commercial judgment even when the defendant becomes aware by other means of the lawsuit and could have taken advantage of procedural rights in the courts of the judgment country.

CHAPTER 4

FREE MOVEMENT

This chapter concerns the free movement of goods, trade in agriculture, transport and the free movement of persons, services and capital. The implementation of free movement rights has not always been easy. The Single European Act of 1987 amended the Treaty of Rome to establish the goal of creating a Europe genuinely "without internal frontiers," leaving customs and other controls solely to points of entry. The target for the completion of this task was the end of December 1992. Hundreds of new legislative acts were adopted in its pursuit, with substantial progress on all fronts.

FREE MOVEMENT OF GOODS

The free movement of goods within Europe is based upon the creation of a customs union. Under this union, the member states have eliminated customs duties among themselves. They have established a common customs tariff for their trade with the rest of the world. Quantitative restrictions (quotas) on trade between member states are also prohibited, except in emergency and other limited situations. The right of free movement applies to goods that originate in the Common Market *and* to those

137

that have lawfully entered it and are said to be in
"free circulation."

Measures of Equivalent Effect

The establishment of the customs union has been
a major accomplishment, though not without difficulties. The member states not only committed
themselves to the elimination of tariffs and quotas
on internal trade, but also to the elimination of
"measures of equivalent effect." The elastic legal
concept of measures of equivalent effect has been
interpreted broadly by the European Court of Justice and the Commission to prohibit a wide range of
trade restraints, such as administrative fees
charged at borders which are the equivalent of
tariffs. Charges of equivalent effect to a tariff must
be distinguished from internal taxes that are applicable to imported and domestic goods. The latter
must be levied in a nondiscriminatory manner (Article 90), while the former are prohibited entirely
(Articles 23, 25). There has been a considerable
amount of litigation over this distinction.

The elasticity of the concept of measures of an
equivalent effect is even more pronounced in the
Court's judgments relating to quotas. This jurisprudence draws upon an early Commission directive
(no longer applicable) of extraordinary scope. In this
directive (No. 70/50), the Commission undertook a
lengthy listing of practices that it considered illegal
measures of equivalent effect to quotas. It is still
occasionally referenced in Commission and Court of
Justice decisions. The directive's focus was on na-

tional rules that discriminate against imports or simply restrain internal trade.

Cassis Formula

This "effects test" soon found support from the ECJ. In the famous *Dassonville* case, the Court of Justice ruled that Belgium could not block the importation via France of Scotch whiskey lacking a British certificate of origin as required by Belgian customs law. The Court of Justice held that any national rule directly or indirectly, actually or potentially capable of hindering internal trade is generally forbidden as a measure of equivalent effect to a quota. However, *if* European law has not developed appropriate rules in the area concerned (here designations of origin), the member states may enact "reasonable" and "proportional" (no broader than necessary) regulations to ensure that the public is not harmed.

This is commonly called the *"Cassis* formula," after the "Cassis de Dijon" case, in which a German *minimum* alcoholic beverage rule was held unreasonable. Products meeting reasonable national criteria, the *Cassis* formula continues, may be freely traded. The *Cassis* formula is also the origin of the "mutual reciprocity" principle used in significant parts of the legislative campaign for a Europe without internal frontiers.

The *Cassis* decision suggests use of a Rule of Reason analysis for national fiscal regulations, public health measures, laws governing the fairness of commercial transactions and consumer protection. Environmental protection and occupational safety laws of the member states have been similarly treated. Under this approach, for example, a Danish "bottle bill" requiring use of only *approved* containers was unreasonable. However, the Danes' argument that a deposit and return system was environmentally necessary prevailed. This was a reasonable restraint on internal trade recognized by the Court under the *Cassis* formula for analyzing compelling state interests.

Under *Cassis,* national rules requiring country of origin or "foreign origin" labels have fallen as measures of effect equivalent to quotas. So have various restrictive national procurement laws, including a "voluntary" campaign to "Buy Irish." Minimum and maximum retail pricing controls can also run afoul of the Court's expansive interpretation of measures of equivalent effect. Compulsory patent licensing can amount to a measure of equivalent effect. Where demand for the patented product was satisfied by imports from another member state, the U.K. could not compulsorily require manufacturing within its jurisdiction. Member states may not impose linguistic labelling requirements so as to block trade and competition in foodstuffs. In one instance, a Belgian law requiring Dutch labels in Flemish areas was nullified as in conflict with the Treaty of Rome. These cases vividly illustrate the extent to which litigants are invoking the Treaty of Rome and the *Cassis* formula in attempts at overcoming commercially restrictive national laws.

There are cases which suggest that "cultural interests" may justify national restrictions on European trade. For example, British, French and Belgian bans on Sunday retail trading survived scrutiny under the *Cassis* formula. And British prohibitions of sales of sex articles, except by licensed sex shops, are compatible. However, national marketing laws (e.g., prohibiting sales below cost), when applied without discrimination (especially market access discrimination) as between imports and domestic products, are not considered to affect trade between the member states. In the remarkable *Keck* decision signaling a jurisprudential retreat, the ECJ held that marketing rules may not be challenged under the traditional *Cassis* formula. As to what constitutes "marketing rules," deceptive trade practices laws ordinarily fall outside the scope of *Keck*, while national laws regulating sale outlets and advertising of goods may be embraced.

In recent years, member state regulations capable of being characterized as governing "marketing modalities" or "selling arrangements" have sought shelter under *Keck*. For example, the French prohibition of televised advertising (intended to favor printed media) of the distribution of goods escaped the rule of reason analysis of *Cassis* in this manner, but the Swedish ban on magazine ads for alcoholic beverages did not since it discriminated against market access by imports. Some commentators see in *Keck* and its progeny an unarticulated attempt by the Court to take subsidiarity seriously. Others are just baffled by its newly found tolerance for trade distorting national marketing laws. But the Court of Justice has poignantly refused to extend *Keck* to the marketing of services.

The Court has made it clear that all of the Rule of Reason justifications for national regulatory laws are temporary. Adoption of Common Market legislation in any area would eliminate national authority to regulate trading conditions under *Dassonville, Cassis* and (presumably) *Keck*. All of these judicial mandates, none of which are specified in the Treaty of Rome, acutely demonstrate the powers the Court of Justice to expansively interpret the Treaty and rule on the validity under European law of national legislation affecting internal trade in goods.

ARTICLE 30 AND THE PROBLEM OF NONTARIFF TRADE BARRIERS

The provisions of the Treaty of Rome dealing with the establishment of the customs union do not adequately address the problem of nontariff trade barriers (NTBs). As in the world community, the major trade barrier within Europe has become NTBs. To some extent, in the absence of a harmonizing directive completely occupying the field, this is authorized. Article 30 of the Treaty of Rome permits national restraints on imports and exports justified on the grounds of:

(1) public morality, public policy ("ordre public") or public security;

(2) the protection of health and life of humans, animals or plants;

(3) the protection of national treasures possessing artistic, historical or archeological value; and

(4) the protection of industrial or commercial property.

Article 30 amounts, within certain limits, to an authorization of nontariff trade barriers among the EU nations. This "public interest" authorization exists in addition to but somewhat overlaps with the Rule of Reason exception formulated under Article 28 in *Dassonville* and *Cassis* (above). However, in a sentence much construed by the European Court of Justice, Article 30 continues with the following language: "Such prohibitions or restrictions shall not, however, constitute a means of arbitrary discrimination or a disguised restriction on trade between member states."

Case Law

In a wide range of decisions, the Court of Justice has interpreted Article 30 in a manner which generally limits the ability of member states to impose NTB barriers to internal trade. Britain, for example, may use its criminal law under the public morality exception to seize pornographic goods made in Holland that it outlaws, but not inflatable sex dolls from Germany which could be lawfully produced in the United Kingdom. Germany cannot stop the importation of beer (e.g., Heineken's from Holland) which fails to meet its "pure standards."

This case makes wonderful reading as the Germans, seeking to invoke the public health exception of Article 30, argue all manner of ills that may befall their populace if free trade in beer is allowed. Equally interesting have been the unsuccessful Italian health protection arguments against free trade in pasta made from common (not durum) wheat, and the similar failure of French standards' arguments against free trade in foie gras.

But a state may obtain whatever information it requires from importers to evaluate public health risks associated with food products containing additives that are freely traded elsewhere in the Common Market. This does not mean that an importer must prove the product healthful, rather that the member state seeking to bar the imports must have an objective reason for keeping them out of its market. Assuming such a reason exists, the trade restraint may not be disproportionate to the public health goal. A notable ECJ opinion invalidated a French public health ban on U.K. beef maintained after a Commission decision to return to free trade following the "mad cow" outbreak.

An unusual case under the public security exception contained in Article 30 involved Irish petroleum products' restraints. The Irish argued that oil is an exceptional product always triggering national security interests. Less expansively, the Court acknowledged that maintaining minimum oil supplies did fall within the ambit of Article 30. The public policy exception under Article 30 has been con-

strued along French lines (ordre public). Only genuine threats to fundamental societal interests are
covered. Consumer protection (though a legitimate
rationale for trade restraints under *Dassonville* and
Cassis), does not fall within the public policy exception of Article 30.

INTELLECTUAL PROPERTY RIGHTS AS EUROPEAN TRADE BARRIERS

A truly remarkably body of case law has developed around the authority granted national governments in Article 30 to protect industrial or commercial property by restraining imports and exports.
These cases run the full gamut from protection of
trademarks and copyrights to protection of patents
and know-how. There is a close link between this
body of case law and that developed under Article
81 concerning restraints on competition. See Chapter 7.

Trade restraints involving intellectual property
arise out of the fact that such rights are nationally
granted. Owners of intellectual property rights
within Europe are free under most traditional law
to block the unauthorized importation of goods into
national markets. There is thus a strong tendency
for national infringement lawsuits to serve as vehicles for the division for the Common Market. Although considerable energy has been spent by the
Commission on developing Common Market rights
that provide an alternative to national intellectual

property rights, some of these proposals have yet to be fully implemented. See Chapter 5.

Exhaustion Doctrine

The European Court of Justice has addressed these problems under Article 30 and generally resolved against the exercise of national intellectual property rights in ways which inhibit free internal trade. In many of these decisions, the Court acknowledges the existence of the right to block trade in infringing goods, but holds that the *exercise* of that right is subordinate to the Treaty of Rome. The Court has also fashioned a doctrine which treats national intellectual property rights as having been *exhausted* once the goods to which they apply are freely sold on the market. One of the few exceptions to this doctrine is broadcast performing rights which the Court considers incapable of exhaustion. Records, CDs, and cassettes embodying such rights are, however, subject to the exhaustion doctrine once released into the market. Such goods often end up in the hands of third parties who then ship them into another member state.

The practical effect of many of the rulings of the Court of Justice is to remove the ability of the owners of the relevant intellectual property rights to successfully pursue infringement actions in national courts. When intellectual property rights share a common origin and have been placed on goods by consent, as when a licensor authorizes their use in other countries, then infringement actions to protect against trade in the goods to which the rights apply are usually denied. This may not be the case, however, when voluntary trademark assignments that are not anticompetitive are involved. In such cases, the ECJ has demonstrated some concern for consumer confusion when trade in parallel goods occurs.

It is only when intellectual property rights do not share a common origin or the requisite consent is absent that they stand a chance of being upheld so as to stop trade in infringing products. Compulsory licensing of patents, for example, does not involve consensual marketing of products. Patent rights may therefore be used to block trade in goods produced under such a license. But careful repackaging and resale of goods subject to a common trademark may occur against the objections of the owner of the mark. And compulsory licensing cannot be conditioned upon import bans applicable to the beneficiary licensee. Such bans offend the free movement of goods law and unfairly create investment incentives.

Centrafarm Case

An excellent example of the application of the judicial doctrine developed by the Court of Justice in the intellectual property field under Article 30 can be found in the *Centrafarm* case. The United States pharmaceutical company, Sterling Drug, owned the British and Dutch patents and trademarks relating to "Negram." Subsidiaries of Sterling Drug in Britain and Holland had been respectively assigned the British and Dutch trademark rights to Negram. Owing in part to price controls in the UK, a substantial difference in cost for Negram emerged as between the two countries. Centrafarm was an independent Dutch importer of Negram from the UK and Germany. Sterling Drug and its subsidiaries brought infringement actions in the Dutch courts under their national patent and trademark rights seeking an injunction against Centrafarm's importation of Negram into The Netherlands.

The Court of Justice held that the intellectual property rights of Sterling Drug and its subsidiaries could not be exercised in a way which blocked trade in "parallel goods." In the Court's view, the exception established in Article 30 for the protection of industrial and commercial property covers only those rights that were specifically intended to be conveyed by the grant of national patents and trademarks. Blocking trade in parallel goods after they have been put on the market with the consent of a common owner, thus exhausting the rights in question, was not intended to be part of the package of benefits conveyed. If Sterling Drug succeeded, an arbitrary discrimination or disguised restriction on regional trade would be achieved in breach of the language which qualifies Article 30. Thus the European Court of Justice ruled in favor of the free movement of goods within the Common Market even when that negates clearly existing national legal remedies.

While the goal of creation of the Common Market can override national intellectual property rights where internal trade is concerned, these rights apply fully to the importation of goods (including gray market goods) from outside the Common Market. In *Silhouette*, for example, an Austrian manufacturer's trademark rights blocked imports of its sunglasses from Bulgaria. North American exporters of goods subject to rights owned by Europeans may therefore find entry challenged by infringement actions in national courts. On the other hand, Levi Strauss successfully cited *Silhouette* to keep low-price made in the USA Levi's out of the EU.

NTBS AND THE SINGLE MARKET

Nontariff trade barrier problems have been the principal focus of the campaign for a fully integrated Common Market. Many legislative acts have been adopted or are in progress which target NTB trade problems. There are basically two different methodologies being employed. When possible, a common European standard is adopted. For example, legislation on auto pollution requirements adopts this methodology. Products meeting these standards may be freely traded in the Common Market. Traditionally, this approach (called "harmonization") has required the formation of a consensus as to the appropriate level of protection.

Once adopted, harmonized standards must be followed. This approach can be deceptive, however. Some harmonization directives contain a list of options from which member states may choose when implementing those directives. In practice, this

leads to differentiated national laws on the same so-
called harmonized subject. Furthermore, in certain
areas (notably the environment and occupational
health and safety), the Treaty of Rome and certain
directives expressly indicate that member states
may adopt laws that are more demanding. The
result is, again, less than complete harmonization.

Under Article 95, added by the Single European
Act of 1987, most single market legislation was
adopted by qualified majority voting in the Council.
Notable exceptions requiring a unanimous vote included new laws on taxation, employment and free
movement of persons. However, if a measure is
adopted by a qualified majority, the public interest
exceptions to free internal trade specified in Article
30 apply. This may provide an escape clause for
member states that were outvoted in the Council on
single market legislation. Indeed, Article 95 extends
the scope of Article 30 to include "major needs"
relating to national protection of the working or
natural environments. The Commission must be
notified of any member state use of such an exception, which it or another member state can then
challenge directly before the European Court as an
"improper use." In doing so, the Commission need
not adhere to the lengthy procedures (see Chapter
3) used with Article 226 prosecutions of member
states.

Harmonization Principles

Many efforts at the harmonization of European
environmental, health and safety, standards and

certification, and related law have been undertaken. Nearly all of these are supposed to be based upon "high levels of protection." Some have criticized what they see as the "least common denominator" results of harmonization of national laws under the campaign for a Europe without internal frontiers. One example involves the safety of toys. Directive 88/378 permits toys to be sold throughout the Common Market if they satisfy "essential requirements." These requirements are broadly worded in terms of flammability, toxicity, etc. There are two ways to meet these requirements: (1) produce a toy in accordance with private CEN standards (drawn up by experts); or (2) produce a toy that otherwise meets the essential safety requirements. Local language labeling requirements necessary for purchaser comprehension have generally, though not always, been upheld.

The least common denominator criticism is also raised regarding the second legislative methodology utilized in the internal market campaign. The second approach is based on the *Cassis* principle of mutual reciprocity. Under this "new" minimalist approach, European legislation generally requires member states to recognize the standards laws of other member states and deem them acceptable for purposes of the operation of the Common Market. However, major legislation has been adopted in the area of professional services. By mutual recognition of vocational diplomas based upon at least three years of courses, virtually all professionals have now obtained legal rights to move freely in pursuit of their careers. This is a remarkable achievement.

PRODUCT STANDARDS

An important part of the battle against nontariff trade barriers (NTBs) in the European Union involves product testing and standards. More than half of the legislation involved in the single market campaign concerned such issues. Since 1969, there has been a standstill agreement among the EU states to avoid the introduction of new technical barriers to trade. A 1983 directive (No. 83/89) requires member states to notify the Commission of proposed new technical regulations and product standards. The Commission can enjoin the introduction of such national rules for up to one year if it believes that a Union standard should be developed, and failures to notify can invalidate national rules. The goal is to move from different sets of regulatory approvals to one unified Union system embodying essential requirements on health, safety, the environment and consumer protection. Goods that meet these essential requirements will bear an "CE mark" and can be freely traded. Manufacturers will self-certify their compliance with relevant EU standards. Design and production process standards generally follow the ISO 9000 series on quality management and assurance. Firms must maintain a technical file documenting compliance and produce the file upon request by national authorities.

Standards Bodies

Private regional standards bodies have been playing a critical role in the development of this system. These include the European Committee for Standardization (CEN), the European Committee for Electrotechnical Standardization (CENELEC), and the European Telecommunications Standards Institute (ETSI). Groups like these have been officially delegated the responsibility for creating thousands of technical product standards. They have been turning out some 150 common standards each year. For example, directives on the safety of toys, construction products and electromagnetic compatibility have been issued. These directives adopt the so-called "new approach" of setting broad, exclusive standards at the Union level which if voluntarily met guarantee access to every member state market. Under the "old approach", which still applies to most standards for processed foods, motor vehicles, chemicals and pharmaceuticals, EU legislation on standards is binding law. The technical specifications and testing protocols of these directives must be followed and (unlike the new approach) the member states may add requirements to them. Under either approach, goods meeting Union standards will bear a CE mark. North American producers have frequently complained that their ability to be heard by European standards' bodies is limited. They have had little influence on EU product standards to which they must conform in order to sell freely in the Common Market.

FREE MOVEMENT OF PEOPLE— EU CITIZENSHIP

There has been increasing attention on the creation of what it is called a "People's Europe." This focus is multidimensional. It includes traditional Free Movement Rights of Workers (below), the self-employed, and their families, and of professionals and others operating in the services sector. The "People's Europe" has been expanded to include general rights for nonworkers, such as students, the retired, and others to reside anywhere. The Maastricht Treaty on European Union formally introduced the idea of European citizenship and brought with it a selected bundle of civil rights. These include the right to run for office and vote wherever resident in local and European Parliament elections, and the right to be represented abroad diplomatically by other member state consular or embassy services. European Community passports have replaced national passports, and driving licenses have been standardized. In 2004, EU health insurance cards were introduced to facilitate access to "necessary" care when traveling in other member states.

Schengen Accord

Dismantling border controls over the free movement of people within Europe, a goal of the campaign for a Europe without internal frontiers, has not proven to be an easy task. The Benelux states, Germany, Italy, Spain, Greece, Portugal and France agreed to remove their internal frontier controls on people under the 1990 "Schengen Accord." This accord is the product of intergovernmental agreement, not regional legislation. As such, the Schengen Accord was an early harbinger of what is often called a "variable speed" Europe or "Europe á la carte." At this writing, only Ireland and the United Kingdom do not participate in the Accord. The ten new member states entering in 2004 will be transitioned into the Schengen Accord with the right of free movement for their peoples delayed until 2011.

The Schengen Accord covers such sensitive issues as visas, asylum, immigration, gun controls, extradition and police rights of "hot pursuit." The main points of contention were cross-border traffic of immigrants and criminals, especially terrorists and drug dealers. These issues were resolved largely by promises of greater intergovernmental cooperation. In December of 1990, for example, the Council reached agreement on a directive that will make drug money laundering a crime in all member states. In addition, the member states have reached agreement on an External Borders Convention covering mutual recognition of visas and a limited right of free movement for non-EU nationals legally resident in Europe. Substantial ratification of the Dublin Asylum Convention also promised greater uniformity in that area.

Justice and Home Affairs

One focus of the Maastricht Treaty on European Union of 1993, established as a separate "pillar" outside the Treaty of Rome, was cooperation on justice and home affairs. The member states committed their interior ministries to coordinate their laws on asylum, immigration, frontier controls, crime, customs, terrorism and drugs. Under the Amsterdam Treaty of 1999, much of the Schengen Accord and other European policies on visas, asylum, immigration and free movement of persons were brought under the Treaty of Rome (Title IV), subject to opt out rights for Denmark, Britain and Ireland. This transfer had the notable effect of conveying jurisdiction in these areas to the European Court of Justice. The separate pillar on justice and home affairs was essentially reduced to police and judicial cooperation in criminal matters (e.g., the EUROPOL Convention), but opened to the possibility of ECJ judicial review.

GENERAL RIGHTS OF RESIDENCE

A general right of free movement for purposes of residence throughout the Union has been recognized since 1990 and benefits students, retirees and the populace at large. This right should be distinguished from the free movement rights of workers. The chief concern about a general right of residence is coverage for health and social welfare purposes, and a possible run towards those states with more generous programs. Council Directive 90/364 extends a general right of residence to all member state nationals and their families (including cohabitants) provided they do not become a burden on the public finances of the host country. Spouses and dependent children (even those who are *not* nationals) are entitled to work in the country where the nonworking member state spouse has taken up residence. These principles also apply to employees and the self-employed who have retired.

All member state nationals and their families seeking to exercise their right of residence in another member state must demonstrate sufficient financial resources and health insurance coverage. "Sufficiency" for these purposes connotes resources in excess of the level which would trigger social assistance in the host state. Retired persons must prove that they receive a disability, retirement or old age pension meeting this criterion. Students have a general right of residence for educational purposes provided they can show sufficient resources and enrollment in the host state. The student's family may accompany him or her and work in that state. All general rights of residence are subject to exceptions based upon public policy, health or safety.

Students

Students seeking vocational training in another member state cannot be subjected to discriminatory tuition fees not charged to nationals. In one decision, the Court of Justice took a broad view of "vocational training" under Article 151 of the Treaty of Rome. Any form of education which prepares for qualification in a particular trade, profession or employment is included. This is the case regardless of age or the level of the training, and even if the study program involves some general education. A French national, for example, was therefore entitled to train in strip cartoon arts without paying special fees at a Belgian city academy.

Tens of thousands of students are now exchanged under the ERASMUS now SOCRATES program each year. It has been extended to students from EFTA and many Central European countries. The Rome Treaty was amended by the 1993 Maastricht Accord to authorize cooperative action and "incentive measures" on education, vocational training, youth, cultural and public health affairs. The Amsterdam Treaty of 1999 added employment incentives to this authority. These provisions explicitly rule out harmonization by regional mandate in these fields and thus reflect the growing trend toward "subsidiarity."

FREE MOVEMENT OF WORKERS, THE SELF–EMPLOYED AND THEIR FAMILIES

The foundations of the Treaty of Rome include the free movement of persons, services and capital. These are often referred to in economic literature as "factors of production." Their inclusion in the Treaty of Rome distinguishes the Treaty from others which merely create customs unions.

Freedom of movement for workers is secured in Article 39 and by an extensive range of legislative acts which have implemented this right. Whereas, for example, North Americans must obtain work permits in order to undertake employment within the Europe, this is not required of citizens of the member states nor Iceland, Liechtenstein and Norway under the European Economic Area treaty. They may seek employment on the same basis as nationals of the state where the job is located. In other words, workers from such countries enjoy "national treatment."

This right has caused renewed interest by North Americans in becoming "dual nationals." Irish and Italian "laws of return" ordinarily permit emigrants born in Europe *and* their children or grandchildren to obtain Irish and Italian citizenship. British subjects who are patrials may generally do likewise. Although the U.S. government discourages dual citizenship status for Americans, the benefits of being a European national under the Treaty of Rome make this status quite attractive. Dual nationals with one member state citizenship may not be denied their rights by another member state. For example, an Argentinian/Italian was entitled to reside and enter business in Spain.

Social Advantages

The right of expatriate European workers to bring their families, obtain social services, housing, education and pensions in a nondiscriminatory manner is all provided in a wealth of law on "social advantages." There is no regional social security system. Rather, European law assures equal treatment of claims made against national systems covering health care, old age, unemployment, taxation, housing, family benefits and workers' compensation.

The exercise of the right of free movement by workers cannot be subject to the issuance of restrictive residency or entrance permits. They can be required within a reasonable time to report their presence to the host member state. A valid identity card from their home state is all that is required to prove a worker's right to reside elsewhere. Part-time and probationary workers (such as teachers seeking licensure) are included, as are the unemployed who actively seek work. In one decision, the European Court of Justice even struck down a longstanding Greek law restricting ownership of land to Greeks as contrary to the free movement rights of the Treaty of Rome. In another widely known decision, free movement rights were extended to professional athletes.

In the early years, many Italian workers moved north into the factories of West Germany and to a lesser extent France as the rebuilding of the European economy took place. Membership was eagerly sought in later years by Greece, Portugal and Spain and more recently nations of Central Europe so as to acquire these rights for their expatriate workers. Prior to membership, such workers were subject to much less liberal national laws on guest workers. These national laws continue for the most part to govern the rights of the large number of Turkish and Slavic employees in Germany, North Africans in France and Commonwealth citizens in Britain. Special employment rights (but not national treatment) have been given to Turkish workers under the "Ankara Agreement", which acknowledges Turkey's associate status with the European Union.

Free Movement Exceptions

The only blanket exception to the regime of free movement of workers is established in Article 39(4) of the Treaty of Rome. Employment in the "public service" of member states is exempted. The public service, for these purposes, involves jobs with official authority, including the judiciary, the police, defense forces and tax inspectors. Licensed attorneys fall outside the public service, even though they may be required in order to litigate in national courts. Municipal positions are included when there is participation in the exercise of public power, which was the case for example in Brussels with the city architect but not city hospital nurses. Secondary school teachers are not part of the public service, and such positions are therefore open to competition, but may be subject to language requirements.

Member states may restrict the free movement of workers from other states on grounds of public policy (ordre public), public security or public health. These provisions have been litigated extensively. In a long series of decisions, the European Court has evolved rules which limit the power of member states to expel or deny admission to workers whose past conduct is objectionable. Only when that conduct is effectively combatted if engaged in by its own nationals may restraints on expatriate workers be applied. Public policy reasons for limiting the free movement rights of workers must be based on the existence of a genuine and serious threat affecting fundamental societal interests. Past criminal convictions, alone, are insufficient.

Reverse Discrimination

The Common Market law prohibiting discrimination against workers from member states does not reach national laws that discriminate against a country's own citizens regarding free movement and employment. In other words, "reverse discrimination" can occur when European law protects the rights of workers from other states but national law denies similar rights to workers of that nation. Conversely, when a worker has exercised the right to employment elsewhere in the region, he or she is entitled to rely on the Treaty of Rome upon returning home.

RIGHT OF ESTABLISHMENT— PROFESSIONALS

The right to go into business as a self-employed person in another member state is secured by Article 52 of the Treaty of Rome. This is known as the "right of establishment." Many entrepreneurs, for example, have used this right to open restaurants throughout the Common Market. Cuisine in Britain is thought by some to have greatly benefited from this freedom. The right of self-establishment carries with it nearly the same bundle of national treatment rights and exceptions associated with employed workers. It is also subject to the *Cassis* formula.

Implementation of the right of establishment for professionals is anticipated in Article 47 by the issuance of legislation mutually recognizing diplomas and national licenses. Medical doctors, dentists, veterinarians, architects and many others have benefited from these provisions and the substantial implementing law that now accompanies them. For example, the Council has adopted directives about freedom to supply services in the case of travel agents, tour operators, air brokers, freight forwarders, ship brokers, air cargo agents, shipping agents, and hairdressers. It has been relatively easy to deal with those professions (e.g., medicine and allied professions) in which diplomas and other evidence of formal qualification relate to equivalent competence in the same skill. It did, however, take 17 years to negotiate the directive on free movement of veterinarians. And litigation over the implementation of these directives continues. It took a Commission prosecution to remove the French requirement that doctors and dentists give up their home country professional registrations before being licensed in France.

Diploma Directives

Typically, European law on the right of establishment creates minimum professional training standards which, if met, will result in mutual recognition. Substantial variations in training may trigger special admissions requirements, such as time in practice, an adaptation period or an aptitude test. A major single market directive applies this approach to virtually all professionals receiving diplomas based upon a minimum of three years of study. A subsequent directive requires mutual recognition of certificates and diplomas awarded for less than three years study, which applies to master degrees (LLMs). Mutual recognition in this instance means that access is gained to host country professional bodies. This is different from the home country licensing method of mutual recognition used for banking, insurance and investment advisors. Even in the absence of such legislation, professional disqualification on grounds of nationality is prohibited.

LEGAL SERVICES

Considerable difficulty has been encountered in lifting restrictions within member states on the freedom to provide legal services. For example, within the legal profession there may be only a small amount of training or required knowledge held in common by a "lawyer" from a civil law jurisdiction (e.g., an avocat from France) and a "lawyer" from a common law jurisdiction (e.g., a solicitor from England). As a result, the initial directive relating to lawyers' services took a delicate approach to the question of freedom to temporarily provide legal services in other member states and stopped short of dealing with a right of establishment.

This 1977 directive allows a lawyer from one member state, under that lawyer's national title (e.g., abogado, rechtsanwalt, barrister), to provide services in other member states. This includes the right to appear in court without local co-counsel unless representation by counsel is mandatory under national laws. Once retained, a local lawyer need not actually conduct the litigation. It is sufficient that the local attorney is retained to "act in conjunction with" the proceedings. But the legal services directive cannot be used so as to circumvent national rules on professional ethics, particularly where a dual nationality lawyer has been disbarred and then moves to another state.

Directive 77/249 gave rise to lawyer identity cards issued under the auspices of *Commission Consultative des Barreaux Européans* (C.C.B.E.), which was charged to propose a specific directive about a right of establishment for lawyers. However, the mutual recognition of diplomas accomplished in Council Directive 89/48 applies to lawyers. The maximum adaptation or training period allowed under this directive is three years. In 1997, the long-awaited right of establishment directive was adopted. It mirrors much of the prior law, but makes it easier (than under the diploma directive) to join the local bar after three years of sustained practice in the host state.

Right of Establishment for Lawyers

The C.C.B.E. adopted a common Code of Conduct for lawyers in 1988. It is hoped that this Code will ultimately become binding in all member states. It seeks to harmonize rules of conduct on confidentiality, conflicts of interest, segregation of client funds and malpractice insurance. In other areas, the Code does not harmonize, but rather provides choice of law rules to resolve conflicting national approaches to advertising, contingent fees and membership on boards of directors. The host country rules in these areas will apply to lawyers providing services across borders under Directive 77/249. Home country rules apply as to general fee arrangements.

Admission to the practice of law is still governed by the rules of the legal profession of each member state. Several European Court judgments have upheld the right of lawyer applicants to be free from discrimination on grounds of nationality, residence or retention of the right to practice in home jurisdictions. For example, a Greek lawyer who had a doctorate in German law and had worked for some time advising on Greek and European law in Munich was denied admission to the German bar. On appeal, the Court of Justice held that Article 43 obligates member states not to impede the movement of lawyers. The member state must compare an applicant's specific qualifications with those detailed by national law. Only if the applicant does not meet all the necessary qualifications may the host state require additional courses or training. Some EU jurisdictions allow multi-professional practices, but a Dutch ban on practicing law in full partnership with accountants was upheld primarily because of the absence of strict codes of ethics for accountants.

By joining the bar in another country, or by continuously providing services under home country licenses, lawyers acquire the right to establish themselves in more than one nation. See Directive 98/5 on rights of establishment for lawyers. The multinational law firm, pioneered by Baker and McKenzie in the United States, has relatively few regional counterparts in Europe. Attorneys from member states are establishing affiliations and sometimes partnerships which reflect and service the economic, political and social integration of Europe. These "European law firms" often compete with existing branches of North American multinational firms for the lucrative practice of Common Market law.

In professional fields, the real barrier to movement of people across borders is language. In some instances, linguistic requirements for jobs are lawful despite their negative impact on free movement rights. As much as Europe may succeed in its campaign for truly establishing an integrated market, the language barriers will remain. Although younger generations are increasingly multilingual, a professional who cannot speak to his or her clients or students is unlikely to succeed in another member state.

FREEDOM TO PROVIDE AND RECEIVE SERVICES ACROSS EUROPEAN BORDERS

The freedom of nonresidents to provide services within other parts of Europe is another part of the foundations of the Treaty of Rome. The freedom to provide services (including tourism) implies a right to receive and pay for them by going to the country of their source. Industrial, commercial, craft and professional services are included within this right, which is usually not dependent upon establishment or registration in the country where the service is rendered. In other words, the freedom to provide or receive services across borders entails a limited right of temporary entry into another member state.

The Council has adopted a general program for the abolition of national restrictions on the freedom to provide services across borders. This freedom is subject to the same public policy, public security and public health exceptions applied to workers and the self-employed. The Council's program has been implemented by a series of legislative acts applicable to professional and nonprofessional services. As with the right of self-establishment, discrimination based upon the nationality or nonresidence of the service provider is generally prohibited even if no implementing law has been adopted.

In parallel with law developed in connection with the free movement of goods, member state governments may require providers of services from other states to adhere to public interest rules under the *Cassis* formula. These rules must be applied equally to all service providers operating in the nation, and only if necessary to ensure that the out-of-state provider does not escape them by reason of establishment elsewhere. In other words, if the rules (e.g., ethics) of the country in which the service provider is established are equivalent, then application of the rules of the country where the service is provided does not follow. Following *Cassis*, and notably not *Keck*, the Court of Justice has affirmed member state marketing controls over the sale of lottery tickets (social policy and fraud interests) and over "cold calling" solicitations for commodities futures. Telemarketing in most other areas is forbidden, except with prior consumer consent, under a 1977 directive.

Financial Services

Bankers, investment advisors and insurance companies have long awaited the arrival of a truly common market. Their right of establishment in other member states has existed for some time. The right to provide services across borders without establishing local subsidiaries was forcefully reaffirmed by the Court of Justice in a 1986 decision largely rejecting a requirement that all insurers servicing the German market be located and established there.

Legislative initiatives undertaken in connection with the single market campaign create genuinely competitive cross-border European markets for banking, investment and insurance services. Licensing of insurance and investment service companies and banks meeting minimum capital, solvency ratio and other requirements (as implemented in member state laws) is done on a "one-stop" home country basis. Banks, for example, cannot maintain individual equity positions in non-financial entities in excess of 15 percent of their capital funds and the total value of such holdings cannot exceed 60 percent of those funds. They can participate in and service securities transactions and issues, financial leasing and trade for their own accounts.

Member states must ordinarily recognize home country licenses and the principle of home country control. For example, Council Directive 89/646 ("the Second Banking Directive" now codified as Directive 2000/12) employs the home country single license procedure to liberalize banking services throughout Europe. However, host states retain the right to regulate a bank's liquidity and supervise it through monetary policy and in the name of the "general good." Similarly, no additional insurance permits or requirements may be imposed by host countries when large industrial risks (sophisticated purchasers) are involved. However, when the public at large is concerned (general risk), host country rules still apply.

Reciprocity and the United States

Unless there is "effective market access" under United States law for European firms, U.S. companies entering Europe after 1992 may be unable to obtain the benefits of common service markets. This problem is generally referred to as the "reciprocity requirement." It is this kind of requirement that gave the campaign for a Europe without internal frontiers the stigma of increasing the degree of external trade barriers. Many outsiders, in rhetoric which sometimes seems excessive, refer to the development of a "Fortress Europe" mentality and threat to world trading relations.

There was a rush by non-member state bankers, investment advisors and insurers to get established before January 1, 1993 in order to qualify for home country licenses. North Americans and others have been particularly concerned about the reciprocity requirement. Since state and federal laws governing banking, investment services and insurance are restrictive, and in no sense can it be said that one license permits a company to operate throughout the United States, one result of European integration has arguably been reform of U.S. regulatory legislation. Since 1994 the United States has noticeably relaxed its rules on interstate banking and largely repealed the Glass–Steagall Act limitations on universal banking.

CAPITAL MOVEMENTS AND THE EUROPEAN MONETARY SYSTEM

The Treaty of Rome is also concerned with the free movement of money. "Current payments" associated with import/export transactions in goods and services, as well as wage remittances, are routinely made and protected. This includes money taken abroad to make payment for tourist, medical, educational or business travel services. But it does not include the unsubstantiated export of banknotes.

The free movement of *capital* goals of the Treaty of Rome were much delayed. In fairness, the Treaty initially just required member states to be "as liberal as possible" in granting exchange control authorizations for investment capital transfers. This provision acknowledged the sensitivity of the member states' concerns about disequilibriums in balance of payments and currency values. It was not until the implementation of the single market campaign that legislative acts firmly entrenched the right of individuals and companies to move capital across borders without substantial limitation. The capital movements directive (88/361) allows some retention of member state controls over the purchase of vacation or retirement homes by nationals. National prohibitions against the purchase of real estate or investment in European companies by outsiders are also possible.

This capital movements legislation, when combined with the various banking and investment services reforms, supports a remarkable new financial sector in Europe. It also supports the EURO replacing national currencies. In moving toward monetary union, the member states created the

European Monetary System (EMS). When the EMS was established in 1979, member states deposited 20 percent of their gold and dollar assets with the European Monetary Cooperation Fund in exchange for an equivalent amount of European Currency Units (ECUs). This fund is used as a non-cash means of settlement between central banks undertaking exchange rate support.

ECONOMIC AND MONETARY UNION, A COMMON CURRENCY

The legal basis for the European Monetary System and European Currency Units was substantially advanced by the addition to the Treaty of Rome of Article 98 in the Single European Act of 1987. This article committed the member states to further development of the EMS and ECU, recognized the cooperation of the central banks in management of the system, but specifically required further amendment of the Treaty if "institutional changes" were required. In other words, a common currency managed by a central bank system was *not* part of the campaign for a Europe without internal frontiers.

Draft plans for such developments surfaced in the Commission using the U.S. Federal Reserve Board as a model. Britain, always concerned about losses of economic sovereignty (what greater loss is there?), proposed an alternative known as the "hard ECU." This proposal would have retained the national currencies but added the hard ECU as competitor of each, letting the marketplace in most instances decide which currency it preferred.

In December of 1989, the European Council (outvoting Britain) approved a three stage approach to economic and monetary union (EMU). Stage One began July 1, 1990. Its focus was on expanding the power and influence of the Committee of Central Bank Governors over monetary affairs. This Committee was a kind of EuroFed in embryo. It was primarily engaged in "multilateral surveillance." Stage One also sought greater economic policy coordination and convergence among the member states.

Stage Two anticipated the creation of a European Union central banking system, but functioned with the existing national currencies in the context of the EMS and ERM. Stage Two was a learning and transition period. In October of 1990, it was agreed (save Britain) that Stage Two would commence January 1, 1994. This deadline was actually met, and the European Monetary Institute was installed in Frankfurt. It was the precursor to the European Central Bank.

Stage Three involved the replacement of the national currencies with a single currency, the EURO, managed by a European Central Bank. In December of 1991, agreement was reached at Maastricht to implement Stage Three no later than Jan. 1, 1999 with a minimum of seven states. Britain and Denmark reserved a right to opt out of Stage Three.

All member states had to meet strict economic convergence criteria on inflation rates, government deficits, long-term interest rates and currency fluctuations. To join the third stage, a country was supposed to have an inflation rate not greater than 1.5 percent of the average of the three lowest member state rates, long-term interest rates no higher than 2 percent above the average of the three lowest, a budget deficit less than 3 percent of gross domestic product (GDP), a total public indebtedness of less than 60 percent of GDP, and no devaluation within the ERM during the prior two years. These criteria will likewise govern admission of the new member states from Central Europe into the EURO zone.

European Central Bank

It was also agreed at Maastricht that in the third stage the European Central Bank (ECB) and the European System of Central Banks (ECSB) would start operations. The ECB and ECSB are governed by an executive board of six persons appointed by the member states and the governors of the national central banks. The ECB and the ECSB are independent of any other European institution and in theory free from member state influence. Their primary responsibility is to maintain price stability, specifically keeping price inflation below two percent per year. In contrast, the U.S. Federal Reserve has three primary responsibilities: maximum employment, stable prices and moderate long-term interest rates.

The main functions of the ECB and ECSB are: (1) define and implement regional monetary policy; (2) conduct foreign exchange operations; (3) hold and manage the official foreign reserves of the member states; and (4) supervise the payments systems. The ECB has the exclusive right to authorize the issue of bank notes within the Common Market and must set interest rates to principally achieve price stability. The Court of Justice may review the legality of ECB decisions. The ECB works closely with the Ecofin Council's broad guidelines for economic policy, such as keeping national budget deficits below 3 percent of GDP in all but exceptional circumstances (2 percent decline in annual GDP). If the Ecofin considers a national government's policy to be inconsistent with that of the region, it can recommend changes including budget cuts. If appropriate national action does not follow such a warning, the Ecofin can require a government to disclose the relevant information with its bond issues, block European Investment Bank credits, mandate punitive interest-free deposits, or levy fines and penalties. By 2004, half the Euro states were under threat of sanctions for failure to comply with the 3 percent budget deficit rule.

EURO Zone

The economic performance of member states in 1997 became the test for admission to the economic and monetary union. Since both France and Germany had trouble meeting the admissions criteria, this opened a window for much more marginal states such as Belgium, Italy and Spain to join immediately. Greece also subsequently qualified for the EURO zone. As expected, Denmark, Britain and Sweden opted out of initial participation in the common currency. The Danes did so by voting No in a year 2000 national referendum. The Swedes voted similarly in 2003.

On January 1, 1999, the participating states fixed the exchange rates between the EURO and their national currencies. National notes and coins were removed from the market by July 2002 as the EURO was installed. The EURO has been used for most commercial banking, foreign exchange and public debt purposes since 1999. It has also been adopted (voluntarily) by the world's securities markets, and by Monaco, San Marino, the Vatican, Andorra, Montenegro and Kosovo.

The arrival of the EURO has important implications for the United States and the dollar. For decades, the dollar has been the world's leading currency, although its dominance has been declining since the early 1980s. Use of the Deutsche Mark and Yen in commercial and financial transactions, and in savings and reserves, had been steadily rising. The EURO is likely to continue the dollar's decline in all of these markets. It is certainly the hope of many Europeans that they have successfully created a rival to the dollar.

COMMON TRANSPORT POLICY

A common transport policy is another objective that the Treaty of Rome outlines. Despite its critical role in the free movement of goods and people within the Common Market, transportation was an area in which the Treaty's aspirations long remained unfulfilled. Trade restraints in road, rail and air transportation within the Europe abounded. Indeed, the level of frustration with the lack of integration in this field was reflected in a 1985 lawsuit filed by the Parliament against the Council before the European Court of Justice seeking to force the Council to fully implement the Treaty's goals for a more common and integrated transportation market. The Court found that there had indeed been a "failure to act" by the Council which had to be remedied within a reasonable time. There have been important reforms in the transport field since then.

Road Transport

After much delay, progress has been made in road transportation. Legislation has abolished discriminations arising from different (but still regulated) rates and from conditions applied to like goods in like circumstances. European law also deals with common rules for international road carriage, restrictions upon drivers' hours, and installation of tachograph that record such hours. The latter requirement caused a furor in Britain because it stopped drivers from "moonlighting" extra runs. Differences among the member states about road taxes, safety requirements, noise levels, and truck weights and dimensions have mostly been resolved. In 1988, a Council directive vastly increased the number of authorizations of interstate carriage of goods. Since 1993, such authorizations are unlimited, though subject to qualitative licensing controls. In this area, the Council seriously addressed its obligations under the 1985 Court of Justice judgment of inaction.

Maritime Transport

Council regulations on maritime transport services move in the same direction (especially by removing so-called national flag reservations), but fail to deal with "cabotage" (transport within one member state). European competition law rules apply, as do its antidumping rules. See Chapters 6 and 7. This represents the first application of dumping law in the services sector.

Air Transport

Air transport has been a tougher nut to crack. Market-sharing, profit pooling and other restrictive cartel practices have long victimized Europe's flying public. Not surprisingly, many of the airlines are governmentally owned. In the so-called "Nouvelles Frontieres" case, the Court of Justice struck a blow for greater competition and consumer benefit by legitimizing European and national law enforcement actions against restrictive airline practices.

Price fixing by air carriers (including on flights to and from Europe) is unlawful unless specifically exempted by the Commission.

Since these decisions, Commission threats of prosecutions combined with legislation of a market-liberalizing character have made some headway at flying friendlier skies in Europe. Early in 1992, the Council adopted the Third Package of Liberalization measures on air transport. Under this package, airlines have substantial freedom to set ticket prices, operating throughout the region under a single license issued by national authorities employing common financial and safety criteria. Each airline is able to acquire freight and passengers in other nations (cabotage rights). National authorities may regulate flights and prices to and from non-member countries, and within their internal markets. National authorities may also intervene if they deem fares unreasonably low or high, with the airline retaining a right to appeal such interventions to the Commission. The Council also issued a series of additional regulations on airline license criteria, market access, consumer protection and competition. Gradually, the Third Package of Liberalization has had an impact. Airline competition has improved; discounter Ryanair for example is successfully adapting the Southwest Airlines formula to the EU market.

CHAPTER 5

INTERNAL POLICIES

Some of the most dramatic surrenders of national sovereignty to European institutions occur in pursuit of internal policies. If a truly common market is to result, many national economic policies must be coordinated or conformed to regional standards. Much of the "acquis communautaire" that new member states must implement in their national legal systems is found in EU policy programs. This chapter selectively provides illustrations of such efforts under Treaty of Rome to minimize the trade distorting impact of national economic laws. Taxation is an excellent and perhaps the most difficult example.

TAXATION

If each government were to legislate freely and differently on taxation, the operation of the Common Market would clearly be affected. Article 90 of the Treaty of Rome forbids discriminatory or protective taxation based on nationality or the origin of products. The goal of this article is to prohibit the use of tax laws as a trade barrier and ensure that goods which compete are equally taxed. The practical effect of Article 90 is to convey substantial powers of judicial review over national tax law and policy to the European Court. France, for example, has repeatedly found its annual car taxes under such review. France based this tax on a power rating scale the practical effect of which was to tax all French autos at a lesser rate than some imports. This tax system was twice held invalid under Article 90 of the Treaty of Rome.

Value-Added Tax

Sales taxes and what Europeans refer to as "turnover taxes" can also have a trade distorting impact. Each member state now has a turnover tax generally referred to as the value-added tax (VAT). This was not always the case. Britain, for example, had to switch from a sales tax to a VAT upon joining. The VAT is a cumulative multi-stage tax system encountered in virtually every transaction of goods *or services* throughout the region. United States attorneys might ponder what their clients' reactions would be if they added service taxes to their fees. The Sixth VAT Directive adopted in 1977 was particularly notable. It established a uniform basis for VAT assessment governing territorial application, taxable transactions, the place of taxable transaction, chargeable events and the chargeability of the tax, applicable rates and exemptions, deductions, and persons liable for VAT and their obligations.

Although harmonization has been achieved as to the nature of the required tax system (the VAT), differing national levels of VAT taxation continue to distort trade relations. Britain, for example, has generally charged one uniform VAT rate of 15 to 17.5 percent but zero rated a number of "necessities." Italy, on the other hand, had three levels of VAT with luxuries taxed at times as high as 38 percent. Furthermore, each country established tax collection points at its borders in order to assure the collection of the proper amount of VAT for particular products in accordance with national law (the "destination principle"). These "tax frontiers" probably represented the most significant NTB in the Common Market prior to 1993.

Many considered the ability of the Europeans to achieve a consensus as to the proper levels of VAT and excise taxation, or at least to reduce the degree of differences in such taxation among the member states, to be the litmus test of the campaign for a fully integrated market. Late in 1992, the Council formally agreed to the Commission's proposed interim VAT system scheduled to last through 1996. Agreement was reached on moving to alignment of VAT rates. At this point, Denmark and Sweden have the highest 25 percent VAT rates with Luxembourg the lowest at 15 percent. Since 2003, VAT is collected on Internet sales and services, including digital downloads. The tax frontier was eliminated by imposing VAT reporting and collection duties on importers and exporters using the destination principle on VAT rates. Customers must obtain a VAT registration number which must be given to their cross-border suppliers. The suppliers report these numbers and transactions to the relevant national tax authorities, all of whom are electronically linked.

The harmonization of VAT rules inside Europe has had a wide ranging impact. Regarding the taxation of boats, for example, it used to be that a buyer or importer for personal use could gain VAT exemption by exporting the boat every 6 to 12 months to another country. This was commonly done. However, a 6 months VAT exemption limit for the entire Union has been imposed since 1993. This means that VAT exemption can be had only by leaving the region for 6 months, a much more difficult requirement given European geography and most boater preferences.

Excise Taxes

Excise duties are another example of the potential for trade distortion through taxation. Excise taxes on imported liquor, for example, must be levied at the same rate, on the same basis and by the same methods as domestic competitors. Low alcohol cheap wines imported into Britain thus cannot be taxed more than beer. Nor can France discriminate in taxation of wine versus grain spirits. But the prohibition against discriminatory internal taxation does not apply where there are no similar or competing national products.

The excise tax frontier has been eliminated by moving to a system of interlinked bonded warehouses between which goods can move easily. To help prevent smuggling from low-tax to high-tax member states, the Council agreed to "presumption of fraud" limits on duty-paid imports. These limits are 110 liters of beer, 90 liters of wine, 800 cigarettes, and 10 liters of spirits. An individual must prove, if challenged by a customs official, that imports above these limits are for private consumption rather than for resale. The UK, Denmark and Ireland, countries which have high excise tax rates, use the presumption.

As with the VAT, excise taxation continued to follow the destination principle. The Commission prefers taxation on the basis of origin principles. Under the destination method, goods are shipped within the Common Market net of tax and incur VAT upon entry into the importing country. An origin-based system applies VAT to exported goods before they are shipped, thus collecting tax revenues in the country where the value was added.

Corporate Taxes and Interest Income

Corporate taxation has also received attention, but remains less than uniform throughout the Common Market. There are directives on taxation of cross-border mergers, taxation of dividends from subsidiaries to parents, and a convention on arbitration of transfer pricing disputes. Some discriminatory corporate tax measures have been struck down by the Court of Justice. In 1997, a voluntary Code of Conduct on Corporate Taxation was adopted. This Code seeks to avoid use of "predatory" tax incentives to attract investment, although Ireland gets to keep its 12 percent income tax rate on manufacturers. By 2003, an agreement on passing along withholdings or reporting payment of bank interest to the recipient's home country was agreed upon, with nonmember Switzerland included. This is expected to particularly hit Germans with bank accounts in Luxembourg and Switzerland, but also covers Monaco, Liechtenstein, Andorra and San Marino.

COMPETITION POLICY—GOVERNMENT SUBSIDIES

Europe's competition policy is a natural consequence of its Common Market. The dismantling of internal tariffs, quotas and measures of equivalent effect opens up traditionally sheltered national markets to competition through trade in goods and services. Having created the playing field, so to speak, the Treaty of Rome seeks through its rules on competition to ensure that the field is as level as possible for all who participate. These rules are of two basic types: business competition (antitrust) and government subsidies. The primary business competition rules originate in Articles 81–86 of the Treaty of Rome. They are of such enormous importance to all who do business in Europe that Chapter 7 is devoted exclusively to them.

Subsidies by governments are one of the most intractable of world and Common Market trade problems. In the first place, there are subsidies everywhere. For example, most tax laws (including the Internal Revenue Code) are littered with subsidies. Secondly, identification and calculation of the amount of subsidy can be extremely difficult. Years have been spent just cataloging subsidies. The Commission has concluded that the member states spend billions annually on state subsidies.

Much of this aid goes to "crisis industries" that are declining, but a reasonable amount is targeted at growth sectors, technology development and general support. Moreover, subsidies are almost endemic where the member states own or are heavily invested in enterprises. Some enterprises have been acquired by governments out of bankruptcy in order to save jobs. Some have been established for strategic, prestige or capital requirements' reasons. Others have simply been nationalized as a matter of social policy. In recent years, there has been a trend (but not a stampede) towards privatization of enterprises owned by European governments. Neither nationalization nor privatization is mandated or controlled by the Treaty of Rome.

The Commission has taken the position that any action by a member state as an owner that is different from what a private investor would do can violate the subsidy or competition law rules of the Treaty of Rome. Such actions may include cash payments, debt write-offs, acceptance of rates of return that are below market, implied or express guarantees of loans, cheap financing, new equity capital in circumstances a private investor would avoid, and dividend waivers. In adopting this position, the Commission is relying heavily upon Article 87 of the Treaty of Rome.

Treaty Rules

Article 87(1) declares every national "aid" (subsidy) that distorts or threatens to distort competition by favoring certain businesses or goods incompatible with the Common Market. For example, state aids intended to benefit workers but implemented through a reduction in public charges to textile corporations in Italy were caught within Article 87(1). The impact of the subsidy, not its purposes, determines its character. French textile industry aids financed partly by import levies were similarly prohibited because of their discriminatory impact. Though the money may be private in origin, a state aid exists when that money is distributed through a public body. Provision of subsidies through state-owned enterprises are also caught. Investment subsidies that strengthen the position of a company in the Common Market fall within Article 87(1) as threats to the distortion of competition.

Article 87(2) declares the following subsidies *compatible* with the Treaty of Rome: (a) social aid granted to individuals without discrimination as to the origin of goods; (b) natural disaster aid; and (c) economic aid required to compensate for the division of Germany. Furthermore, Article 87(3) lists a number of aids which *may* be compatible with the Common Market if approved by the Commission. These include regional subsidies to promote development in areas of high unemployment or abnormally low standards of living, subsidies for important projects of common European interest, subsidies to preserve cultural heritage, and subsidies to remedy serious disturbances in the economy of a member state. Also included are subsidies to facilitate the development of certain economic activities or areas (e.g., shipbuilding) provided they do not adversely affect trading conditions to an extent contrary to the common interest. Finally, any subsidy may be lawful if approved by the Council acting by qualified majority vote.

Commission Enforcement

The Commission is charged in Article 88 with keeping all state aids under "constant review," which it does mostly by way of a reporting system. The duty of member state governments to report on the provision of subsidies to industry has been repeatedly upheld by the European Court. If a subsidy is not compatible with the Common Market per Article 87 or is being misused, the Commission may render a decision to that effect against the member state unless the Council unanimously approves of the aid. Such Commission decisions terminate the ability to receive further state aid payments. Absent compliance, the Commission can enforce its decision by bringing an action *directly* before the European Court of Justice. The Commission need not follow the more deliberate procedures established in Article 226 for ordinary prosecutions of member states not adhering to their regional obligations.

Certain patterns have emerged in the law on state subsidies. Regional development aids are generally supported, especially since the Single European Act of 1987 made elimination of regional economic disparities a priority. The whole of Greece, Portugal and Ireland, for example, have been treated as underdeveloped regions for subsidy law purposes. Indeed, the Community itself engages in the same subsidies under its Regional Policy. Sectoral industrial aids to ease unemployment and modernize smokestack industries (coal, steel, textiles, shipbuilding) have generally been allowed. Production and marketing subsidies have generally been disallowed. Research and technological development subsidies, especially for energy saving projects, often pass muster. Since environmental protection subsidies violate the polluter must pay principle of the Environmental Policy, these are not frequently approved.

The Commission's role relative to national subsidies has gradually changed over the years from prosecutorial watchdog against discriminatory and anticompetitive aids to coordinator of national subsidy policies and levels. In this capacity, the Commission can find itself negotiating specific subsidy amounts or refunds with national governments, e.g., French subsidies to Alstom, France Telecom, Bull and Air France. A "one time, last time" rule tries to limit major subsidies to once in a decade. The power of prosecution under Article 87 remains. No member state, for example, may match another nation's subsidy. The Court of Justice has affirmed the power of the Commission to order refunds of offending national subsidies. Many have suggested authorizing the Commission to levy fines and penalties against member states that fail to adhere to European law on subsidies.

PROCUREMENT

Article 94 of the Treaty of Rome empowers the Council of Ministers, acting on Commission proposals, to issue directives for the "approximation" (better known as "harmonization" or "coordination") of national laws directly affecting the establishment or operation of the Common Market. Such directives must be adopted unanimously within the Council. Since a vast number of national laws affect the Common Market, the potential scope of Article 94 is very broad. This scope, over the years since 1957, was not fully exploited principally because of the unanimous Council voting requirement. Indeed, by 1986 and a Community of twelve nations, innovative legislation under Article 94 became quite difficult to obtain. That is why one major thrust of the 1987 Single European Act was the inclusion of Article 95. It specifies qualified majority voting in the Council of Ministers for much of the single market legislative agenda. Qualified majority voting procedures also apply to directives used to harmonize national laws (e.g., subsidies) distorting the conditions of competition in the Common Market.

Harmonization of national laws of concern to the Common Market is critical to advancing European integration. Harmonization can, for example, remove many of the barriers to free movement previously discussed in Chapter 4, including those expressly permitted by Article 30 and the *Dassonville/Cassis* and *Keck* line of cases discussed in Chapter 4. It can do the same for the public security exceptions to the free movement of workers and the self-employed, as well as to the freedom to provide services across borders. Harmonization is critical to removal of the tax and nontariff trade barrier (NTB) frontiers, a central focus of the campaign for a Europe without internal frontiers. In addition, harmonization can reach out to areas not specifically treated in the Treaty of Rome but which are of consequence to the functioning of the Common Market. A good example is government procurement law.

Every government, at whatever level, tends to favor local producers when spending the taxpayers' money. Various "Buy American" laws permeate much of the military and civil procurement of the federal, state and local governments in the United States. The governments of European nations are no different. Nevertheless, through a long series of harmonizing directives issued by the Council and aggressive decisions of the European Court, the effects of Buy French, Buy Greek and Buy Greater London Council types of laws are slowly being overcome. For example, one Court opinion struck down a program of public advertisements urging consumers to voluntarily buy only goods marked with a "Guaranteed Irish" symbol. This program combined private and governmental funds and officials. It was declared a measure of equivalent effect to a quota hindering regional trade in breach of Article 28.

Procurement Directives

The Council has issued a series of directives intended to open up government procurement to competitive bids. The first focus of this effort was on tendering procedures for public works projects. Discriminations on the basis of nationality which amount to the equivalent of trade quotas are prohibited under an early 1969 directive. Discriminatory procedural rules concerning the award of public works and construction contracts are standardized in a 1971 directive.

The second focus of the effort to combat discriminatory government procurement is on supply contracts for goods and services to member governments, their regional and local subdivisions, public agencies and the like. A 1977 directive requires most public supply contracts to be announced in advance in the Official Journal. The announcement must also include the criteria for selection of bidders or suppliers, which may not be discriminatory. This directive does not apply to purchases of military supplies, but covers purchases of nonmilitary supplies used by military forces. Certain national governmental monopolies, e.g., water, gas and electricity, were excluded from its application. A 1980 directive amended these rules to bring them into conformity with the 1979 GATT Code on Government Procurement. The GATT Code liberalized government procurement rules on an international basis. The 1980 directive, nevertheless, maintained a margin of preference for local enterprises seeking governmental supply contracts within Europe.

The early procurement legislation did not live up to expectations. Purchasing entities and public authorities undertaking construction projects continued to give preference to domestic suppliers and contractors. A survey revealed the most common and serious breaches of the procurement rules: (1) failure to advertise contracts in the Official Journal; (2) abuse of the exceptions permitting single tendering; (3) discriminatory administrative, financial or technical requirements in tenders, especially the insistence on compliance with national standards even when regional law does not allow this; (4) illegal disqualification or elimination of bidders or applicants from other Member States, for example by discriminatory selection criteria; and (5) discrimination at the award stage.

It was reported in late 1986 that approximately 98 percent of all procurement contracts went to national suppliers. Single tendering (unpublicized, noncompetitive contract awards) and selective supplier arrangements (unpublicized, selectively competitive contract awards) continue to hurt efforts at overcoming buy-local preferences. Other problems exist with exemptions from regional procurement law for special needs such as "speed of delivery," "security" and "particular specifications." Procedural and substantive reforms of the existing directives were developed by the Commission in 1986. These reforms covered notice requirements, longer bid periods, publication of contract awards (who won), use of European specification standards (not national standards), and reduction of exemption industries (energy, transport, water and telecommunications). A legislative simplification of EU procurement rules was accomplished in Directives 2004/17 and 2004/18.

Buy EU

Reform of procurement rules was part of the unified internal market campaign. Early in 1988, the Council adopted a directive tightening up the procedural aspects of the procurement rules so as to reduce single tendering. Under another 1988 directive, public construction bidding was similarly reformed. In 1992, a directive extended the open procurement rules and procedures to most public service contracts. In 1990, a directive was adopted which in 1993 opened up public contracts in the telecommunications, energy, transport and water industries. This directive contains a controversial ''Buy European'' clause which allows public authorities to dismiss bids with less than 50 percent regional content, and gives local suppliers a minimum margin of preference of 3 percent.

Europe indicated that this preferential clause could be dropped if satisfactory agreements were reached within the GATT on amendment of the

Procurement Code. Late in 1991, the United States threatened to retaliate against the Buy European rules of this directive by unilaterally imposing trade sanctions on goods imported into the U.S. market. This threat was announced under Title VII of the Omnibus Trade and Competitiveness Act of 1988. Europe responded by first pointing out the greater degree of procurement preferences accorded under Buy American law.

Negotiations on this issue outside the Uruguay Round led in 1993 to a compromise Memorandum of Understanding. The Europeans agreed not to discriminate against U.S. suppliers, goods or services, and to open certain energy contracts. The U.S. agreed to waive certain federal "Buy American" provisions as applied to bids of European origin and to try to persuade the states to do likewise. No agreement was reached regarding telecommunications procurement. This led first to U.S. procurement sanctions, followed by European retaliation. Germany, however, seemingly broke ranks by negotiating a bilateral telecommunications agreement with the U.S. This resulted in the suspension of the U.S. sanctions as applied to Germany and much consternation within Europe.

Since 1995, Europe and the United States have participated fully in the WTO Procurement Agreement. This has helped reduce transatlantic trade and procurement tensions.

PRODUCTS LIABILITY

Products liability law is one field where Europe acted before the single market campaign to harmonize national rules. Council Directive 85/374 established a regime of strict (no-fault) defective products liability. Prior to the products liability directive, the rules of law on products liability of the individual member states varied greatly. Traditional negligence liability with plaintiff's burden of proof was the rule in Italy, Portugal, Spain and Greece. A presumption of liability shifting the burden of proof to the defendant that bordered on strict products liability governed in Germany, Denmark, the Netherlands, the United Kingdom and Ireland. Absolute strict liability, creating a presumption liability that could not be overcome, was the rule in France, Belgium and Luxembourg.

Strict Liability

Under Council Directive 85/374, the injured person is required to prove damages, the defect and a causal relationship between defect and damages. The term "product" applies to "all movables, with the exception of primary agricultural products and games, even though incorporated into another movable or into an immovable" and specifically includes electricity. Both new and used products are covered. However, the evaluation of whether a product is defective takes place at the time when the "producer" has most recently put the product into circulation. Manufacturers of components are treated as such producers. Producers also include manufacturers of finished products, suppliers of raw materials or component parts and persons who, by putting names, trademarks or other distinguishing features on products, present themselves as producers. Licensors are not generally treated as producers but their licensees are. Thus, department stores and commercial chains will be regarded as producers if they sell products manufactured by others under their own names without referring to actual origin. They will be jointly and severally liable with the actual producer. However, if a department store has had a product specially made under the designation "specially manufactured for ... by ...," the department store should not be regarded as a "producer."

Any person who imports products into the Common Market for distribution in the course of business is deemed a producer. This rule only concerns persons who import products into Europe, not persons who import from one member state to another. The importer's intentions at the time of importation are crucial. If the product was originally imported in the course of business, the importer will be regarded as a producer even if the product is later dedicated to personal use. An importer who originally imported the product for personal use, but later decides to use the product commercially, does not become a producer. The burden of proof that the product is not imported in the course of business rests with the importer. Whether the doctrine of strict products liability applies to retailers is decided by each member state.

A product is defective "when it does not provide the safety which a person is entitled to expect." It is not the injured person's expectations that control, but rather the normal expectations of purchasers of such products. The reasonable expected use of the product is determined when evaluating defects of production, design or the lack of adequate warnings or instruction. The gravity of the potential injury, the probability of the occurrence of injury, and the consumer's awareness of the danger are analyzed to determine whether adequate warnings or instruction have been given.

Exceptions and Defenses

The exception for "primary agricultural products" includes fish products but excludes all products that "have undergone initial processing." The line between primary and initially processed products thus becomes quite important and will no doubt be subjected to judicial interpretation. Moreover, member states can elect to include primary agricultural products under their strict liability regime. Luxembourg appears to be the only nation to do so to date. The products liability directive does not apply to services. However, if a defective product is used when rendering services, the producer may be held strictly liable for any damages. The person rendering services will only be liable if he or she has acted with negligence.

Strict liability is tempered by certain defenses, notably the "state-of-the-art" defense which excludes liability if the manufacturer could not have discovered the defect when the product was made. However, the member states have the option of omitting this defense, which (to date) only Luxembourg and Finland have done. The British version of this defense, implemented in the 1987 Consumer Protection Act, withstood challenge by the Commission before the European Court of Justice.

Strict liability is also tempered in the award of damages by contributory negligence principles. The calculation and types of damages that may be recovered and damages caps are largely left to national law. Thus the award of "pain and suffering" or punitive damages is under member state control, as is the imposition of total limits on recovery. Germany, Spain and Portugal have set such total limits. A three-year statute of limitations ordinarily applies, and a ten-year absolute bar on liability is established in the Council directive on products liability.

For some nations, such as Ireland and Spain, this directive mandated a fundamental switch away from liability systems grounded entirely in negligence principles. France, on the other hand, considered the directive too generous to manufacturers. All three were pursued by the Commission for implementation failures. Nevertheless, Americans who have studied the painstaking manner in which strict products liability doctrine was crafted in state courts are often surprised by the sweeping adoption of comparable law in Europe. One explanation lies in the goal of free movement and a desire to equalize the risks of liability (and the insurance costs) that most often accompany the distribution of goods to the public. There is, also, greater acceptance of the need to compensate accident victims regardless of fault. Moreover, the absence of a well financed plaintiff's bar, contingency legal fees, juries and rules that require each party to pay their own legal costs have made products liability litigation infrequent. These factors facilitated the passage of the products liability directive.

CONSUMER PROTECTION AND CREDIT

The European Union has had a consumer protection and information policy since 1975. Its consumer protection role was recognized in TEU amendments to the Treaty of Rome. The member states, however, may enact more stringent protective measures provided they are compatible with the Treaty of Rome. In addition to products liability (above), EU law covers health and safety product labelling and manufacturing. Foodstuffs, cosmetics, detergents, vehicles, textiles, toys, dangerous substances, medicines, fertilizers, pesticides and animal feed are some of the areas now governed by Union consumer protection law. There is, for example, a directive which fixes the maximum level of pesticide residues on fruits and vegetables. The Commission operates an information exchange network on products that present grave and immediate danger to consumers.

The source member state notifies the Commission of the hazard, and the Commission forwards this information to the other member states.

All products dangerous to humans or the environment are subject to the Union's *dangerous substances directives*. This includes explosives, flammable, toxic and carcinogenic substances. No such products are to be allowed on the market until after a review of their "forseeable risks" and "unfavorable effects" by national authorities. Child-resistant packaging is ordinarily required as is labelling using a common "CE" black on orange-yellow symbol. Any special risks associated with the product and safety advice must be spelled out on the label. Dangerous substances meeting the terms and conditions of this directive may be freely traded within the Union, each nation relying on the authorities of all other EU countries to implement the directive as to manufacturers within their borders.

An EU *product safety directive* has also been adopted Council Directive 92/59 revised by Directive 2001/95 applies to all products not subject to more specific Union law on safety. Suppliers may place only safe products on the market. A safe product does not present any risk, or only risks considered acceptable and consistent with a high standard of protection. In assessing the acceptability of risk, the product's intended or reasonably foreseeable use must be evaluated. The supplier must give the user sufficient information to assess acceptable risks and to monitor the safety of the product. Suppliers will be deemed to meet the general safety requirement if they comply with Union standards or (in their absence) member state safety requirements. The directive requires member states to have the power to impose sanctions for violations, including the power to ban products from the market, but it does not require that consumers be given a damages remedy for unsafe products.

Council Directive 93/13 covers *unfair terms in standardized consumer* contracts concluded after Dec. 31, 1994. Such terms do not bind consumers, and the member states are obliged to take effective measures to ensure their discard by suppliers and sellers. Consumer groups must be allowed to proceed before courts or authorities involved with determinations of unfairness in consumer contracts of general use. Standardized contract terms are considered "unfair" if they evidence bad faith and cause a significant imbalance in the parties' rights and obligations under the contract. A nonexhaustive list of examples of unfair terms is annexed to the directive. These examples include liability limits, seller rights to unilaterally alter the contract without good cause and restraints upon consumer legal remedies. Member states remain free to provide for higher levels of consumer protection against unfair terms in standardized contracts.

Consumer Credit

The Council has adopted two important *consumer credit directives*. Directive 87/102 seeks to insure that consumers receive precise information from creditors as to the true costs of credit. "Consumers" for these purposes do not include business customers. "Creditors," on the other hand, must be acting in the course of a trade, business or profession. The directive applies to "credit agreements" involving loans or deferred payment, but not installment contracts. Leasing agreements, charge cards and other selected contracts are exempted. Directive 90/88 establishes an annual percentage rate of charge (APR) disclosure requirement.

Directive 99/44 concerns the sale of consumer goods and associated guarantees. Basically, the seller must deliver goods conforming to the contract of sale. If nonconformity is discovered within two years, the consumer generally is entitled to free repair or replacement, a price adjustment or contract recision. Final sellers in turn have recourse against producers and intermediate sellers. Directive 98/27 mandates the availability of injunctive relief in connection with eleven consumer rights directives, including for example misleading advertising, medicinal products advertising, unfair contract terms, time shares, distance sales, package travel, product guarantees and off premise sales.

SECURITIES

Article 294 of the Treaty of Rome creates a right of national treatment as regards participation in the capital of profit-making companies. In other words, discrimination based upon nationality cannot be practiced when it comes to corporate capital. In addition, several important directives have been adopted in the securities field. These concern admission of securities to stock exchange listings, the issuance of a prospectus, and regular information disclosures by publicly traded firms. Some commentators have suggested that the net result of these directives is a "Common Market Prospectus." Once approved by a member state, a prospectus conforming to European rules can be used throughout the region subject to minimal additional disclosure requirements.

Early Securities Law Directives

The 1989 Prospectus Directive (No. 89/298) created prospectus requirements for nearly all transferable securities publicly offered within a member state. The Prospectus Directive contained a mutual recognition clause. When public offerings were made within short intervals in two or more member states, a prospectus prepared and approved in accordance with this law had to be recognized and accepted in all member states. In 2003, the New Prospectus Directive (below) was adopted, repealing the 1989 directive.

The 1979 Listing Conditions Directive (No. 79/279) established minimum conditions for the admission of securities to a stock exchange listing. These conditions concern the size of the issuer, its history and the distribution of its shares in the market. The directive creates reporting obligations for issuers of listed securities. It provides that if shares of a non-member company are not listed in the issuer's home country or principal market, they may not generally be listed in a Common Market country. However, if the national authorities are satisfied that the absence of a listing "is not due to the need to protect investors," listing may follow. Non–member issuers are required to meet the minimum conditions and obligations of the 1979 Listing Conditions Directive.

The 1980 Listing Particulars Directive (No. 80/390) coordinated member state disclosure requirements. Member states had to ensure that securities listings in their territories were accompanied by the release of a disclosure document ("listing particulars"). This document is akin to an SEC registration statement and must enable investors to make an "informed assessment" of the financial position and prospects of the issuer. This directive thus imposed a general obligation to disclose material facts in the listing application. A 1987 Directive (No. 87/345) applied when applications were made to list securities on two or more exchanges. The listing particulars in such cases followed home state rules and were approved by home state authorities. Other member states had to recognize these documents without requiring approval by their authorities and without requiring additional information. This 1987 directive allowed countries to restrict mutual recognition to listing particulars of issuers having registered offices in a member state. In 2003, the New Prospectus Directive replaced the Listing Particulars Directive.

New Prospectus Directive

The New Prospectus Directive (No. 2003/34) covers all securities offered to the public or admitted to trading on a regulated market. The prospectus must provide all necessary information for investors to make informed assessments in an "easily analyzable and comprehensible form." Either a single or "subdivided" prospectus can be used. A subdivided prospectus consists of three documents: (1) a registration; (2) a securities note; and (3) a summary note. Once a subdivided prospectus is approved, the registration is valid for 12 months. Thus only the security and summary notes need to be revised in subsequent offerings. The prospectus must be prepared according to International Accounting Standards.

Home country registration by issuers of securities results in sending notices of approval to host state authorities who are bound to honor them. Translation requirements are minimized. Exemptions cover government bonds, small issues and qualified sophisticated buyers. The prior "mutual reciprocity" approach is abandoned. That said, an EU-wide securities and exchange commission has not been created, and whether the New Prospectus Directive will gain marketplace adherents remains to be seen.

Mutual and Pension Funds

Council Directive 85/611 on open-end investment companies ("unit trusts" or mutual funds) was implemented in 1985. It allows marketing in other member states based upon home country authorization meeting the minimum standards of the directive. There is no "reciprocity rule" in the Unit Trust Directive that might hinder North American mutual fund companies wishing to operate in Europe. The Unit Trust Directive controls the structure, obligations, investment policies and disclosure obligations of unit trusts and investment companies. With certain exceptions, such entities may only invest in transferable securities listed on a Common Market stock exchange, traded on a regulated market in a member state, or traded on an approved exchange or regulated market in a non-member state. Unit trusts and investment companies must repurchase or redeem units from holders upon request. Directive 2001/107 regulates the prudential management and access to market of UCITs.

Council Directive 2003/41 concerns pension funds. High levels of protection for members and beneficiaries are required. Cross-border administration of pension schemes is facilitated using mutual recognition principles along with customized investment strategies following the "prudent person principle." Whether to use pay-as-you-go or funded pension schemes is left to member state discretion.

Market Abuses and Inside Trading

In 1988, the Council adopted an "anti-raider" directive requiring disclosure of the acquisition or disposal of 10 percent or more of a publicly listed company. Securities "market abuses," including stock-buy programs, market manipulations, public disclosure of inside information, investment recommendations and disclosure of conflicts of interest, are covered in Directive 2003/6. Until 1988, only three of the member states had laws regulating insider trading. Nevertheless, a directive on insider trading was finalized in 1989. This directive (No. 89/592 now contained in 2003/6) prohibits trading on the basis of inside information "with full knowledge of the facts" by primary and secondary insiders. Specifically, this prohibition applies to any person who possesses inside information from membership in the structure of the issuer, share ownership, or access to information through employment, professional or other duties. Persons who possess inside information, the source of which "could not be other than" one of the previously enumerated persons, are also covered. Disclosure of inside information to third parties outside the normal course of employment or professional duties, and procurement of securities by others on the basis of such information is prohibited.

Inside information is defined as nonpublic information "of a precise nature" which if made public would be "likely to have a significant effect on the price" of securities. Many perceive that the insider trading directive closely parallels U.S. securities law principles. However, unlike U.S. law, the European directive only applies to securities traded on markets regulated by "public bodies" that operate regularly and are accessible directly or indirectly to the public. The directive specifically permits member states to exclude transactions without a professional intermediary undertaken outside a regulated market. One concern with the directive is that it allows member states to choose which types of penalties apply to insider trading violations.

In 1991, the United States Securities and Exchange Commission (SEC) and the Commission signed a joint communiqué intended to improve bilateral and multilateral cooperation in the securities law field. Information exchange, cooperative approaches to financial integrity of issuers, and securities market oversight are covered by this communiqué.

COMPANY LAW

Article 293 of the Treaty of Rome obliges member states to enter into negotiations with each other about equal protection of citizens, abolition of double taxation, mutual recognition of firms and companies, the possibility of international mergers, and simplification of enforcement of judgments. Article 293 was the backdrop against which member states signed in 1968 a Convention on Mutual Recognition of Companies and Other Bodies Corporate. This Convention sought to ensure that Treaty benefits extend to such legal personae. Unfortunately, it never achieved full ratification by the member states. Article 43 on the right of establishment entitles companies based in one member state to set up agencies, branches or subsidiaries in other member states, even when this avoids paid-in capital requirements. In the absence of an EU convention on legal personalities, nothing in the right of establishment permits a company to freely transfer its place of incorporation (seat) and administrative center to another member state without home state permission where that is required. In this case, the British Daily Mail newspaper sought to change to Dutch citizenship to take advantage of lower taxes.

However, two decisions of the European Court of Justice, *Überseering* and *Inspire Art,* hold that a company formed under the laws of one member state of the European Union may move or establish its entire operations to or in any other member state. The other member state may not impose any restrictions on or deny the legal capacity of such a company even if there is no connection to the member state in which it was formed other than statutory registration. The Court explicitly clarified that it does not constitute an abuse of the principle of freedom of establishment if the purpose is to circumvent the application of the stricter company laws of the member state in which the company is operating through its branch by forming the company in another member state with more liberal laws. It further stated that all questions relating to the company's status (liability of limited partners and managing directors, capital requirements etc.) must be governed by the law of incorporation of the company. It is widely thought that these decisions will avoid restrictive Germany company law rules by, for example as in *Uberseering*, incorporation in the Netherlands.

Company Law Directives

The Council has adopted a number of non-controversial coordination directives under Article 44 advancing Union company law. These in theory seek to avoid the race to the bottom problems associated with Delaware corporate law in the United States. The first directive sets out requirements for disclosure, validity and nullity of share capital companies. The ECJ has ruled that the listing of grounds for nullifying the formation of a company found in the First Company Law Directive 68/151 exhausts all such possibilities. Grounds for nullification based upon the Spanish Civil Code requirement of "causa" could not be utilized since that Code must be construed in conformity with Directive 68/151. The second deals with the classification, subscription and maintenance of capital of public and large companies. Increases in share capital must be approved by company shareholders with preemptive rights preserved. This obligation is derived from Article 25 of the Second Company Law Directive, which has direct effect in Union law. Companies are generally forbidden from acquiring their own shares. Governmental acts authorizing increases in company capital to ensure survival which prejudice the preemptive rights of shareholders are impermissible under Directive 77/91. The Second Company Law Directive was amended in late 1992 to close a loophole by prohibiting parent companies from buying through subsidiaries more than 10 percent of their own shares when faced with hostile takeovers.

The Third Company Law Directive concerns the internal merger of public companies. Modern procedures for mergers with related and unrelated companies are established. Asset and liability acquisitions and new company formations are allowed. Shareholder rights are specified. The sixth directive governs sales of assets of public companies, including certain shareholder, creditor and workers' rights. The fourth standardizes the treatment of annual accounts (*e.g.,* in their presentation, content, valuation and publication). It requires public presentation of a "true and fair view" of company assets, liabilities, finances, profits and losses. Small and medium-sized firms can publish abridged accounts. All companies must present comparable figures for the preceding year. Valuation of assets and liabilities must be prudent, consistent and reflect the company as a going concern. The fourth directive even details the notes that must accompany annual accounts. In addition, shareholders must be given a report by management annually on the development of the business, future plans, research activities and company purchases of its own shares. There is a permissive provision relating to inflation or current cost accounting. There is some doubt about the degree of relation to similar requirements of the United Kingdom accounting bodies or "generally accepted accounting practices" in the United States. Directive 2001/65 spells out "fair value" accounting rules, notably for derivatives. Regulation 1606/2002 mandated use of International Accounting Standards by publicly traded companies.

The Sixth Company Law Directive adopted in 1982 complements the third directive and addresses the division or "scission" of public limited companies, where they wind up without liquidation. The seventh concerns requirements for consolidated accounts of groups of companies. Consolidated accounts must follow the rules of the fourth directive as supplemented by the seventh. Consolidated accounts are required if an EU firm has legal or *de facto* control over other companies through majority shareholdings, appointment or removal power over management in a subsidiary, the right to exercise dominant influence, or the possibility of shareholder agreements conveying majority voting rights. Consolidated accounts must treat the group as a single enterprise regarding transactions among the companies. The Eighth Company Law Directive provides certain minimum standards and qualifications for auditors of company accounts.

Works Councils

Several controversial proposals for company law directives are in varying stages of evolution. These include a fifth directive on company structure and administration which has been long delayed due to differing views about the functions of single and two-tier boards of directors and officers, and worker representation at these levels. Another controversial topic (the "Vredeling proposal") would have required substantial information sharing between companies and their employees. The 1994 "works council" Directive 94/45 requires councils in companies with more than 1000 employees operating with 150 employees in at least two member states. Workers must be given information on and an opportunity to respond to a broad range of topics including the firm's economic and financial situation, employment, work methods and mergers and layoffs. But the information can be withheld when disclosure might "seriously harm" the functioning of the company or be "prejudicial" to it. Thousands of works councils now operate with little controversy. Directive 94/45 applies to parent companies located outside the EU.

Other less controversial directives are also planned. The ninth directive concerns liability on the part of parent companies for the debts of subsidiaries they effectively control. The tenth directive deals with cross-border company mergers. The eleventh (adopted in 1989) involves disclosure by branches operating in other EU states, and the twelfth (also adopted in 1989) affects single member private limited liability companies. Hostile takeovers, a sensitive area, are the subject of the thirteenth proposed company law directive. This directive would require equal treatment of shareholders and specify permissible defensive measures, and was denied in 2001 by a tie vote in Parliament.

EUROPEAN COMPANIES

An amended proposal for a European Company was submitted by the Commission to the Council in August 1989. Nineteen years had passed since the submission of the first proposal in 1970, and 14 years since the last amended proposal in 1975. In that period, considerable harmonization had been accomplished by way of directives. Finally, late in 2001, a European Company Statute was finalized, taking effect in 2004. Forming a European Company ("Societas Europeae" or SE) is optional. An SE operates on a European-wide basis governed by EU law. A regulation establishes its company law rules, while a directive covers worker involvement in SE. Under the Statute, an SE registered in one member state can freely move its registered office to another. SEs may be privately or publicly traded companies. SE, at least in theory, will remove the need for costly networks of subsidiaries throughout the European Union. Large legal and administrative cost savings are expected to be realized. SE must be registered in the member state where it has its administrative head office, and the Statute does not significantly alter applicable taxation.

Regarding worker participation, the issue that held up the SE proposal for over 30 years, the first duty is to try negotiate agreement on employee involvement. Failing that, Standard Principles attached to the directive require regular reports, consultation and information exchange between management and worker representatives. Such reports must detail business plans, production and sales, management changes, mergers, divestments, potential closures and layoffs, and the implications of all this to workers. In the case of a European Company

created by merger, the Standard Principles apply
when at least 25 percent of the employees had the
right to participate before the merger. However,
member states need *not* implement the directive on
participation for SEs created by mergers, but if so
the SE can be registered only if an agreement with
the employees is reached, or when no employees
were covered by participation rules before the SE
was created.

ENVIRONMENTAL POLICY

For many years, environmental law was a step-
child of European integration. The Treaty of Rome
of 1957 did not expressly authorize or anticipate
such a policy. Clearly, however, differing national
standards on the environment can have a substantial impact on the functioning of the Common Market. As environmental politics (remember the Green
Party) and consciousness came of age in Western
Europe, initial environmental efforts rested on Article 94 (harmonization) and Article 308, the Treaty's
"necessary and proper" powers clause. The first
Environmental Action Program commenced in
1973. Europe is now embarked on its sixth such
program covering 2001–2010. Hundreds of environmental legislative acts have been adopted. The
Commission has noted at length, however, that
there are serious problems with national implementation (or the lack thereof) of regional environmental law.

Policy Principles

There are two basic thrusts to the environmental policy. The first is the establishment of minimum quality standards (e.g., drinking water). The second involves specific emission controls (e.g., the discharge of pollutants into surface and ground water). On emission controls, Europe has proceeded slowly, industry by industry, after first identifying priority problems. The first water emissions directives involved mercury and cadmium discharges. Rules also govern the biodegradability of detergents and the sulphur content of liquid fuels. Among the first air pollution directives, auto emissions and lead content in gasoline have had a high priority.

The procedures for adoption of European environmental legislation and the conclusion of international environmental agreements are unusually detailed. Article 174(3) requires consideration of available scientific and technical data, local environmental conditions, the potential benefits and costs of action or inaction, the economic and social development of Europe as a whole, and balanced development of its regions when preparing environmental policy. Europe can legislate only when action at the regional level will better achieve the objectives at stake than action by individual member states (the "subsidiarity principle").

Waste Management

Waste control directives have targeted oil, PCB and PCT discharges as priorities. Waste management issues have frequently come before the Court of Justice. For example, French law implementing the waste oil directive could not deny the right of oil companies to export wastes to an approved recycling center in another member state. Similarly, existing directives meant that Belgium could not ban the disposal of hazardous waste. But it could prohibit, in the name of environmental protection, importation of general waste products from neighboring countries.

The Single European Act of 1987 added Articles 174–176 to the Treaty of Rome. These articles firmly established environmental policy as an important domain of the region. Indeed, Article 174(2) made environmental protection requirements a mandatory component of *all* European policies. One of the overriding legal principles of environmental policy is that the polluter shall pay. This may mean that national governments are limited in their ability to grant subsidies for environmental protection purposes. Another key principle is that member states may adopt more demanding environmental requirements, provided they are compatible with the Treaty of Rome.

Questions arose as to whether innovative German packaging laws comported with European environmental and trade policy. These laws require acceptance for recycling of transport packaging, secondary packaging (e.g., boxes), and all sales packaging including cans, plastic containers, foil, etc. The duty to take back sales packaging does not apply to manufacturers, distributors and retailers who participate in the "green dot" program. This program involves regular collection of sales packaging at consumers' homes or collection centers. Green dots may appear on products when a company's system meets prescribed quotas for collection and recycling. By 1995, 80 percent of all packaging materials had to be collected and no less than 80 percent of those materials had to be recycled or reused.

Germany's early packaging laws served to stimulate a major environmental directive (No. 94/62). It requires recovery of at least 50 percent of all packaging by weight of which a minimum of 25 percent must be recycled. Member states, like Germany, may exceed these targets assuming distortions of the regional market are avoided. The directive also requires compliance with certain packaging standards. Directive 2000/53 follows the same path on recycling end-of-life vehicles.

Labels, Audits, Impacts and Information

An eco-labelling system to enable consumers to identify environmentally less harmful products has been approved. Using a "cradle to grave" approach, products are evaluated for their impact on the environment throughout their lifespan. Products less damaging to the environment receive the eco-label logo, a flower with stars as petals enclosing the EU's Greek-style "E" symbol. Consumer trade, industry and environmental organizations are consulted on the stringency of the criteria products must meet for the award. Final decisions are taken by a regulatory committee of the member states on the basis of Commission proposals. All products are eligible for the labelling system except beverages, foodstuffs, pharmaceuticals and dangerous substances. National eco-labelling plans coexist with the regional system. Participation in the system is voluntary, but shifts in consumer preferences to environmentally friendly products may spur use of the logo for competitive reasons.

The Commission proposed an "eco-auditing" system for much of European industry in 1991. This voluntary system was adopted by the EU Council in 1993 as part of a broader "eco-management" scheme. Companies may participate on a site-by-site basis by adopting a company environmental policy, conducting an environmental review, introducing an environmental management system, executing an environmental audit, setting environmental performance objectives and preparing an environmental statement after the audit. All of these requirements must be verified by an independent, accredited environmental "verifier." Monitoring and reporting on subsequent environmental conditions are regularly required. The "benefits" of participation, apart from public opinion, include registration and publication of the participants by governments and by the company (but the fact of participation may not be used in advertising or on product packaging). The Commission originally sought a mandatory eco-auditing system. It is conceivable that experience with this voluntary scheme may lead ultimately to that result.

A 1985 Council Directive (No. 85/337) requires an environmental impact assessment for environmentally significant development projects. The Directive aims to "identify, describe and assess in an appropriate manner ... the direct and indirect effects" of such projects on humans, fauna, flora, soil, water, air, climate, landscape, material assets and cultural heritage. The Directive requires developers to provide national authorities with detailed information relating to the project. Such information includes: (1) a description of the project, including information on its site, design, processes and wastes; (2) an outline of the "main alternatives" considered; (3) a description of "the measures envisaged to prevent, reduce and where possible offset any significant adverse effects on the environment"; and (4) a "non-technical" summary. The Environmental Impact Directive does not create substantive environmental protection standards. Rather, it establishes development permission procedures to promote public review at the national level of environmental consequences.

Similarly, the Directive on the Freedom of Access of Information on the Environment (No. 90/313) obliges the member states to create procedures for citizens to obtain environmental information. Under this Directive, national authorities must allow access to "any available information ... on the state of water, air, soil, fauna, flora and natural sites and on activities ... or measures adversely affecting, or likely so to affect these, and on activities or measures designed to protect these." However, national authorities may refuse to provide information where the request may affect foreign relations, national security, public security, commercial and industrial confidentiality, and the information, if disclosed, could increase the likelihood of environmental damage.

International Environmental Agreements

Cooperation within international organizations on the environment is shared between the region and its member states "within their respective spheres of competence." Adoption of international environmental accords is subject to the same procedures regularly used for trade treaties. See Chapter 6. One important indicator of just how sensitive the environmental field is within the Union is provided by Article 175. Under the Single European Act of 1987 (SEA), that article required a unanimous Council vote before any legislative or international action on the environment could be undertaken, specifically reserving to the Council the decision as to when qualified majority voting could be used. Most other authority added to the Treaty of Rome by the Single European Act prescribed qualified majority voting.

This divergence led to litigation over the proper legal basis for environmental legislation. The Court of Justice upheld use of Article 95 (internal market measures) with its qualified majority voting and Parliamentary cooperation rules in a well known decision involving control of titanium dioxide. The Maastricht European Union Treaty altered the SEA to provide regular Parliamentary cooperation on environmental legislation and general use of qualified majority voting by the Council in this field.

Europe is forging ahead in some areas of environmental protection. For example, regarding fluorocarbons and the ozone layer, the Commission has started using "voluntary agreements" with industry. The Commission reached such an agreement with the Federation of European Aerosol Manufacturers in 1989 committing the industry to a 90 percent reduction in the use of CFCs by 1991. This agreement was confirmed in Commission Recommendation 89/349, an act without legal force. Similar results have been achieved on the use of styrofoam in the refrigeration industry. The Commission has also proposed taxing sources of CFCs, carbon dioxide and aircraft noise.

The European Parliament has been a supporter of stronger environmental policies, backing up its commitment with new budgetary allocations and by promoting the creation of a European Environmental Agency in Copenhagen. Its initial task is to function as an information clearinghouse. The EU has also concluded a large number of international environmental agreements, including the Basel Convention on Transboundary Movements of Hazardous Wastes, the Bonn Agreement on the Prevention of Pollution of the North Sea, and the Washington Convention [against] International Trade in Endangered Species of Wild Flora and Fauna. The Council adopted a Resolution in 1993 tightening supervision and control of shipments of waste into and from the region. This Resolution transposes the Basel Convention into European law. One particularly innovative environmental agreement party is the Barcelona Convention on the Mediterranean Sea. This Convention obligates the signatories to select from a menu of options on improvement and protection of the Mediterranean.

BROADCASTING

The EU Council has acted to promote "television without frontiers." Belgium and Denmark voted against this directive (No. 89/552). Each state must admit television broadcasts from the others. The regulation of the content of those broadcasts is generally left to home state control, subject to various rules on rights of reply and advertising. Maximum advertising time limits (generally 15 percent) are established in the television without frontiers directive. This directive also regulates cigarette and childrens' advertising, including a general ban on tobacco advertising. This is not an area where national rules may be more demanding, as Sweden learned when its tougher rules against advertising to children were invalidated.

The broadcasting directive provides that "when practicable," broadcasters (many of which are government-owned) should reserve a majority of their time for programs of European origin. Europeans refer to this language as a "political commitment," not a binding rule of law. Either way, it is more restrictive than meets the eye because broadcast time devoted to news, sports events, games, advertising and teletext services is *excluded* when measuring compliance. Moreover, no member state may reduce the percentage of broadcast time allotted to European works from that which existed in 1988.

The rules of origin for television programs focus on producer citizenship and production costs, not cultural content. A work is "European" if it is made by producers in a member state, supervised and actually controlled by producers there or the contribution of European co-producers to the cost is "preponderant." Many U.S. firms have moved quickly into co-productions intended to qualify as European under the broadcasting directive. This directive, when first proposed, contained an absolute requirement of more than 50 percent European broadcasting content. Intense lobbying by the United States, a major exporter of films and TV shows to Europe, introduced the "when practicable" limitation. Nevertheless, the long-term goal of broadcasting European television productions at least half the time is clearly stated and is being actively pursued. Will "The Practice" survive the cut?

The broadcasting directive is supported by decisions of the European Court of Justice that television signals constitute the provision of a "service" and thus come within the Treaty of Rome. In addition, the launching of the European satellite EU-TELSAT in 1983 made transborder broadcasting possible. The broadcasting directive was one of the few early single market laws to attract headlines in the United States. The entertainment industry is America's second largest source of export earnings after military products and technology. The broadcasting directive caused the United States business community to wake up and become proactive in Europe. They have been supported by Congressional resolutions denouncing the broadcasting directive, and repeated statements by United States Trade Representative (USTR) that it is the "enemy of free trade."

U.S. Reaction

In 1991, the USTR put the European Community on a "priority watchlist" of nations whose intellectual property practices are suspect by U.S. standards. This was done under the "Special 301" trade sanction provisions of Section 182 of the Trade Act of 1974. The USTR is monitoring national implementation of the broadcasting directive to determine whether, and to what degree, American programs are denied access. Since France, Italy, the United Kingdom, Spain and Portugal have enacted broadcast quotas, and the French quota is 60 percent, the potential exists for Section 301 retaliation and exacerbation of the dispute between the U.S. and the European Union.

More balanced observers note that the broadcasting directive reflects the sense of cultural invasion that many Europeans resent and associate with more than just television, for example a McDonald's on every corner. France refers to the United States as a "hyperpower" a country whose power extends beyond economics, defense and technology to domination of attitudes, concepts, language and mode of life. Generally, however, the fear of losing cultural identity within Europe is diminishing as younger generations are educated, travel, intermarry, and take up work around the region. The beginnings of a European "melting pot" are evident, but concern about the cultural influence of "outsiders" is growing and Europe will always be multicultural. These trends affect not just United States broadcasters, but also Japanese exporters, and the racial and ethnic minorities of Europe.

INTELLECTUAL PROPERTY RIGHTS

All of the European Union member states are parties to the Paris Convention on the Protection of Industrial Property (1883). The expression "industrial property" is now usually replaced by "intellectual property." This means that each of them grants national treatment rights to citizens of other member states regarding patents and trademarks. The Paris Convention also gives applicants a one year right of priority to apply in other states for patent rights and a six months right of priority for trademark rights. These priority rights date from the initial home country application. Thus the Paris Convention achieved limited harmonization of EU patent and trademark law.

Patents and Designs

The 1973 European Patent Convention (EPC) established the European Patent Office (EPO) in Munich. It allows applicants to simultaneously apply for national patent rights in any of the contracting countries. These include all of the EU nations, plus a number of other European states. The applicant must meet the requirements for patentability established by the EPC. Challenges to patentability decisions by the EPO can be made within 9 months after granting of the patent. Thereafter, challenges must be made in national courts subject to national patent laws. The EPC basically presents a one-stop opportunity to obtain a basket of national patents in Europe. It does not foreclose the option of individual national patent applications.

The 1975 Community Patent Convention (CPC) still has not come into force. The CPC will allow applications for a Common Market patent valid in any contracting state. The CPC does not, however, permit patenting of biotechnology inventions, although this may well be amended following eventual ratification. A Common Market patent may be granted, revoked or transferred throughout the Union as a whole. Licenses for part of the Union will be possible. It will be an alternative to (but not a replacement for) national patent rights. The CPC should be contrasted with the bundle of national rights obtained through the EPC. However, the CPC will require its signatories to harmonize national patent laws to conform to the Convention's rules on infringement, litigation procedures, exhaustion of rights and other issues. It will create a new Court of Patent Appeals.

Biotechnology patents are mandated by Council Directive 98/44, provided industrial application is possible. The human body and its genes are not patentable, nor are processes for cloning human beings or uses of human embryos for industrial or commercial purposes. Plant variety rights are established in Regulation 2100/94.

The protection of semiconductor topographies is regulated by Council Directive 87/54. This directive was adopted in response to U.S. requirements of reciprocity before EU nationals can obtain comparable U.S. rights under the Semiconductor Chip Protection Act of 1984. Topographies that are original ("not commonplace") are protected for ten years. This protection includes the right to prohibit reproduction of the topography and its commercial exploitation. But exclusivity is not preserved when reverse engineering occurs or a semiconductor product is put on the market by consent. The European Union has not signed the Washington Treaty on protection of microcircuits.

After years of debate, Council Directive 98/71 harmonized national rules on design rights, an area of intellectual property rights law with diverse coverage throughout the EU. Design rights are possible for jewelry, cars, furniture, consumer electronics, machinery, tools, spare auto parts and other products. Such rights last from five to 25 years, and may be used to preclude Common Market trade.

Trademarks

Late in 1993, the Council adopted a regulation creating "Community Trademarks." Businesses operating in the European Common Market may now elect to process applications for such marks through the Union's new Trademark Office in Alicante, Spain. This presents a streamlined alternative to seeking national trademark registration, in each member state. Any words or symbols capable of distinguishing goods or services are registrable even if exclusively descriptive. Colors may also be distinctive. Community Trademarks may be opposed whenever there is a likelihood of confusion, there are prior national registrations of the marks that have been genuinely used, or various nonregistrable grounds (e.g., genericism) are present. Community Trademarks are valid for 10 years and may be renewed. Any failure to use a Community mark for 5 years can cause protection to be withdrawn. Hundreds of thousands of Community marks have been issued, many to U.S. businesses. There is a Board of Appeal within the Trademark Office, followed by what have been numerous appeals to the European Court of First Instance.

In addition, the Council has adopted Directive 89/104. This directive seeks to harmonize some aspects of EU trademark law, but not trademark registration procedures. A summary of its highlights follows. The directive applies to individual trademarks, service marks, collective marks, and guarantee or certification marks which are the subject of a registration or an application for registration in the member states. It does not cover trademark rights acquired through use, which is possible in Italy, Ireland and the United Kingdom. A trademark may consist of any "sign" capable of being represented graphically. This includes words, personal names, designs, letters, numerals, and the shape of goods or their packaging, provided that such signs are capable of distinguishing the goods or services of one firm from those of others. It may therefore include such things as musical jingles or screen layouts/user interfaces for computer programs (in each case to the extent that third party rights are not infringed).

Article 3 distinguishes between absolute grounds for refusal or invalidity of marks (*e.g.,* marks devoid of distinctive character, contrary to public policy or accepted principles of morality) and relative grounds (*e.g.,* a sign of high symbolic value, particularly a religious symbol). Allowance is made for registered marks which acquire a distinctive character through use. Member states are also permitted to continue to refuse registration on grounds already in force prior to adoption of the directive. Article 4 provides that registration of a mark which is identical or confusingly similar to one registered nationally or as a regional trademark, or a well known but unregistered mark, is not allowed.

A common set of infringement criteria are contemplated in Article 5 of the directive. These criteria include presentation of the use of registered trademarks on different classes of goods if detrimental to the distinctive character of the mark. Article 7 provides that the principle of the exhaustion of rights applies. Licensing of marks for limited use or for limited areas is generally permissible. Article 9 states that where a proprietor for an earlier trademark has acquiesced for a period of five successive years to the use of a later trademark registered in good faith in that member state while being aware of such use, he or she is no longer entitled to apply for a declaration that the trademark is invalid or to oppose the use of the later trademark. This provision resembles adverse possession. Furthermore, trademark rights can be revoked if the owner has not put the mark to genuine use for five years absent valid reasons for non-use. Use of the mark on exported goods will meet the genuine use requirement.

Copyrights

In November of 1992, the Council adopted Directive 92/100 on minimum 50–year rental and lending rights for copyrighted works. This directive requires the member states to provide authors' and producers' rights to allow or prohibit the rental or lending of original or copied copyrighted works, such as records, videos or films. The concepts of "rental" and "lending" are broadly defined to include any "direct or indirect economic or commercial advantage." Libraries that loan such works to the public at charges which do not exceed operating costs are not deemed to have an "advantage" and therefore are not caught within Directive 92/100.

The member states may override a refusal to lend for cultural promotion and other activities provided they remunerate the rights' holder, but cannot override a refusal to rent. Even when there is an assignment of rental rights to record or film producers, the original holder retains an equitable right to remuneration that cannot be waived. Performers and broadcasters obtain exclusive rights to authorize or deny the fixation of their works and their reproduction and distribution. When broadcasters use sound recordings, a mandatory remuneration scheme is triggered with the funds shared between the record producers and the performers. A number of exceptions to these exclusive rights may be granted, including private, reportorial, teaching, scientific and ephemeral use.

Late in 1993, the Council adopted Directive 93/83 in order to harmonize copyright and related rights for satellite and cable TV transmissions. The primary goal is to insure payment for the holders of such rights. For satellites, commencing in 1995, broadcast rights must be obtained in the country of origin not destination. Prior contracts must be adapted to this rule by the end of 1999. For cable TV, broadcast rights must be negotiated through cooperative bodies representing various categories of rights holders. Unreasonable refusals by broadcasters to retransmit programs by cable were arbitrated until 2003.

The Council also adopted Directive 93/98 in order to harmonize the duration of copyrights and related rights (e.g. photographs and posthumous works). As from July 1, 1995, all works subject to copyright protection in the Union will last for 70 years after the death of the author. The term is 50 years for neighboring rights. For audiovisual and cinematic works, there was some dispute about who is "the author." Copyright protection for these works will extend for 70 years from the death of the last survivor of the following persons: the principal director, the author of the script, the author of the dialogue and the composer of the music. Directive 2001/84 harmonizes the law of monetary resale rights for artists ("droit de suite").

Directive 2001/29 draws upon the WIPO Copyright Treaty of 1996 and corresponds to the U.S. Digital Millennium Copyright Act of 1998. The Directive is Internet driven, and outlaws possession, making or providing all tools capable of circumventing technological measures intended to protect copyrighted material. In other words, "hackers" beware. Likewise, tampering with copyright management information (that is to say, encryption devices) is prohibited under Directive 2001/29. Remedies may vary among the member states, but must be "effective." Some EU members have enacted criminal sanctions, others have limited relief to damages.

TRIPs

The European Union adheres to the WTO Agreement on Trade–Related Intellectual Property Rights (TRIPs), thereby generating substantial uniformity in intellectual property law. The TRIPs Code covers the gamut of intellectual property. On copyrights, there is protection for computer programs and databases, rental authorization controls for owners of compute software and should recordings, a 50–year motion picture and sound recording copyright term, and a general obligation to comply with the Berne Convention (except for its provisions on moral rights).

On patents, the Paris Convention (1967) prevails, product and process patents are to be available for pharmaceuticals and agricultural chemicals, limits are placed on compulsory licensing, and a general 20–year patent term from the date of application is created. United States law, which previously granted 17 year patents from the date of issuance, has been amended to conform. For trademarks, internationally prominent marks receive enhanced protection, the linking of local marks with foreign trademarks is prohibited, service marks become registrable, and compulsory licensing is banned. In addition, trade secret protection is assisted by TRIPs rules enabling owners to prevent unauthorized use or disclosure. Integrated circuits are covered by rules intended to improve upon the Washington Treaty. Lastly, industrial designs and geographic indicators of alcoholic beverages (e.g., Canadian Whiskey) are also part of the TRIPs regime.

Infringement and anticounterfeiting remedies are included in the TRIPs, for both domestic and international trade protection. There are specific provisions governing injunctions, damages, customs seizures, and discovery of evidence. Directive 3295/94 implements the Union's remedies against counterfeit and infringing goods, but criminal sanctions are not mandatory.

COMPUTER SOFTWARE, DATABASES AND DATA PRIVACY

Two areas of technology law of particular interest to U.S. firms have been legislated amidst controversy and a blitz of American lobbying. Council Directive 91/250 requires member states to protect computer programs by copyright, something not all EU jurisdictions did. However, its rules on "decompilation" (reverse engineering) for purposes of interoperability with an independently created program are liberal by U.S. standards. There is a specific right to "observe, study or test the functioning of the program in order to determine the ideas and principles that underlie any element of the program." However, decompilation may not be used for the development, production and marketing of a substantially similar computer program. The directive takes no position on the patentability of computer software.

Directive 96/9 protects databases. It creates exclusive rights to databases not otherwise copyrightable.

Council Directive 95/46 concerns data privacy. It details extensive rights for individuals concerning the processing of personal data, including website registrations. Individuals have broad rights to be informed of proposed usages, deny disclosure, require corrections, and, particularly, to object to "direct marketing" use of their data. Violation of these rights can result in public prosecutions and private actions by e-commerce consumers in their country of residence. The directive prohibits the transfer of personal data to non-EU countries unless they ensure "an adequate level of protection" of EU-sourced data. The adequacy of United States protection has been hotly debated. By agreement in 2000, U.S. companies processing EU data may seek "safe harbor" from the directive by submitting to U.S. Federal Trade Commission jurisdiction over approved self-regulating U.S.-based privacy organizations (e.g. BBB Online). A goodly number of firms, including Microsoft, have done so.

E–COMMERCE

The European Union began considering the advent of the "Information Society," and the need to establish a Pan–European information technology infrastructure with the 1994 white paper on "Growth, Competitiveness and Employment: the Challenges and Courses for Entering into the XXIst Century" prepared by former European Commission Vice–President Martin Bangemann. The Bangemann Report led to the establishment of an Information Society Project (now Promotion) Office within the EU, and a series of actions plans to promote the Information Society in Europe. These plans were intended to formulate strategies to change the existing regulatory and legal framework, technical infrastructure, and the cultural attitudes necessary to promote the Information Society. This led most recently to the eEurope Initiative to further accelerate the development of an European Information Society.

The EU efforts to coherently address the impact of technology on European society as a whole results in a very different approach to many of the issues raised by E–Commerce than that seen in the United States for example. It is an approach which is inherently multinational, and characterized by a conscious effort to harmonize or approximate legal rules throughout the different member countries in the EU. At the same time it is an approach which also consciously seeks to identify and remove barriers to the development of E–Commerce and other Information Society services. Although only one aspect of the broader European Information Society initiatives, measures related to E–Commerce have been central to the various EU action plans. These measures include the 1997 European Initiative on Electronic Commerce, which focused on primarily on developing infrastructure and protecting consumers' economic and legal interests; the related 1997 Distance Selling Directive; the 1999 Electronic Signature Directive; and most recently the Electronic Commerce Directive in 2000. There are also several other important measures aimed at particular issues, such as Data Privacy Directives (above), which have a significant impact upon online transactions but which would not themselves be considered as "enabling" legislation for E–Commerce transactions.

SOCIAL POLICY—OCCUPATIONAL SAFETY, THE SOCIAL FUND AND SOCIAL CHARTER

The Treaty of Rome is dominated by economic affairs. Nevertheless, Europe has always sought to provide for some of the concerns of the human beings who are impacted by the winds of economic change. The Treaty of Rome seeks to improve working conditions and standards of living on a harmonized basis. The right of nationals to move freely to take up employment has previously been discussed in Chapter 4. Europe's social policy builds upon this basic right. Article 144, for example, led to the enactment of social security legislation to insure coverage for those who exercise their right to move freely to work.

A major impetus came in 1987 with the addition of Article 138 by the Single European Act. This article focuses on health and safety in the working environment. Acting by a qualified majority vote, the Council in cooperation with the Parliament is empowered to issue directives establishing minimum requirements in this field. It has done so, for example, on visual display units, heavy load handling and exposure to biological agents and carcinogens. More generally, Council directives now establish minimum safety and health requirements for most workplaces, equipment used by workers, and protective devices. Article 138 specifically requires such directives to avoid imposing administrative, financial and legal constraints that would hold back the creation and development of small and medium-sized enterprises. Like the 1987 Treaty amendments creating the Environmental Policy, Article 138 allows member states to maintain or introduce more stringent legal rules on working conditions, provided these are compatible with the Treaty of Rome.

The European Social Fund comes out of the regional budget. It is used to pay up to 50 percent of the costs of the member states under their vocational retraining and worker resettlement programs. European rules have substantially harmonized these programs. Unemployment compensation is also funded when plants are converted to other production for workers who are temporarily suspended or suffer a reduction in working hours. They retain the same wage levels pending full re-employment. Commission Decision 83/516 extended the operation of the European Social Fund to promoting employment among those under age 25, women who wish to return to work, the handicapped, migrants and their families, and the long-term unemployed.

Social Charter

The single market campaign has a social dimension. Labor unions have been especially concerned about the prospect of "social dumping," the relocation of companies to states with weaker unions and lower wages. There is no regional legislation on minimum wages and none is expected in the near future. One response to these concerns led to the Charter of Fundamental Social Rights For Workers, adopted in 1989 by 11 member states less Britain through the European Council. The Charter proclaims the following fundamental social rights for workers:

(1) freedom of movement and choice of occupations;

(2) fair remuneration (sufficient to have a decent standard of living);

(3) improved living and working conditions (e.g., paid leave);

(4) adequate social security benefits;

(5) free association in unions, including the right *not* to join, and the right to strike;

(6) nondiscriminatory access to vocational training;

(7) equal treatment for women and men;

(8) development of rights to access to information, and rights of consultation and participation;

(9) satisfactory health and safety conditions at work;

(10) for the young, a minimum employment age of 15, substantial limitations on night work for those under 18, and start-up vocational training rights;

(11) for retirees, the right to assistance "as needed" and a decent standard of living; and

(12) for the disabled, assistance to integrate socially and professionally.

The Charter was to be implemented immediately by the member states in "accordance with national practices." In addition, for each item listed above, regional legislation was anticipated.

Adoption of this legislation was slow chiefly because Britain held a veto power in the Council over employment matters under the Single European Act. The Commission, however, drafted a number of Social Action Program legislative measures. One such measure guaranteeing minimum maternity leave benefits of 14 weeks at statutory sick pay rates was adopted by the Council in 1992. A woman's employment cannot be terminated because she is pregnant. In addition, pregnant women are entitled to switch from night work, exempted from work detrimental to their health, and entitled to take paid leave for pre-natal check-ups. This directive required substantial improvements to existing legislation in Ireland, Portugal and the United Kingdom. Unpaid parental leave rights are detailed in Directive 96/34.

From the Social Protocol to the Social Chapter

In December 1991 at the Maastricht Summit agreement was reached, save Britain, on a "social policy protocol" facilitating adoption by the other eleven member states of laws by qualified majority vote governing many areas which bridge workers' interests and company operations. Some suggested that the "social protocol" would have been more accurately labeled a "workers' rights protocol". It focused on working environment issues including conditions of labor, health and safety, disclosure of information, sex discrimination, and worker consultation. The "social protocol" thus overlapped considerably with the Social Charter.

Despite its repeated opposition to development of a "social dimension," the United Kingdom under Conservative rule adopted or implemented over half of the measures noted in the Social Charter. What the Conservatives consistently objected to were rules relating directly to the employee-employer relationship, not worker benefits such as pregnancy leave or health or safety measures. Nevertheless, the Court of Justice repeatedly ruled against Britain in litigation challenging the adequacy of its implementation of worker-related directives (e.g., on collective redundancies (mass layoffs) and transfers of enterprises). And, in a major decision, the Court ruled over vehement objection that the "working time" directive (No. 93/104) was properly adopted by qualified majority vote on the basis of Article 138's authorization of worker health and safety law. This ruling had the practical effect of avoiding Britain's Social Protocol opt out rights. The directive creates, inter alia, a minimum right to four weeks of paid vacation. Subsequently, the United Kingdom under the Labour Party administration of Prime Minister Blair opted into the region's Social Policy and the 1999 Amsterdam Treaty repealed the Social Protocol.

As amended, Articles 135–145 of the Treaty of Rome (the "social chapter") embrace social goals reflecting the Social Charter. There is express authority for EU legislation on worker health and safety, work conditions, information and consultation of workers, and gender equality. Qualified majority voting and co-decision Parliamentary powers are generally used. However, there is no authorization for EU action on matters of pay, and rights of association, strike and lock-out. EU legislation can occur by unanimous vote on social security, co-determination, worker protection upon termination and employment of third country nationals.

REGIONAL POLICY

The Treaty of Rome is premised upon the opening of national markets to competitive trade. The Treaty, especially as amended by the Single European Act in 1987, recognizes that some areas of the Union will not succeed under these conditions. These "less developed" parts of the EU benefit from the Regional Policy. Since 1987, the basic provisions on Regional Policy are located in Articles 158–162 of the Treaty of Rome under the title "economic and social cohesion."

The Regional Policy operates in conjunction with other programs, notably in agriculture, the Social Fund and coal and steel, to facilitate the growth and development of its poorer parts. The Mezzogiorno in Southern Italy was an early target for regional aid which now extends to most of Portugal, Greece and Ireland, as well as parts of the remaining member states. Some aid comes in the form of Union authorization for national subsidies. Other aid comes directly from the nonprofit European Investment Bank (EIB). The EIB is funded by the Union and the capital market. It has financed a large number of regional development projects.

Article 158 commits the Union to the goal of reducing the disparities between its regions and the "backwardness" of its least-favored regions. A region is least-favored if its per capita GDP is less than 50 percent of the EU average. A major step toward this goal accomplished by the Single European Act was formal recognition of the European Regional Development Fund. This fund has operated since 1975 in addition to, and coordinated with, those that function under the Union's Common Agricultural Policy and its Social Policy. The Regional Development Fund targets structural adjustment and conversion of declining industrial regions with aid grants. Its monies have gone a long way toward convincing the poorer regions of the Union that the campaign for a fully integrated market will bring some benefit to them. Regional development has often become the grease that insures a unanimous vote whenever needed to move the Common Market closer to a full reality.

Expanded economic aid to the least developed members of the Union was accomplished under the "cohesion funds" of the Maastricht Treaty on European Union and the European Economic Area agreement with the EFTA states (less Switzerland). Extensive and difficult negotiations over retention of such funds preceded the 2004 expansion in membership of the European Union which took in numerous states less developed than even the poorest EU member. Countries like Poland, Latvia and Slovakia (for example) are going to receive substantial regional development funds, possibly at the expense of Spain, Greece and Ireland (for example).

EQUAL PAY AND EQUAL TREATMENT

Article 141 is a prominent element in European social policy. It is derived from International Labor Organization Convention No. 100 which three states, including France, had adopted by 1957. The French were rightfully proud of this tradition of nondiscrimination between the sexes on pay. They also appreciated that gender-based inequality in pay in other member states could harm the ability of their companies to compete. Article 141 thus enshrines the principle that men and women shall receive equal pay for equal work. For these purposes, "pay" is defined as wages or salary, and any other consideration in cash or kind, received directly or indirectly respecting employment. "Equal pay without discrimination based on sex" means that piece rate payment must be calculated on the same units of measurement and that time rates must be equal for the same job.

Equal Pay

Article 141 has been the subject of voluminous legislation and litigation. It applies, quite appropriately, to the European Community as an employer. Early on, the Court of Justice decided that the Article 141 on equal pay for equal work is directly effective law. This decision allowed individuals to challenge pay discrimination in public and private sector jobs. The ruling was applied prospectively by the Court of Justice so as to avoid large numbers of lawsuits for back pay.

In the famous *Defrenne* case, a flight attendant for Sabena Airlines was able to allege illegal discrimination in pay and pension benefits (as a form deferred pay) to stewards and stewardesses on the basis of Article 141 law before a Belgian work tribunal. European law in this area enshrines the principle of "comparable worth," a most controversial issue in United States employment law. Furthermore, women who are paid less than men performing work of less worth may claim relief. The hard question is how to determine what constitutes "equal work" requiring equal pay under Article 141, or what "women's work" is worth more than that being done by men (again requiring pay adjustments). For example, does secretarial work equal custodial work? Is the work of an airline attendant worth more than that of an airline mechanic?

In determining equal or greater values, most states favor a job content approach. Content is determined through job evaluation systems which use factor analyses. For example, in Great Britain a job is broken down into various components such as skill, responsibility, physical requirements, mental requirements and working conditions. Points or grades are awarded in each of these categories and totaled to determine the value of the job. Different factors may be balanced against each other. In Ireland, the demand of physical work can be balanced against the concentration required in particular skills. This is known as the "total package" approach. The equal job content approach relies on comparisons. This raises the question of which jobs should be deemed to be suitable for comparison. The member states have taken different approaches to this question. In Britain the comparison must be drawn from the same business establishment. In contrast, the Irish Anti–Discrimination Pay Act provides for "comparisons in the same place," and "place" includes a city, town or locality. This approach is designed to ensure that legitimate regional differences in pay are not disturbed.

Pay Differentials

Employer defenses also vary from member state to member state. In Ireland, employers may justify a variation if they can show "grounds other than sex" for a disputed variation in pay. In Britain, employers will succeed if they can prove a "genuine material factor which is not the difference of sex." In Germany, the employer can prove that "material reasons unrelated to a particular sex" justify the differential. A further consideration in the implementation of equal pay laws has been the existence of pre-existing wage schedules set by collective agreement. In Britain and Italy, courts have held that collective agreements relating to pay cannot be changed or altered except where direct discrimination can be shown. But the European Court has indicated that where significant statistics disclose an appreciable difference in pay between jobs of equal value (here women in speech therapy and men in pharmacy) Article 141 requires the *employer* to show that the difference is based on objectively justified factors unrelated to sex discrimination. The fact that separate collective bargaining processes are used does not alter this burden.

The burden of proving "objectively justified economic grounds" for pay differentials is on the employer. When a woman succeeds a man in a particular position within a company, she is entitled to equal pay absent a satisfactory explanation not based upon gender. The same is true of part-time (female) workers doing the same job as full-time (male) workers. Free travel to employees upon retirement cannot go only to men. And "pay" includes retirement benefits paid upon involuntary dismissal, which cannot be discriminatory. It also includes employer-paid pension benefits which cannot be for men only. Mobility, special training and seniority may be objectively justifiable grounds for pay discrimination.

Comparable Worth

Council Directive 75/117 complements Article 141. It makes the principle of equal pay apply to work of *equal value* (to the employer), a principle now expressly incorporated in Article 141 since 1999. This mandates establishment of nondiscriminatory job classifications to measure the comparable worth of one job with another. The Commission successfully enforced Directive 75/117 in a prosecution before the European Court of Justice against the United Kingdom. The Sex Discrimination Act of 1975, adopted expressly to fulfill Article 141 obligations, did not meet European standards because employers could block the introduction of job classification systems. Danish law's failure to cover nonunionized workers also breached the equal pay directive. But its implementation under German law, notably by constitutional provisions, sufficed to meet regional standards.

Equal Treatment

The principle of equal pay for equal work has been extended to *equal treatment* regarding access to employment, vocational training and promotion, and working conditions (e.g., retirement deadlines). This directive prohibits discrimination based upon sex, family or marital status and extends to the self-employed. Equal treatment is limited by three exceptions. Member states may distinguish between men and women if: (1) sex is a determining factor in ability to perform the work; (2) the provision protects women; or (3) the provision promotes equal opportunity for men and women. Discrimination is also permitted in "occupational activities" for which workers of only one sex are appropriate.

Equal treatment must be extended to small and household businesses. Dutch Law compulsorily retiring women at age 60 and men at age 65 violated the directive. Women cannot be refused employment because they are pregnant even if the employer will suffer financial losses during maternity leave. Maternity and adoption leave benefits for women, however, need not be extended to men. The dismissal of a woman because of repeated absences owing to sickness is lawful provided the same absences would lead to the dismissal of men.

Affirmative Action

Predictably, questions of "affirmative action" have arisen in the context of Article 141 law. A controversial decision of the Court of Justice invalidated a Bremen regulation giving women of equal qualifications priority over men where women made up less than half the relevant civil service staff. While not strictly a quota, the Court found that Bremen had exceeded the limits of the equal treatment directive in promoting equality of opportunity. Specific reservation of University professorships for women in Sweden likewise fell upon ECJ review. Sweden now uses increasing targets for women in full professorships. Article 141(4) of Treaty of Rome, as amended by the Amsterdam Treaty in 1999, attempts to address such issues. It allows member states to maintain or adopt "measures for specific advantages" in order to make it "easier" for the "under represented sex" to pursue vocational activity or to prevent or compensate for "disadvantages" in professional careers.

Gender and Other Discrimination

Equality also governs social security entitlements such as disability or caring for the disabled pay. Social security benefits cannot be based upon marital status. Women police officers cannot be denied arms when men are not, even in the interest of "public safety" and "national security." Equal treatment requires the elimination of preferences based upon gender in laws governing collectively bargained employment agreements. In addition, the Council adopted a declaration in December 1991 endorsing the Commission's recommended Code of Practice on sexual harassment. This Code rejects sexual harassment as contrary to equal treatment law. Council Directive 2002/73 codifies this approach, emphasizing protection of employee dignity. But both the equal pay and equal treatment directives fail to cover significant categories of women workers; part-time, temporary and home workers. Additional legislation in these areas can be expected.

There is a trend within the jurisprudence of the Court of Justice towards recognition of a broad human right of equality before the law. This is evidenced in a number of Article 141 cases, reliance upon the European Human Rights Convention in developing general principles of EU law (see Chapter 2), and in revised Articles 2, 3 and 13 of the Treaty of Rome (1999). Transsexuals and homosexuals have begun to benefit from this trend. But the Court notably refused to require equal employer travel benefits for same sex partners under Article 141 law and likewise the Court of Justice refused to recognize such partners as the equivalent of marriage for household allowance purposes. Revisions of the 1976 equal treatment directive emphasizing an approach called "gender mainstreaming" are in progress. Directive 2000/43 broadly provides for equal treatment irrespective of racial or ethnic origin. Directive 2000/78 more narrowly prohibits employment discrimination on grounds of religion or belief, disability, age or sexual orientation.

COMMON AGRICULTURAL POLICY

The Treaty of Rome establishes the basic principles governing what is perhaps the most controversial of all regional policies, the Common Agricultural Program (CAP). The inclusion of agricultural trade in the Treaty of Rome was a critical political element. For many reasons, including the desire for self-sufficiency in food and the protection of farmers, free trade in agricultural products is an extremely sensitive issue. When the Common Market was established in 1957, France and Italy had substantial farming communities, many of which were family based and politically powerful. Both countries envisioned that free trade in agricultural products could threaten the livelihoods of these people. The solution, as outlined in the Treaty of Rome, was to set up a "common organization of agricultural markets."

The objectives of the CAP stated in the Treaty of Rome include the increase of productivity, the maintenance of a fair standard of living for the agricultural community, the stabilization of markets and the provision of consumer goods at reasonable prices. It has not proved possible to accommodate all of these objectives. Consumer interests have generally lost out to farmers' incomes and trading company profits. Target prices for some commodities (e.g., sugar, dairy products and grain) are established and supported through market purchases at "intervention levels". "Variable import levies" (tariffs) are periodically changed to ensure that cheaper imports do not disrupt CAP prices. External protection of this type is also extended to meat and eggs. Fruit, vegetables and wine are subject to quality controls which limit their flow into the market. Wine and agricultural products are subject to regulated designations of origin.

Regulatory Controls

In recent years, perhaps the most controversial "common organization" has been for bananas. The Europeans import bananas under a complex quota system adopted in 1993 that favors former colonies and dependencies. Internally and externally those affected have gone bananas over this regulation. Several challenges originating from Germany failed before the European Court of Justice, but in the end the United States, Mexico, Ecuador, Guatemala and Honduras prevailed in the World Trade Organization. After suffering "authorized retaliation" in the form of tariffs on EU exports, the Europeans have promised to adjust their "common organization" for bananas by replacing its quotas with non-preferential tariffs.

The European Agricultural Guidance and Guarantee Fund (better known by its French initials as FEOGA) channels the agricultural budget into export refunds, intervention purchases, storage, and structural adjustment. Agricultural policy regulations cannot discriminate against like or substitute products. But the bias towards producers, not consumers, in the CAP has been consistently upheld by the Court of Justice.

Agricultural goods, like industrial products, can trigger free movement litigation. These issues are often raised under Articles 28–30, covered in Chapter 4. In one case, for example, the Court of Justice suggested that British animal health regulations were a disguised restraint on trade in poultry and eggs. As with industrial goods, if the real aim is to block imports, such regulations are unlawful measures of equivalent effect to a quota. On the other hand, the United Kingdom could establish a Pear and Apple Development Council for purposes of technical advice, promotional campaigns (not intended to discourage competitive imports), and common quality standards for its members. But it could not impose a mandatory fee to finance such activities.

Apart from variable tariff protection, CAP quality control regulations can serve to keep foreign agricultural products from entering the European market. For example, the ban on beef hormones adopted by qualified majority vote in the late 1980s stirred opposition internally. In the United States, the beef hormones legislation was vehemently opposed by the White House, but accepted by the renegade Texas Department of Agriculture which offered as much hormone-free beef as Europe would buy. The Texas offer delighted the Commissioner on Agriculture who rarely has a U.S. ally and is said to have wired: "I accept."

A veritable maze of legislation and case law governs the CAP. For many years, special agricultural "monetary compensation amounts" (MCAs) were collected at national borders, greatly contributing to the failure to achieve a Europe without internal trade frontiers. It was not until 1987 that firm arrangements were realized to dismantle the MCA system. In most years, the net effect of the CAP is to raise food prices in Europe substantially above world price levels. The CAP has meant that agriculture is heavily subsidized. Indeed, it continues to consume the lion's share of the regional budget and at times seems like a spending policy that is out of control.

The Common Agricultural Policy does include a variety of "structural" programs intended to reduce the size of the farm population, increase the efficiency of its production and hold down prices. These programs have involved retirement incentives, land reallocations, and training for other occupations.

There has been a gradual reduction in the number of farmers over the years. In 1988, the Council adopted rules designed ultimately to reduce agricultural expenditures by linking total expenditures to rates of economic growth, establishing automatic price cuts when production ceilings are reached, and creating land set-aside and early retirement programs for farmers.

France and Italy, in the early years, became major beneficiaries of CAP subsidies. West Germany, with a minimal agricultural sector, was the primary payor under the program. It, in turn, principally benefitted from the custom union provisions establishing free trade in industrial goods. Hence a basic tradeoff was established in 1957 by the Treaty of Rome. France and Italy would receive substantial agricultural subsidies out of the Common Market budget while West Germany gained access for its industrial goods to their markets. Britain, like Germany, sees itself as a net payor under the CAP. It has repeatedly been able to negotiate special compensatory adjustments as a consequence. Greece, Spain, Portugal and Ireland, on the other hand, looked forward eagerly to membership as a means to CAP subsidies. So too the countries of Central Europe await CAP subsidies with great expectations. These countries, along with unified Germany, Austria, Sweden and Finland (whose agricultural subsidies were actually *reduced* upon joining the CAP), are often the least efficient producers of agricultural products. As such, they stand to lose the most if the CAP is substantially replaced by market forces.

International Ramifications

In the main, however, like the United States until recently, the Europeans seemed unable to stabilize the level of agricultural subsidies. This resulted in overproduction ("butter mountains," "wine lakes") and frequent commodity trade wars. A significant amount of fraud to obtain CAP subsidy payments has occurred. Others legitimately farm marginal land with lots of fertilizer polluting this environment. The excess produce is stored, used in social welfare programs and frequently "dumped" in cheap sales abroad.

Despite its incredible cost, over half the EU budget, the CAP remains one of the political and economic cornerstones of European integration. In 1992 the Council of Agricultural Ministers agreed as an internal matter to cuts in support prices of 29 percent for cereals, 15 percent for beef and 5 percent for butter. Farmers received direct payments representing the income lost from the price cuts. Further price cuts and direct payments were agreed in 1999. It was hoped that these reductions would reduce export subsidies on agricultural goods and international trade tensions. They also supported the argument that the extraordinary level of European subsidization of agriculture was simply not sustainable.

European agricultural trade restraints are of enormous consequence to North American exporters. Equally significant are its "export refunds" on agricultural commodities, refunds that affect the opportunities of North American exporters in other parts of the world. The United States has argued (at times successfully) that these refunds violate the GATT/WTO rules on subsidies, while at the same time increasing its own export subsidies on agricultural goods. The result for many years was an agricultural "trade war" between the U.S. and Europe. Each side sought to outspend the other on agricultural export subsidies in a market that has been wonderful to buyers.

External protests from North America notwithstanding, the CAP is unlikely to disappear. Major attempts at a resolution or at least diminishment of the agricultural trade war were undertaken in the Uruguay Round of GATT negotiations during the late 1980s and early 1990s. Late in 1992, both sides announced the resolution of a number of longstanding subsidies' disputes (notably on oilseeds) and a compromise on contested agricultural trade issues. Agreement was reached on 20 percent mutual reduction in internal farm supports and a 21 percent mutual reduction on export subsidies measured on a volume basis over 6 years using a 1986–90 base period. After a year of French protests and further negotiations, this agreement was formally incorporated into the WTO accords.

Tensions between Europe and the United States on agricultural trade have of late diminished (though hardly disappeared), but the U.S. Farm Bill of 2002 threatens to reignite them. The really big issue looming on the CAP horizon is enlargement of the European Union to include Hungary and Poland, among others. Each enlargement of the Union plugs more farmers into the extraordinary CAP subsidy system and the ten new members admitted in 2004 will gain full payments by 2013. The Amsterdam and Nice Treaties notably failed to resolve ongoing disputes over agricultural reform. A last minute deal in 2002 capped costs at their 2006 level plus 1% a year starting in 2007. In theory this will force a gradual winding down of CAP subsidies. One wonders just how much longer European taxpayers will continue to pay for the CAP.

CHAPTER 6

EXTERNAL TRADE LAW

Articles 131–134 of the Treaty of Rome concern external commercial relations. This is referred to as the Common Commercial Policy, and it covers both imports and exports. Article 133 provides some illustrative examples of the wide scope of this policy, including tariffs, quotas, trade agreements, export controls, dumping and subsidies. The European Court of Justice has ruled that the member states cannot enact external commercial policy laws without "specific authorization." However, as the following materials make clear, surrendering national sovereignty over external commercial relations is a most sensitive area.

COMMON CUSTOMS LAW

The Europeans have adopted a Common Customs Code. It took effect Jan. 1, 1994. The Code gathers together basic customs rules previously distributed among some 25 individual directives and regulations. The Code includes coverage of customs clearance procedures, customs warehouses and free trade zones, duty free entry for processing and re-export, duty free re-entry of components that have been processed abroad, classification, valuation, origin, payment and customs' bonds. Customs appeals must be allowed to a national court capable of referring questions of Customs Code law to the European Court of Justice. The EU follows the 1999 Kyoto Convention on modernized customs procedures.

Tariffs

The Common Customs Tariff (CCT), now called the Combined Nomenclature (CN), has been steadily reduced over the years as a result of the GATT tariff Rounds. After the Tokyo Round (1978), European tariffs on manufactured goods dropped on average to about 8 percent, and after the Uruguay Round (1995) to about 4 percent. Member states may not alter the common customs tariff by unilaterally imposing additional duties. The CN is supplemented by tariff rate quotas, tariff preferences, antidumping and other special duties, all of which are reported in the "Taric." These duties are established by regional law, but it is the member states that apply the rules and collect the tariffs. These revenues are forwarded by the national customs' services to the Commission less an administrative charge. Litigation concerning European customs law tends therefore to originate in national tribunals as importers dispute classification, valuation and origin issues. These issues are then typically referenced to the Court of Justice for resolution under Article 234.

The Combined Nomenclature details a tariff schedule that makes two fundamental distinctions.

Goods admitted into the Common Market are subject to either "Autonomous" or "Conventional" duties. The Autonomous Duties represent the original 1968 CCT tariffs and are higher than the Conventional Duties which are the Union's current most-favored-nation (MFN) tariffs as negotiated within the GATT/WTO. For most exports, including nearly all those from the United States and Canada, the MFN rates of duty are applied. The various duty free entry programs to which Europe subscribes will almost never apply to goods originating in either Canada or the United States.

New members are always phased into the customs union rules and tariffs over a transitional period. Portugal and Spain, for example, were not fully aligned until the end of 1992. The same approach is being used with the ten new member states that joined in 2004. United States exporters to any one of the member states pay the same customs duties, regardless of the port of entry. Once U.S. goods enter a member state in principle they may be freely traded inside the Common Market.

Classification

Europe follows the Customs Cooperation Council harmonized nomenclature in its customs classification system. This generally corresponds to the classifications found in the Harmonized Tariff System (HTS) adopted by the United States in 1988. Starting in 1993, a binding tariff classification system based upon mutual recognition of classification decisions made by national customs authorities was instituted. Whenever an importer requests and obtains such a "BTI" decision, it applies to imports of the same product in all other member states. This process reduces the number of divergent tariff classifications, particularly regarding trade sensitive textiles and electronics.

Valuation

The valuation of goods for purposes of assessing the CN is done according to the GATT/WTO Customs Valuation Code. This means that in most instances arms-length transaction value is the basis for tariff assessments, subject to various adjustments. One notable difference between European and U.S. implementation of the Valuation Code concerns international freight and insurance charges. Unlike the United States, such charges are included in the customs value of goods subject to its common external tariff. Purchasing agents' commission are not included in customs values for purposes of collecting the common external tariff, nor are export permit or quota charges, weighing charges, and separately invoiced internal transport charges.

Rules of Origin

As a general matter, the Customs Code determines the origin of goods based upon where the "last substantial process or operation" that was economically justified was performed and resulted in a new product or represented an important stage in manufacture. A process is "economically justi-fied" if it adds value or provides commercial advantages. A process or operation is "substantial," for these purposes, only if the resulting product has its own properties and composition. Cleaning, grinding, grading and packaging a raw material do not meet this standard. If this technical approach to origin is insufficient, a "value added" analysis is pursued. This analysis focuses on the value added to the product in the claimed country of origin. Ten percent is insufficient to confer country of origin status.

Rules of origin are critical to duty free entry of goods from Cotonou Convention, Mediterranean Basin or GSP developing nations. Generally speaking, the rules of origin associated with these programs focus on changes in tariff classifications as the determining factor. But many unique product-specific rules of origin are also created, and these often stress value added approaches. The most generous of these rules of origin apply to Cotonou exports where, for example, any European contribution may be counted as from a Cotonou nation for purposes of value added calculations. Special rules of origin and content requirements apply to high-technology products like printed circuit boards, integrated circuits and the like. These rules often have the effect of transferring technology and production to Europe. EFTA exports may be freely traded under rules of origin that emphasize a change in tariff category.

The many variations on the origin of goods contained in European trade agreements make these rules particularly complex. A product from one country that fails to meet one of the specialized or preferential rules of origin governing entry into the Common Market will be judged under the general rule of origin discussed above.

Counterfeit Goods

The common customs law of the Europe also includes Council Regulation 3842/86 targeting counterfeit goods. Such goods may not be imported nor freely circulated. They are subject to seizure by national customs authorities. The definition of counterfeit goods contained in this regulation refers to goods bearing marks without authorization. Thus the regulation does not apply to trade in "gray market goods" (those produced abroad under license). The Commission also operates a computerized, encoded data network known as the Customs Information System (CIS) to help combat fraud and illegal trading (especially in drugs). Customs officials at all points of entry and exit may communicate with each other, central authorities and the Commission.

Quotas

Until the completion of the internal market on January 1, 1993 a complicated system of import quotas for individual member states existed for various products, notably for automobiles from Japan as well as bananas. The elimination of controls at the Union's internal borders necessitated a harmonization of all European Union import and cus-

toms quotas. Regrettably this has not always resulted in a liberalized access to the EU market, but in a
number of cases the Union has introduced new
regimes which make it more difficult to export to
the European Union. A particularly prominent example is the Common Market Organization for bananas,[1] which although incompatible with the
GATT according to the findings of GATT/WTO panels, was upheld by the European Court of Justice.[2]
It resulted in a discriminatory foreclosure of the
Union market for Latin American bananas which
before could be imported freely into Germany and
the Benelux countries. Since the exporters of bananas most adversely affected by the EU regime of
trade restraints are U.S. multinationals, the United
States was authorized by the WTO to retaliate
against EU exports and did so by imposing substantial tariffs. Finally, in 2001, settlement of the "bananas dispute" was reached, with the EU promising
to replace its quotas with a nonpreferential tariff
scheme.

GENERALIZED TARIFF PREFERENCES (GSP)

Europe participates in the generalized system of
tariff preferences (GSP) initiated under the GATT/
WTO to give duty free access to industrial markets
for selected goods coming from the developing

1. Council Regulation 404/93 and Commission Regulation
1442/93.

2. Germany v. Council (1994) Eur.Comm.Rep. I–4973 (Case
C–280/93).

world. This policy is implemented in the common customs tariff regulations and is especially favorable to goods from countries with strong anti-drug, labor rights and environmental regimes. Poland and Hungary were added to the GSP program in 1990 in recognition of restructuring and developmental problems in their economies. Most of Central Europe has been similarly treated prior to membership. South Africa became a beneficiary as of 1995.

Approximately 150 non-European developing nations now benefit from the GSP trade preferences of the EU, including China. Burma was suspended from the EU program in 1997 for human rights concerns. Since 1998, goods from South Korea, Hong Kong and Singapore no longer qualify. Similarly, the Four Dragons were "graduated" (i.e., no longer treated as developing nations) out of the United States' GSP program in 1989. Burma was suspended from the EU program in 1997 for human rights concerns. In 2001, the EU began phasing in complete duty and quota free access for the world's poorest 48 countries.

The European system of generalized tariff preferences is selectively applied when about 130 "sensitive products" are involved. In other words, there are limitations (quotas and tariff ceilings) on duty free access to the Common Market if the goods compete with European manufacturers. However, these GSP limitations do not apply to products already receiving duty free access under the Cotonou Convention or the Mediterranean Policy. Thus, nations that are covered by the latter trade rules still obtain some margin of preference over other third world GSP beneficiaries.

ANTIDUMPING DUTIES

Another part of the Common Commercial Policy concerns unfair trading practices applied to goods exported to the Common Market. The two most important areas of law here concern the dumping and subsidies rules embodied in Council Regulation 384/96. Similar rules apply to unfair shipping services used to bring goods to Europe. In recent years, the number of antidumping proceedings has risen substantially. Some of these proceedings involve goods from nonmarket economy states (NMEs). Apart from NMEs, Japanese and United States exports have most frequently been involved in antidumping proceedings. Many of these proceedings are settled by promises of the exporters to raise prices and refrain from "dumping." The standing of most exporters and complainants to challenge Commission dumping decisions has been affirmed by the European Court. Such persons would otherwise lack any possible judicial remedy. Importers, on the other hand, have remedies in the national courts of the member states and are therefore generally unable to challenge Commission dumping decisions directly before the European Court.

Dumping involves selling abroad at a price that is less than the price used to sell the same goods at home (the "normal" or "fair" value). To be unlawful, dumping must threaten or cause material injury to an industry in the export market, the market where prices are lower. Dumping is recognized by most of the trading world as an unfair practice (akin to price discrimination as an antitrust offense). Dumping is the subject of a special GATT/ WTO code which establishes the basic parameters for determining when dumping exists, what constitutes material injury and the remedy of antidumping tariffs. Such tariffs amount to the margin of the dump, i.e., the difference in the price charged at home and (say) Europe.

Dumping Determinations

"Normal value" is first defined as the comparable price actually paid or payable in the ordinary course of trade for the like product intended for consumption in the exporting country or country of origin. The Commission usually considers all sales made in the period under investigation (typically 12 months). However, only sales made in the ordinary course of business enter into the calculation. Transactions between related or compensated parties may not be considered in the ordinary course of trade unless the Commission believes they are comparable to arms-length dealings. Sales below cost, for example, are regularly excluded from the Commission's determination of normal value and may trigger "constructed value" determinations.

If there are no sales of the like product in the ordinary course of trade on the domestic market of the exporting country or such sales are inadequate to permit a proper comparison, the Commission turns to (1) the "comparable price" of the product as exported to another surrogate country or (2) its constructed value. The constructed value methodology is often used. It involves calculation of production costs plus a reasonable profit. The costs of production include materials, components and manufacturing costs, as well as sales, administrative and other general expenses. The Commission need not follow the exporter's accountings in making these calculations. A profit margin of 10 percent or more has been utilized.

If the goods are from nonmarket economies, a status some Central and Eastern European nations have finally escaped, the Commission has three options for determining normal value. These are utilization of a price derived from the sale of a like product in a market country, a constructed value price based on the costs of a producer in a market country or (if needed) the price actually paid adjusted to include a reasonable profit margin.

Once a normal value for the goods is established by the Commission, the "export price" is determined. This is defined as the price actually paid or payable for the product sold for export to Europe. Relatively speaking, this calculation is less controversial except when the producer sells through its own subsidiary. In such cases the Commission practice has been to calculate the export price on the basis of the price at which the good is first resold to an independent buyer, and deductions (adjustments) are made both for direct and indirect expenses. The normal value, however, is adjusted only for costs which are directly related to the sales. As a result, the export price is necessarily inferior to the normal value. This asymmetrical approach has repeatedly been upheld by the European Court of Justice. In addition, certain adjustments must be made to the normal value and export prices so calculated. These adjustments reflect differences in physical attributes, import charges, indirect taxes and selling expenses. The object of making these adjustments is to arrive at comparable "ex-factory" price calculations.

The dumping margin is the difference between the adjusted normal value and the adjusted export price. It is established by the Union institutions by comparing a weighted average normal value with individual export transactions, thus excluding so called negative dumping margins, i.e. the effect of export sales above the normal value upon the calculation of a weighted average export price. This margin ultimately determines the maximum extra duty the importer must pay provided there also is material injury to a European industry and the Commission decides that imposing the duty would be in the Community's interest. This "public interest" determination typically pits consumer against industrial interests. The manufacturers usually win out, but occasionally the consumers' interest in lower-priced imports prevails. The precise amount of the antidumping duty is supposed to represent only that which is necessary to remove the injury.

Common Market dumping duties are imposed prospectively, applying in most cases to all future imports during the next five years. Settlements of antidumping investigations frequently result in the raising of prices by exporters.

Critiques

Although much of this law on antidumping duties is consistent with the GATT/WTO code, and therefore generally conforms to United States law on the subject, some interesting twists have been applied. One of the most controversial is the so-called "screwdriver plant regulation" aimed mostly at Japanese exporters. These exporters, when faced with antidumping duties on top of the common customs tariff, began to assemble consumer electronics and other products inside Europe using Japanese made components plus a screwdriver. The net effect of the Commission's response was to reimpose dumping duties on these products unless at least 40 percent of the components originate outside the source country (Japan). Similar results were achieved in certain cases when Japanese goods assembled in the United States were exported to Europe. In one case, the goods had actually qualified as American for purposes of U.S. procurement rules. This origin was rejected by the European Commission. The Japanese successfully challenged the screwdriver regulation within the GATT.

Some have asserted that the Europe employs a double standard when calculating export prices and normal values for dumping law purposes. They claim that the Commission has cloaked itself in the technical obscurity of the law so as to systematically inflate normal values and deflate export prices, thereby causing more dumping to be found. Use of asymmetrical methods to reach these determinations has been upheld by the European Court. Additional criticism has been levied against the Commission's refusal to disclose the information upon which it relies in making critical dumping law decisions. Consumer groups have not traditionally been granted access to non-confidential files accumulated by the Commission in antidumping proceedings. However, by amendment, consumers and consumer organizations have been granted the right to inspect all non-confidential information made available to the Commission by any party to an investigation.

COUNTERVAILING DUTIES

The internal trade problems associated with member state "aids" (subsidies) to enterprises located inside the Common Market have already been discussed in connection with competition policy. See Chapter 5. Many of the same problems re-emerge in the context of the Common Commercial Policy. This time, however, the source of the subsidies are governments located *outside* the Common Market. The types of "subsidies" subject to "countervailing duties" are in dispute internationally. Many subsidies, especially export subsidies, are treated as an unfair trading practice under the GATT/WTO. As with dumping, there is a separate code which creates the ground rules in this area. This code (as revised after the Uruguay Round) is implemented as a matter of Common Commercial Policy (Council Reg. 2026/97). Once again, European law therefore generally parallels similar law in the United States. European regulations prohibit export subsidies. In addition, certain specific domestic manufacturing, production and transportation subsidies can also be countervailed if they (like export subsidies) threaten material injury to a European industry.

The Court of Justice has said that the concept of a countervailable subsidy presupposes the grant of an economic advantage through a charge on the public account. For a domestic subsidy to be countervailable, it must have "sectoral specificity" (seek to grant an advantage only to certain firms). For an export subsidy to be countervailable, it must specifically benefit the imported product. As with dumping proceedings, the Commission makes these judgments provisionally and the Council renders final judgment (issued as a customs regulation). The amount of the extra duty corresponds to the amount of the subsidy. Relatively few external subsidy proceedings have been pursued under European law.

ESCAPE CLAUSE PROCEEDINGS AND VOLUNTARY TRADE RESTRAINTS

European commercial policy regulations establish common rules for imports and exports. These rules authorize "safeguard" or "escape clause" measures to curb exports in the face of shortages, or to curb surging imports that threaten serious injury to similar products of the region. Special rules apply to escape clause proceedings when the imports are from state-trading countries. This body of law is derived from the WTO Safeguards Agreement and found in Council Regulation 3285/94. Its counterparts in U.S. law are found in Sections 201 and 406 of the Trade Act of 1974. Use of escape clause relief triggers a duty to compensate WTO trade partners.

The protective measures authorized by the European escape clause regulations may include tariffs, quotas and, more controversially, agreements with exporting nations to voluntarily control the flow of certain goods. Such "voluntary export restraints" (VERs) have been used on consumer electronics, machine tools, food products and steel imports. After much effort, and adherence to the WTO escape clause agreement, Europe has greatly reduced its dependence upon VERs as a means of protection against import competition. Unlike the United States, Europe has generally refrained from frequent invocation of escape clause relief.

FOREIGN COUNTRY TRADE BARRIERS

Another area of the Common Commercial Policy was commenced in 1984 in response to efforts (ultimately withdrawn) by the Reagan Administration at limiting participation of European licensees of United States technology in the Siberian natural gas pipeline project. This was sometimes called the "new commercial policy." It has been replaced by the Trade Barriers Regulation embodied in Council Regulation 3286/94. This regulation covers situations not subject to escape clause, dumping or subsidy proceedings. It concerns "obstacles to trade" by foreign *countries* and roughly approximates Section 301 of the U.S. Trade Act of 1974.

Regulation 3286/94 applies when countries engage in practices that are incompatible with international agreements, e.g., the GATT/WTO agreements. Actionable conduct can be found if nations create or maintain obstacles to trade that adversely effect European exporters (market access complaints) and are subject to a right of action under international trade law. International dispute settlement procedures (mostly WTO) or unilateral retaliatory measures can result. The latter can include raising tariffs, suspending trade concessions or imposing quotas.

TRADE RELATIONS

The Europeans have traditionally adopted a united front within the GATT/WTO and empowered the Commission to represent them. This representation creates much more bargaining power over tariffs and other issues with Canada, the United States and Japan than European nations ever had individually. Throughout the GATT negotiating "rounds," most recently the Uruguay Round, Europe has become a force to be reckoned with. Indeed, many attribute the failure of the Uruguay Round to reach closure on time in 1990 to European recalcitrance over agricultural trade barriers necessary to the preservation of its Common Agricultural Policy.

U.S.–EU Trade

Trade between the United States and the Common Market is voluminous, roughly in balance and yet fractious. While the focal point in recent years has been agricultural trade, especially the problems of export subsidies and nontariff trade barriers (notably Europe's banana quotas, beef hormone bans and freeze on GMO (genetically modified organism) approvals), there are many contentious issues. For example, Airbus subsidies are said to threaten Boeing, and the single market legislative campaign to erect a "Fortress Europe" in banking, insurance, broadcasting, data privacy and other areas. There is continuing concern in North America that Europe may turn inward and protective.

Europe, for its part, has begun imitating the United States' practice of issuing annual reports voicing *its* objections to U.S. trade barriers and unfair practices. Extraterritorial U.S. jurisdiction has been a constant complaint, including the Helms–Burton Cuban LIBERTAD and the Iran–Libya Sanctions Acts. These reports have also targeted Section 301 of the Trade Act of 1974. The Europeans perceive Section 301 as a unilateral retaliatory mechanism that runs counter to multilateral resolution of trade disputes through the GATT/WTO. This perception has not stopped them from partially duplicating this mechanism in their law against foreign country trade barriers (above). Nevertheless, since the United States has been taking the bulk of its trade disputes to the WTO under its Dispute Settlement Understanding, the Europeans have less to complain about on this score.

Trade relations between the EU and the U.S. have improved in limited ways under the Transatlantic Economic Partnership Program (1995). Nevertheless, deep underlying conflicts remain. It is this author's view that NAFTA and the EU are competing with good reason for possession of the world's largest market. Larger markets bring greater leverage in intergovernmental trade negotiations, economies of scale and improved "terms of trade" (pay less for imports, receive more for exports), and enhanced abilities to exercise global economic leadership. Europe's 2004 expansion from 15 to 25 member states may be matched or bettered by the proposed Free Trade Area of the Americas encompassing 33 nations. And so the struggle for market power will continue.

Japan–EU Trade

Europe's trade relations with Japan are less voluminous, less in balance and (at least superficially) less fractious than with the United States. Japan runs a growing surplus, but the amount is smaller than the huge surplus it accumulates in trading with the States. Many Europeans speak quietly and with determination about their intent to avoid the "United States example" in their trade relations with Japan. Less quietly, some national governments have imposed quotas on the importation of Japanese autos and instituted demanding local content requirements for Japanese cars assembled in Europe. The Commission, for its part, has frequently invoked antidumping proceedings against Japanese goods and demonstrated a willingness to create arcane rules of origin that promote its interests at the expense of the Japanese.

TRADE AGREEMENTS

Article 300 of the Treaty of Rome establishes the procedures used in the negotiation of most international trade agreements. Basically, the Commission proposes and then receives authorization from the Council to open negotiations with third countries or within an international organization. When the Commission reaches tentative agreement, conclusion or ratification must take place in the Council after consulting the Parliament. The Council votes by qualified majority on Common Commercial Policy agreements. These include most GATT/WTO agreements. The Council votes unanimously on association agreements and on international agreements undertaken via Article 308 (e.g., environmental conventions prior to 1987). The Commission cannot characterize an international agreement as "merely administrative" so as to avoid Treaty rules and procedures and conclude agreements on its own.

The Treaty on European Union amended Article 300 to provide that the Council must also vote unanimously on international agreements covering areas where a unanimous vote is required to adopt internal rules. See Chapter 2. Parliament's role in international agreements was expanded by the TEU. Its assent must now be obtained for association agreements, agreements with important budget implications and agreements entailing amendment of legislation adopted under co-decision (Parliamentary veto) procedures. The Council is also authorized to take emergency measures to cut off or reduce trading with other nations for common foreign or security policy reasons.

An opinion of the European Court as to the compatibility with the Treaty of Rome of the proposed agreement and the procedures used to reach it may be obtained in advance at the request of the Commission, Council or a member state. There are no public proceedings when such opinions are sought. Use of this advance ruling procedure may forestall judicial review at a later date of the compatibility of international agreements with the Treaty of Rome. This lesson was vividly made when the Court of Justice rejected the final draft of the 1991 European Economic Area Agreement. This rejection sent the Agreement back for renegotiation and a new set of dispute settlement procedures which subsequently met with ECJ approval.

ERTA and WTO Agreements Cases

Article 133 of the Treaty of Rome conveys the power to enter into international commitments under the Common Commercial Policy. This may also be the case by *implication* even when there is no express Treaty authorization to enter into international agreements necessary to achieve internal Common Market objectives. The well known *ERTA* decision of the European Court regarding transport holds the scope of the trade agreements power to be coextensive with all *effective* surrenders of national sovereignty accomplished under the Treaty of Rome.

More recently, the Court of Justice revisited the *ERTA* doctrine in an opinion reviewing the Uruguay Round trade agreements. The European Community had long represented the member states in the GATT and exclusively negotiated these agreements. But the General Agreement on Trade in Services (GATS) and the Agreement on Trade–Related Aspects of Intellectual Property (TRIPS) raised special concerns since the Treaty of Rome and *ERTA* were ambiguous as to whether the Community or the member states or both had the power to conclude these agreements.

The Court of Justice, in the complex *WTO Agreements* opinion, ruled that the Community had exclusive power regarding trade in goods agreements (including agriculture) based on Article 133 authorizing the Common Commercial Policy. While the cross-frontier supply of services not involving movement of persons also fell under Article 133, all other aspects of the GATS did not. Regarding TRIPS, only the provisions dealing with counterfeit goods came under the Community's exclusive Article 133 authority. Noting that the effective surrender of national sovereignty over intellectual property is not (yet) total and that internal trade in services is not "inextricably linked" to external relations, the Court ruled the competence to conclude GATS and TRIPs was jointly shared by the Community and the member states. Likewise, they share a duty to cooperate within the WTO in the administration of these agreements and disputes relating to them.

Member State Involvement

As a rule, member states may not negotiate trade treaties in exclusively regional fields. They may do so on a transitional basis in areas where the Community lacks authority or (less clearly) has not effectively implemented its authority. For example, in the early 1970s there was no effective regional energy policy. Thus, the International Energy Agreement achieved through the Organization for Economic Cooperation and Development (OECD) in 1975 after the first oil shocks is not an Community agreement. In contrast, the Community clearly had competence in the field of export credits for goods. OECD arrangements in this area are exclusively the province of the Community with no residual or parallel authority in the member states. Likewise, in 2002 the ECJ ruled that bilateral "open skies" aviation agreements between eight individual member states and the United States were illegal incursions into an exclusively EU domain.

The *ERTA* and to a lesser degree the *WTO* decisions of the European Court, combined with the expanding internal competence of the Community, leave less and less room for national governments to enter into trade agreements. However, recognizing the sensitivities involved, "mixed agreements" negotiated by the Commission (acting on a Council mandate) and representatives of the member states are frequently used. Both the Community and the member states are signatories to such accords. This has been done with the "association agreements" authorized by Article 310 (below), certain of the GATT/WTO Codes, the Ozone Layer Convention and the Law of the Sea Convention. The Court of Justice has upheld the validity of mixed international agreements and procedures, but suggested that absent special circumstances their use should not occur when the Community's exclusive jurisdiction over external affairs is fully involved. In other words, mixed procedures should be followed only when the competence to enter into and implement international agreements is in fact shared between the Community and its member states. The Treaty of Nice (2003) makes it clear that trade agreements relating to cultural and audiovisual services, educational services, and social and human health services are shared competences.

Article 307 of Treaty of Rome indicates that most treaties the member states reached prior to joining continue to be valid even if they impact on areas now governed by regional law. Many bilateral treaties of Friendship, Commerce and Navigation fall within this category despite their impact on immigration, employment and investment opportunities.

Member states are, however, required to take all appropriate steps (e.g., upon renewal) to eliminate any incompatibilities between national trade agreements and the Treaty of Rome.

Trade agreements and other international treaties of the European Community are subject to judicial review by the Court of Justice as "acts" of its institutions. Moreover, such agreements are binding on the member states which must ensure their full implementation. When the European Court holds international agreements "directly effective" law, individuals may rely upon them in national litigation. See Chapter 3. The direct effects doctrine has led to cases where citizens end up enforcing trade agreements despite contrary law of their own or other member state governments.

ASSOCIATION AGREEMENTS—MEDITERRANEAN POLICY, CENTRAL AND EASTERN EUROPE

Association Agreements

Article 310 of the Treaty of Rome authorizes association agreements with other nations, regional groups and international organizations. The Council must act unanimously in adopting association agreements. Since the Single European Act of 1987, association agreements also require Parliamentary assent (which it threatened to withhold from renewal of the Israeli association agreement unless better treatment of Palestinian exports was achieved). The network of trade relations established by association agreements covers much of the globe. Those who are "associated" with Europe usually receive trade and aid preferences which, as a practical matter, discriminate against nonassociates. Arguments about the illegality of such discrimination within the GATT/WTO and elsewhere have typically not prevailed.

Article 310 indicates that association agreements involve "*reciprocal* rights and obligations, common action and special procedures" (emphasis added). This reciprocity requirement mirrors GATT law on nonpreferential trading and free trade area agreements. See Chapter 1. Nevertheless, European association agreements usually establish wide-ranging but not necessarily reciprocal trade and economic links. Greece for many years prior to membership was an associate. Turkey still is and has been since 1963. These two agreements illustrate the use of association agreements to convey high levels of financial, technical and commercial aid preliminary to membership. Turkey now has a customs union agreement. Another type of association agreement links the EFTA nations with the European Community. These agreements originally provided for industrial free trade and symbolized an historic reconciliation of the EEC and EFTA trading alliances in 1973. A much broader European Economic Area agreement governs most remaining trade relations. See Chapter 1.

Mediterranean Policy

Still another type of association agreement involves pursuit of the "Mediterranean Policy." This policy acknowledges the geographic proximity and importance of Mediterranean basin nations to Europe. The Med is viewed as a European sphere of influence. Most of these association agreements grant trade preferences (including substantial duty free entry) and economic aid *without* requiring reciprocal, preferential access. Agreements of this type have been concluded with Algeria, Morocco, Tunisia, Egypt, Jordan, Lebanon, Syria, Israel, the former Yugoslavia, Malta, Cyprus and the Palestinian autonomous territories. In 1995 Europe and these partners declared an intent to create a Mediterranean industrial free trade zone by 2010.

Central and Eastern Europe

Because the Soviet Union and its European satellites refused for many years to even recognize the European Community, some bilateral trade and cooperation agreements between those nations and the member states continued in place. It was not until 1988 that official relations between the Community and COMECON were initiated. As democracy took hold, first generation trade and aid agreements were concluded with nearly every Central and East European nation, including many nations formerly part of the Soviet Union.

The Community has advanced to second generation "association agreements" with many of these countries. These are known as "Europe Agreements." They anticipate substantial adoption of EC law on product standards, the environment, competition, telecommunications, financial services, broadcasting and a host of other areas. Free movement of workers is not provided. Free trading is phased in over a ten-year period with special protocols on sensitive products like steel, textiles and agricultural goods. More fundamentally, Europe Agreements are clearly focused on the eventual incorporation of these countries into the Union.

International Agreements

In addition, the European Community has a host of other association agreements based upon most-favored-nation trading, not preferential access. These include agreements with Sri Lanka, Pakistan, Bangladesh, India, the ASEAN group (Thailand, Vietnam, Laos, Burma, Singapore, Malaysia, The Philippines, Brunei, and Indonesia), the Andean Pact (Bolivia, Colombia, Ecuador, Venezuela, Peru), and MERCOSUR (Paraguay, Argentina, Uruguay, Brazil). In 1990, a Cooperation Agreement was signed with the Gulf Council of Arab nations. Very significantly, Mexico and the European Union reached a *free trade* agreement in 2000. Mexico, with its NAFTA membership, thus becomes a production center with duty free access to the world's two largest consumer markets.

THE LOMÉ/COTONOU CONVENTIONS

The Treaty of Rome, in a section entitled the "association of overseas territories and countries," was intended to preserve the special trading and development preferences that came with "colonial" status. In 1957, France, Belgium, Italy and The Netherlands still had a substantial number of these relationships. Article 184 completely abolished (after a transitional period) tariffs on goods coming from associated overseas territories and countries. There is no duty on the part of these regions to reciprocate with duty free access to their markets for European goods. Although some territories continue to exist (e.g., French territories like Polynesia, New Caledonia, Guadaloupe, Martinique, etc.), most of the once associated overseas colonies are now independent nations. This is true as well for most of the former colonies of Britain, Denmark, Portugal and Spain.

As independence arrived throughout Asia, Africa and elsewhere, new conventions of association were employed as a form of developmental assistance. The first of these were the Yaoundé Conventions (1964 and 1971) with newly independent French-speaking African states. These conventions were in theory free trade agreements, but the African states could block trade in almost any goods and Europe protected itself from agricultural imports that threatened its Common Agricultural Policy. A healthy dollop of financial and technical aid was thrown into the bargain.

Participating ACP States

When Britain joined in 1973, it naturally wished to preserve as many of the Commonwealth trade preferences as it could. The Yaoundé Conventions were already in place favoring former French colonies south of the Sahara. The compromise was the creation of a new convention, the first Lomé Convention (1975), to expand the Yaoundé principles to developing Caribbean and Pacific as well as English-speaking African nations. The fourth Lomé Convention (1990) governed trade and aid between Europe and a large number of African, Caribbean and Pacific (ACP) states. Lomé IV was replaced in 2000 by the Cotonou Agreement, which will operate for 20 years.

The Cotonou nations presently include: Angola, Antigua & Barbuda, Bahamas, Barbados, Belize, Benin, Botswana, Burkina Faso, Burundi, Cameroon, Cape Verde, Central African Republic, Chad, Comoros, Congo, Djibouti, Dominica, Dominican Republic, Equatorial Guinea, Eritrea, Ethiopa, Fiji, Gabon, Gambia, Ghana, Grenada, Guinea, Guinea Bissau, Guyana, Haiti, Ivory Coast, Jamaica, Kenya, Kiribati, Lesotho, Liberia, Madagascar, Malawi, Mali, Marshall Islands, Mauritania, Mauritius, Micronesia, Mozambique, Namibia, Niger, Nigeria, Niue, Palau, Papua New Guinea, Rwanda, St. Kitts & Nevis, St. Lucia, St. Vincent & The Grenadines, Samoa, Sao Tomé & Principe, Senegal, Seychelles, Sierra Leone, Solomon Islands, Somalia, South Africa, Sudan, Suriname, Swaziland, Tanzania, Togo, Tonga, Trinidad & Tobago, Tuvalu, Uganda, Vanuatu, Zambia and Zimbabwe.

Perhaps the most important feature of this lengthy listing is the developing nations that are *not*

Cotonou Convention participants. Unless they fall within the Mediterranean Policy, they are apt to perceive the Convention as highly discriminatory against their exports and economic interests.

Contents

Unlike the Yaoundé Conventions, the Lomé Conventions did not create (even in theory) reciprocal free trading relationships. While the Lomé states retained substantial duty free access to the Common Market, Europe obtained no comparable benefit. This one-sided trading relationship has been continued temporarily under the Cotonou Agreement through 2008. By that time, a mutual free trade agreement is anticipated, to be implemented before 2020. A variety of "development" preferences focusing on poverty reduction are extended by the Cotonou Convention. These include expensive purchasing obligations on sugar, for example. There is no free movement of persons as between the ACP states and the Community. However, whenever such persons are lawfully resident and working in the other's territories, they must be given national treatment rights.

Most significantly, the Cotonou nations participate in two innovative mechanisms designed to stabilize their agricultural and mineral commodity export earnings. These programs are known as STABEX and MINEX (also known as SYSMIN). STABEX covers (*inter alia*) ground nuts, cocoa, coffee, cotton, coconut, palm, rawhides, leather and wood products, and tea. MINEX deals with copper, phosphates, bauxite, alumina, manganese, iron ore, and tin. These programs are an acknowledgment of the economic dependence of many Cotonou nations on commodity exports for very large portions of their hard currency earnings.

Some have argued vigorously that STABEX and MINEX perpetuate rather than relieve this dependence. Both programs provide loans and grants in aid to nations who have experienced significant declines in export earnings because of falling commodity prices, crop failures and the like. The greater the dependency and decline, the larger the financial transfers. These sums are not, for the most part, tied to reinvestment in the commodity sectors causing their payment nor to the purchase of European products or technology. In a world where most development aid is tied (i.e., must usually be spent on the donor's products or projects), STABEX and MINEX represent a different approach. Many Latin American nations have lobbied the United States to create similar mechanisms for their commodities.

The Lomé IV Convention (1990) added several new features carried over under the Cotonou Agreement (2000). The European Community now financially supports structural adjustments in ACP states, including remedies for balance of payment difficulties, debt burdens, budget deficits and public enterprises. Cultural and social cooperation, trade in services and environmental issues are also addressed. For example, an agreement not to ship toxic and radioactive waste was reached. The Convention builds upon earlier provisions by specifying protected human rights such as equal treatment, civil and political liberty, and economic, social and cultural rights. Financial support is given to ACP nations that promote human rights.

DUTY FREE ACCESS TO THE COMMON MARKET

The end-game so far as exporters are concerned is unlimited duty free access to the world's largest market. Except for raw materials, few North American exports will qualify for such treatment. However, subsidiaries based in developing or EAA/EFTA nations may achieve this goal. This is possible because of the Community's adherence to the GSP program, its Mediterranean basin trade agreements, the Lomé/Cotonou Conventions and the free trade treaties with EAA/EFTA. It may also be possible to ship goods produced in Central and East European nations duty free into the Common Market under "second generation" Europe Agreements. All of these topics have been previously discussed. There are, of course, exceptions and controls (quotas, NTBs) that may apply under these programs. Nevertheless, the Common Market is so lucrative that careful study of its external trade rules is warranted.

Such studies can realize unusually advantageous trade situations. For example, many developing nations are Cotonou Convention participants or GSP beneficiaries. The goods of some of these nations are also entitled to duty free access to the United States market under the U.S. version of the GSP program, the Caribbean Basin Economic Recovery Act (1983), the Andean Trade Preference Act (1991), or various U.S. free trade agreements. A producer strategically located in such a nation (e.g., Jamaica) can have the best of both worlds, duty free access to Europe and the United States. Since 2000, this ideal outcome is most significantly available via Mexico. Mexico is both a member of NAFTA and has an EU free trade agreement.

COMMERCIAL AGENTS

Council Directive 86/653 coordinates member state laws regarding self-employed commercial agents. The directive defines a commercial agent as a "self-employed intermediary who has continuing authority to negotiate the purchase or sale of goods on behalf of another person (the principal), or to negotiate and conclude such transactions on behalf of and in the name of that principal." This directive was inspired by existing French and German law. In Denmark and Britain new legislation was required for its implementation. From a United States perspective, the directive is remarkably protective of the agent. While not an external trade law per se, Directive 86/653 is particularly significant because many North American firms first do business in Europe through commercial agents.

Directive 86/653 establishes various rights and obligations for commercial agents and principals, e.g., the agent's duty to comply with reasonable instructions and the principal's duty to act in good faith. In the absence of an agreed compensation, customary local practices prevail (and if none, reasonable remuneration). Compensation rights before and after the effective period of the agency contract are specified. Directive 86/653 also establishes when the agent's commission becomes due and payable, as well as the conditions under which it is extinguishable. For example, the agent is entitled to a compensation on all transactions in which he or she participated. Moreover, transactions that have been concluded during the term of the agreement with third parties the agent previously procured as customers for the principal fall within this rule. The agent is also entitled to a compensation on transactions with customers located in his or her area of responsibility or for whom the agent is an exclusive representative.

Termination Rights

An important element concerns the notice and termination rights of the agent. Agency agreements for fixed periods of time that continue to be performed by both parties upon expiration become contracts for an indefinite period. Minimum notice requirements of one month per year of service up to three years, and optional notice requirements up to six months for six years are created. The member states must provide for either a right of indemnification or for damages compensation. The agency agreement cannot waive or otherwise "derogate" these rights. The indemnity cannot exceed one year's remuneration but does not foreclose damages. The indemnity is payable if the agent has brought in new customers or increased volumes with existing customers to the substantial continuing benefit of the principal and is equitable in light of all circumstances.

The right to damages as a result of termination occurs when the agent is deprived of commissions which would have been earned upon proper performance to the substantial benefit of the principal. The agent may also seek damages relief when termination blocks amortization of costs and expenses incurred on advice of the principal while performing under the agency contract. The death of the agent triggers these indemnity or compensation rights. They are also payable if the agent must terminate the contract because of age, infirmity or illness causing an inability to reasonably continue service. No indemnity or damages may be had under specified circumstances, including when the agent is in default justifying immediate termination under national law. "Restraint of trade" clauses (covenants not to compete) are permissible upon termination to the extent that they are limited to two years, the goods in question and the geographic area and/or customers of the agent. Such clauses can be made a pre-condition to the payment of an indemnity.

If an agency agreement chooses non-EU law to govern its terms, say for example California law, this choice of law will not override the agent's mandatory damages remedies.

CHAPTER 7

BUSINESS COMPETITION LAW

The primary purpose of European competition policy is preservation of the trade and other benefits of economic integration. The removal of governmental trade barriers unaccompanied by measures to ensure that businesses do not recreate those barriers would be an incomplete effort. For example, competing enterprises might agree to geographically allocate markets to each other, making the elimination of national tariffs and quotas by the Treaty of Rome irrelevant. Similarly, a dominant enterprise in one state might tie up all important distributors or purchasers of its goods through long-term exclusive dealing contracts. The result could make entry into that market by another business exceedingly difficult. By assisting in the formation and maintenance of an economic union, business competition law is an important component in competition policy. It prevents enterprise behavior from becoming a substantial nontariff trade barrier to economic integration.

The secondary purpose of European competition policy is not unique to regional integration. This purpose is the attainment of the economic benefits generally thought to accrue in any economy organized on a competitive basis. These benefits are many. Perhaps most important of all, an economy characterized by competitive enterprise answers the questions of economic organization by maximizing the market desires of its human constituents. A genuinely competitive market is responsive to individual choice and libertarian in a way that acknowledges and promotes diversity. Competition among businesses protects the public interest in having its cumulative demand for goods and services provided at the lowest possible prices and with the greatest possible degree of responsivity to public tastes.

It is in this sense that a competitive economy is said to be guided by the principle of "consumer welfare" or "consumer sovereignty." When, for example, European law prevents competing enterprises from fixing prices for their goods or prevents a dominant enterprise from charging monopoly prices at the consumers' expense, such law helps to realize the economic benefits of competition within the Euro-economy.

The Maastricht Treaty on European Union added provisions to the Treaty of Rome focused specifically on industrial competitiveness. The goal is to promote a system of open and competitive markets by accelerating structural change, encouraging enterprise initiatives, fostering business cooperation and supporting innovation, research and development. However, Article 157 indicates that this authority may not result in "any measure which could lead to a distortion of competition."

NONDISTORTED COMPETITION POLICY

One of the basic tasks identified in the Treaty of Rome is the institution of a "system ensuring that competition in the common market is not distorted." Distorted competition is a broad English translation for the French concurrence faussée. Nondistorted competition is close to the German concept of funktionsfähiger Wettbewerb, but it is not clear to what extent this concept correlates with what Americans call workable or effective competition. There is some suggestion that workable competition is the minimum level required in business competition law analyses. Nondistorted competition is thus a complex, evolving and distinctly European perspective on economic organization. It includes, for example, the heavy hand of agricultural price regulation and subsidies embodied in the Common Agricultural Policy. See Chapter 5. Anticompetitive state regulations, including price controls, are permissible distortions short of requiring or favoring EU competition law violations, or delegations of state economic responsibility to private traders. For example, member states may not approve or require prices fixed in violation of EU competition rules.

Public and private business competition law is only one facet of nondistorted competition policy. Equally, if not at times more important, are a wide range of other concerns and decisions, including notably state aids (subsidies). See Chapter 5. Foremost of these concerns has been the implementation and maintenance of the customs union and rights of free movement which by their very nature promote competition across borders. See Chapter 4. Indeed, the whole of the single market campaign could be said to underwrite more economic competition.

Trade treaties and the Common Commercial Policy are another important element in the competition regime since they heavily influence external competitive pressures. See Chapter 6. Two areas of European law with specific implications for competition policy are government subsidies and procurement. See Chapter 5. In none of these fields of law, however, is there the depth and expansiveness that can be found in competition law under Articles 81 and 82. It is very nearly impossible to avoid contact with this law in doing business with or in Europe. Hence, business competition rules are often the first encounter that the North Americans have with regional law.

The coverage of competition law that follows is selective. No attempt at a comprehensive survey of this vast field has been made or is possible in a Nutshell. The general principles and case and regulatory examples chosen are merely illustrative of the types of legal problems that can be encountered.

ARTICLE 81

Article 81(1) of the Treaty of Rome deals with concerted business practices, business agreements and trade association decisions. When they have the potential to affect trade between member states *and* have the object or effect of preventing, restricting or distorting competition *within* the Common Market, such business activities are deemed incompatible and prohibited. By way of example, Article 81(1) lists certain prohibited activities:

(1) the fixing of prices or trading conditions;

(2) the limitation of production, markets, technical development or investment;

(3) the sharing of markets or sources of supply;

(4) the application of unequal terms to equivalent transactions, creating competitive disadvantages; and

(5) the conditioning of a contract on the acceptance of commercially unrelated additional supplies.

Article 81(1) has been used to review and challenge a wide range of anticompetitive business activities, some of which are not listed above. These activities include joint buying, joint selling, joint ventures and strategic alliances, and data exchanges among horizontal competitors. They also include an even wider range of activities between vertically related suppliers, manufacturers and franchisee/licensee/distributors.

Void Agreements

Article 81(2) voids agreements, decisions and severable parts thereof that are prohibited by Article 81(1). Thus the prohibitions of Article 81(1) against anticompetitive activity are absolute and immediately effective without prior judicial or administrative action.

The open-ended text of 81(1) gives considerable leeway for interpretation and enforcement purposes. It has, for example, been interpreted to cover nonbinding "gentlemen's agreements." Trade association "recommendations" influencing competition are caught. It also generates considerable uncertainty as to the validity of many business agreements, since full market analyses of their competitive and trade impact are often required.

Exemptions

Article 81(3) permits Article 81(1) to be declared inapplicable when agreements, decisions, concerted practices or classes thereof:

(1) contribute to the improvement of the production or distribution of goods, or to the promotion of technical or economic progress; while

(2) reserving to consumers an equitable share of the resulting benefits; and neither

(3) impose any restrictions not indispensable to objectives 1 and 2 (i.e., least restrictive means must be used); nor

(4) make it possible for the businesses concerned to substantially eliminate competition.

The prohibitions of Article 81(1) may be tempered by "declarations of inapplicability" (exemptions) only when the circumstances of Article 81(3) are present. As befits exemptions from broad prohibitions, the terms of 81(3) are narrow and specific. Article 81(3) and Article 81(1) legal issues are often considered simultaneously in the process of analyzing the market impact of restrictive agreements, decisions and concerted practices. Since May 1, 2004, Article 81(3) is directly effective law, opening up the possibility of its application by national courts and authorities as well as the Commission.

REGULATION 17 AND REGULATION 1— COMMISSION INVESTIGATIONS, ATTORNEY–CLIENT PRIVILEGE, SHARED PROSECUTORIAL POWERS

In March of 1962 the Council of Ministers adopted Regulation 17 on the basis of proposals from the Commission. Regulation 17 has been the major piece of secondary law under Articles 81 and 82. Effective May 1, 2004, Regulation 17 is replaced by Regulation 1/ 2003. These regulations establish the scheme of enforcement for competition law. The Commission, for the most part its Competition Directorate–General or department, has a wide range of powers.

Commission Investigations

The regulations confer investigatory powers in the Commission to conduct general studies into economic sectors and to review the affairs of individual businesses and trade associations. The Commission may investigate in response to a complaint or upon its own initiative. These powers are particularly significant because (except in the case of mergers) notification of restrictive agreements, decisions and practices to the Commission, although at times beneficial, is not mandatory. The Commission may request all information *it* considers necessary, and examine and make copies of record books and business documents.

In conducting its investigations, the Commission may ask for verbal explanations on the spot and have access to premises. One author refers to these powers as "dawn raids and other nightmares." Nevertheless, the Court of Justice has affirmed this right of hostile access. Effective May 1, 2004, subject to the issuance of a local court warrant, this right of access extends to private homes and motor vehicles of corporate directors, managers and other staff. In these matters the Commission acts on its own authority provided there are reasonable grounds to believe that relevant books or records are kept in these locations. It must, however, inform member states prior to taking such steps and may request their assistance. The member states must render assistance when businesses fail to comply with competition law investigations of the Commission.

Businesses involved in the Commission's investigatory process have limited rights to notice and hearing. They do not have access to the Commission's files. Any failure on the part of an enterprise to provide information requested by the Commission or to submit to its investigation can result in the imposition of considerable fines and penalties. For example, the Belgian and French subsidiaries of the Japanese electrical and electronic group, Matsushita, were fined by the Commission for supplying it with false information about whether Matsushita recommended retail prices for its products. These sanctions are civil in nature and run against the corporation, not its directors or management.

The Commission has increased the use of its investigatory powers. Several procedural requirements for Commission investigations and hearings have been discussed by the Court of Justice. One notable Court decision upheld the authority of the Commission to conduct searches of corporate offices without notice or warrant when it has reason to believe that pertinent evidence may be lost. Another notable decision permitted a Swiss "whistle blower" who once worked for Hoffmann–La Roche (a defendant in competition law proceedings) to sue the Community in tort for disclosure of his identity as an informant.

Attorney–Client Privileges

Written communications with external EU-licensed lawyers undertaken for defense purposes are confidential and need not be disclosed. Written communications with in-house lawyers are *not* exempt from disclosure, nor are communications with external *non*-EU counsel. Thus communications with North American attorneys (who are not also EU-licensed attorneys) are generally discoverable. For example, the Commission obtained in-house counsel documents from John Deere, Inc., a Belgian subsidiary of the United States multinational. These documents were drafted as advice to management on how to avoid competition law liability for export prohibition restraints. They were used by the Commission to justify the finding of an intentional Article 81 violation and a fine of 2 million ECUs. United States attorneys have followed these developments with amazement and trepidation. Disclaimers of possible nonconfidentiality are one option to consider in dealing with clients. At a minimum, U.S. attorneys ought to advise their clients that the usual rules on attorney-client privilege may not apply.

Shared Powers

Regulation 17 and Regulation 1 envision significant cooperation and information sharing between European and national authorities in the field of competition law. Effective May 1, 2004, enforcement of Articles 81 and 82 will be shared with the competition agencies and national courts of the member states. A new European Competition Network will be established to facilitate cooperative law enforcement and minimize divergent application of competition law principles, with the Commission to act as final arbiter on substantive matters. The principal reason for this sharing of enforcement duties is to allow the Commission to focus its energies on price fixing, cartel arrangements and other serious violations of Articles 81 and 82.

The Court of First Instance has ruled that the Commission can refuse to pursue a competition law complaint if an adequate remedy is available from a national court. This decision supports the Commission's customary practice of decentralized "subsidiarity" in the competition law field. Starting May 1, 2004, national courts may ask the Commission for support regarding Article 81 or 82, with the Commission and national authorities empowered to file opinions with the national courts. Moreover, in all cases affecting member state trade, Regulation 1/2003 permits the Commission to issue ex ante binding decisions determining that a particular agreement or practice does not infringe European competition law. Such decisions would preclude different results at the national level.

COMMISSION PROSECUTIONS AND SANCTIONS

Enforcement Procedures

In addition to its investigatory powers, the Commission is authorized to determine when violations of the competition law provisions occur. This is the source of the Commission's power to render enforcement decisions. A regulation limits the time period in which the Commission may render a decision in competition law cases to five years. All Commission decisions, including enforcement decisions and decisions to investigate, fine or penalize must be published and are subject to judicial review. Since 1989, these appeals are heard by the Court of First Instance.

During interim periods, the Commission has the power to order measures indispensable to its functions. Interim relief should be granted when there is prima facie evidence of a violation and an urgent need to prevent serious and irreparable private damage or intolerable damage to the public interest. La Cinq, a private television service twice denied membership in the European Broadcasting Union, successfully met these criteria. The Court of First Instance rebuked the Commission's refusal to grant provisional Article 82 protection.

Before deciding that a competition law breach has occurred, the Commission issues a statement of "objections." This statement must reveal which facts the Commission intends to rely upon in reaching a decision that a violation has occurred. A hearing can then be requested by the alleged violator(s) or any interested person. These hearings are conducted in private, with separate reviews of complainants and witnesses. The Commission must disclose only those non-confidential documents in its file upon which it intends to rely and are necessary to prepare an adequate defense. After the hearing, the Commission consults with the Advisory Committee on Restrictive Practices and Monopolies, which is composed of one civil servant expert from each member state. The results of this consultation are not made public. Having consulted the Committee, the Commission is then free to render an enforcement decision.

In its enforcement decision, the Commission may require businesses to "cease and desist" their infringing activities. In practice, this power has sufficed to permit the Commission to order infringing enterprises to come up with their own remedial solutions. However, the Commission may not, at least in an Article 81 proceeding, require a violator to contract with the complainant. Daily penalties may be imposed to compel adherence to the order to cease and desist. Commission decisions on violations are also accompanied by a capacity to substantially fine any intentionally or negligently infringing enterprise. When appeals are lodged against Commission decisions imposing fines and penalties, payment is suspended but interest is charged and a bank guarantee for the amounts concerned must be provided.

In the early years, fines and penalties actually levied by the Commission were few, relatively small in amount and frequently reduced on appeal to the Court of Justice. As competition law doctrine has become clearer, these trends have all been reversed. In its more recent decisions, the Court has upheld substantial fines and penalties imposed by the Commission in competition law proceedings and recognized their deterrent value. In 2001, for example, the Commission imposed competition law fines of more than $850 million on European companies for conspiring to fix prices and divide up the vitamins market.

Any complete picture of the development of Article 81 must account for the Commission's informal negotiations as well as its decisions to prosecute infringing activities. Business compliance with Articles 81 and 82 is often achieved short of a formal Commission decision. Word of informal file-closings is occasionally revealed. In *Re Eurofima,* for example, the Commission terminated proceedings without issuing a decision. In the process of responding to complaints from suppliers, the Commission was able to secure termination of infringing conduct from Eurofima, the most important buyer of railway rolling stock in the Common Market. Eurofima also undertook to continue to comply with competition law. The Commission announced these results in a press release.

INDIVIDUAL EXEMPTIONS, NEGATIVE CLEARANCES AND COMFORT LETTERS (PRIOR TO MAY 1, 2004)

Regulation 17 and Regulation 1 not only set up the investigatory and law enforcement machinery for competition law, but also the means to avoid that law. Until May 1, 2004, businesses could forestall enforcement action by the Commission under Article 81 by seeking an individual exemption under Article 81(3), a negative clearance, or both. To do this, they formally notified the Commission of the terms of any existing or proposed agreement, decision or concerted practice falling within the scope of Article 81(1). Notification ordinarily suspended the possibility of fines and established the earliest effective date if an exemption was granted. One notable use of Article 81(3) has been Commission authorization of "crisis cartels," i.e., production restricting arrangements in industries with prolonged overcapacity.

The Commission developed a "comfort letter" practice in connection with the voluminous requests for negative clearances and Article 81(3) exemptions. This practice acknowledged the impossibility of a detailed review of these requests and avoided the delays inherent in the process of reaching formal decisions. Comfort letters were issued only when the businesses concerned wish to have them and only after public notice and limited opportunity to comment. They signaled that the Commission's file was closed without issuance of a negative clearance or an 81(3) exemption. Comfort letters stated that the Commission saw no reason to intervene in opposition to the activities notified. The parties then typically proceeded to implement their agreement. In the absence of a change of circumstances, the Commission could not alter its position and was precluded from fining the recipient. However, national courts were not bound by the comfort letter in their determinations of Article 81 violations.

Businesses in doubt as to the applicability of Article 81(1) to their activities could request a "negative clearance" from the Commission. The Commission granted negative clearances solely on the basis of the factual and legal information then before it. A negative clearance indicated that the Commission saw no grounds at present to intervene, perhaps because the relevant agreement, decision or concerted practice did not perceptibly affect trade between member states, or did not perceptibly restrain competition within the Common Market as Article 81(1) requires.

There was a critical difference between a negative clearance and an individual exemption. The latter admitted an Article 81(1) violation or potential violation, but requested a declaration of inapplicability under the special terms of Article 81(3). The former denied the violation or potential violation of 81(1) because of the terms of that article and the nature of the activities involved. These lines of argument were often pursued simultaneously.

Effective May 1, 2004, the system of Commission notification to obtain individual exemptions and negative clearances outlined in this section was abolished. Thereafter, exemptions from Article 81 are primarily of the "group" or "block" type summarized immediately below. Member State authorities and courts, in addition to the Commission, have the power to recognize individual Article 81(3) exemptions in appropriate circumstances. See Regulation 1/ 2003 replacing Regulation 17 and the content of Article 81(3) discussed above.

ARTICLE 81—GROUP EXEMPTIONS

The Commission received an onslaught of negative clearance requests and Article 81(3) notifications in 1962 when Regulation 17 took effect. The vast majority of the business activities involved in this deluge were in the distribution and licensing areas. As a result, the Commission sought and obtained authorization in 1965 from the Council to formulate, for limited time periods, group "declarations of inapplicability" under Article 81(3). These are commonly known as "group or block exemptions." The Council granted this authorization, noting that Article 81(3) allows "classes" of exempt agreements.

Group exemptions, guidelines and policy announcements issued by the Commission in areas where group exemptions have not yet been promulgated, invite businesses to conform their agreements and behavior to their terms and conditions. In other words, group exemptions rely upon confidential business self-regulation.

After a number of test enforcement decisions and definitive rulings by the Court of Justice, the Commission issued Regulation 67 in 1967. It became the first of a series of group exemptions from Article 81(1). Regulation 67/67 was replaced in 1983 by Regulation 1983/83. These regulations concerned exclusive dealing methods of distribution. Exclusive dealing agreements ordinarily involve restrictions on manufacturers and independent distributors of goods. These restraints concern who the manufacturer may supply, to whom the manufacturer or distributor may sell, and from whom the distributor may acquire the goods or similar goods. Exclusive dealing agreements should be distinguished from agency or consignment agreements where title and most risk remain with the manufacturer until the goods are sold by their retail agents to consumers. The announced policy position is that competition law will not require a manufacturer to compete with its agents. Exclusivity in genuine retail agency agreements is therefore legal.

The group exemptions for exclusive dealing, exclusive purchasing and franchise agreements were replaced in 2000 by Regulation 2790/99, known as the *vertical restraints regulation*. It is accompanied by lengthy vertical restraints guidelines. This regulation and its guidelines are more economic and less formalistic than the predecessors. Supply and distribution agreements of firms with less than 30 percent market shares are generally exempt; this is known as a "safe harbor." Companies whose market shares exceed 30 percent may or may not be exempt, depending upon the results of individual competition law reviews. In either case, no vertical agreements containing so-called "hard core restraints" are exempt. These restraints concern primarily resale price maintenance, territorial and customer protection leading to market allocation, and in most instances exclusive dealing covenants that last more than five years.

A series of Commission regulations have followed the pattern established by Regulation 67. Test cases are initiated by the Commission before the European Court prior to creating a group exemption. Group exemptions now exist for motor vehicle distribution and servicing agreements (Regulation 1400/2002), production specialization agreements among small firms (Regulation 2658/2000), and research and development agreements among small firms (Regulation 2659/2000). The formerly separate group exemptions for patent licensing and know-how licensing have been merged under the technology transfers Regulation 240/96, subsequently replaced by Regulation 772/2004. Additional group exemptions are anticipated in light of the May 1, 2004 modernization reforms of Regulation 17 noted above.

ARTICLE 81—UNDERTAKINGS AND CONCERTED PRACTICES

There can be no violation of Article 81(1) unless there is an agreement between "undertakings," a decision by an association of undertakings or a concerted practice among undertakings. In other words, except for trade association decisions, at least two parties must be involved. Single-firm behavior, including for example market restraints achieved via parent company control of subsidiaries, is not caught. "Undertaking" has been interpreted to mean a functionally independent economic entity. This definition includes profit or nonprofit organizations, and partnerships or sole proprietorships. It generally precludes finding agreements or concerted practices as between parent corporations and subsidiaries.

Concerted Practices

The meaning of "concerted practices" is critical to Article 81(1) and the Commission's special focus on cartel activities. Concerted practices include any kind of informal cooperation between enterprises, and contrast with formal written or oral agreements and decisions. Without such a flexible legal concept, substantial evasion of the reach of Article 81(1) might be achieved by nonbinding but regularly followed business "understandings."

The Commission and the Court of Justice considered the concept of a concerted practice extensively in *Imperial Chemical Industries (ICI)*. This case involved nearly all the producers of aniline dyes in the region when it had only six member states. Three industry-wide price increases between 1964 and 1967 took place over the full range of more than 6000 aniline dye products.

The Commission, acting on information furnished by trade organizations using dyestuffs, found ten producers of aniline dyes in violation of Article 81(1) by concerting on these price increases. Together they held about 80 percent of the regional aniline dyes market. Proof of the concerted practices tendered by the Commission included: (1) the near identity of the price increases in each country;

(2) the uniformity of products covered by the price increases; (3) the exact timing of the increases; (4) the simultaneous dispatch to subsidiaries and representatives of price increase instructions that were nearly identical in form and content; and (5) the existence of informal contacts and occasional meetings between the enterprises concerned. The Commission decided these circumstantial facts warranted its conclusion that a concerted price fixing practice took place.

On appeal, the Court of Justice affirmed. The Court distinguished the concept of concerted practice from an agreement or decision under Article 81(1): "A form of coordination between undertakings which, without going so far as to amount to an agreement properly so called, knowingly substitutes a practical cooperation between them for the risks of competition." The Court added that while independent parallel behavior by competitors did not fall within the concept of a concerted practice, the fact of such behavior could be taken as a strong indicator of a concerted practice where it produced market conditions, especially price equilibrium, different from those thought ordinarily to prevail under competition. The cartel's defense of "conscious parallelism" on prices was therefore another piece of evidence affirming the Commission's enforcement decision. The sum total of the evidence on which the Commission relied to find a concerted practice was explicable, in the eyes of the Court, only by convergent intentions of producers to increase prices and avoid competitive conditions in the aniline dyes market.

The impact of the concept of concerted practice in European competition law depends on the evidence available to prove cooperative business behavior. It is a legal standard rooted in fact more than law. And it has proved useful in combating other Common Market cartels. In another case, for example, the Court of Justice reaffirmed *ICI* and then laid down a general warning against competitor cooperation and contact. It held that the competition rules *inherently* require that each enterprise independently determine its activities in the Common Market. Direct or indirect contact with the object or effect of influencing the market conduct of an actual or potential competitor, the disclosure of courses of market conduct of an actual or potential competitor or the disclosure of courses of market conduct intended for adoption by others, is prohibited. But a more recent decision indicates that quarterly price announcements, simultaneously released and identical in amount, may not constitute a concerted practice if other plausible explanations exist. Expert testimony suggesting that parallel pricing can be a rational response to market forces may provide the necessary explanation. However, the Commission believes that oligopolies can be attacked using Article 82 and a theory of collective abuse of a dominant position (below).

ARTICLE 81—COMPETITIVE IMPACT

Article 81(1) only applies when an agreement, decision or concerted practice has as its object *or* effect the prevention, restriction or distortion of competition within the Common Market. Distinctions can be drawn as between preventing, restraining and distorting competition, but the sweep of this language basically creates a legal and conceptual net in which most activities of competing enterprises may be examined by the Commission. The manner in which the Commission has cut official holes in this net through exemptions and policy announcements has already been discussed. Nevertheless, since there is a sense in which nearly all actions by enterprises affect their competitive position in the marketplace, the language of Article 81 grants expansive administrative power. That said, the Court of Justice has imposed a "rule of reason" test when evaluating competitive impact. Only those restraints which are "sufficiently deleterious" to competition in the context in which they appear are prohibited and void.

Grundig Case

Restraints of competition by enterprises may take place at different levels of economic activity. Restraints involving competition among firms operating at the same level in the production or distribution process are known as horizontal restraints. Businesses operating at different levels may restrain competition between themselves and third parties (vertical restraints). In *Grundig,* the Court of Justice declined to follow the recommendations of its Advocate General and affirmed that both horizontal and vertical restraints are embraced by Article 81(1). This decision involved a German manufacturer of consumer electronics that established an exclusive dealing agreement with Consten, a French distributor. In other words, *Grundig* was a vertical restraints case.

The agreement was made prior to the adoption of Regulation 67/67. As part of the agreement, Grundig undertook not to deliver its products directly or indirectly to anyone else in France. Grundig also contracted to similar territorial restraints with its other Common Market dealers outside of France. Consten agreed to sell only in its French territory. The result was that no dealer or wholesaler of Grundig products in Europe could sell outside its contracted territory. To strengthen this absolute pattern of territorial distribution, Grundig assigned the French trademark "GINT" to Consten. GINT was placed on all products delivered to Consten in addition to the usual "GRUNDIG" mark.

When prices in France were 20 to 25 percent above those in Germany, a French firm began competing with Consten by importing Grundig products bearing the GINT mark from a renegade German wholesaler. Consten then sued the importer in the French courts for infringement of GINT and violation of French law on unfair competition. The importer replied that the Grundig–Consten contract and the GINT assignment were void under Articles 81(1) and 81(2). Meanwhile, Grundig notified its series of exclusive dealing agreements to the Commission and sought Article 81(3) exemptions for them. The Cour d'Appel de Paris stayed the proceedings under French law.

The Commission found the entire agreement prohibited by Article 81(1) and denied an 81(3) exemption. Although not restrictive of competition as between Grundig and Consten, the agreement was restrictive as between Consten and third-party sellers of Grundig products. It amounted, the Commission said, to absolute territorial protection in France from the competition of parallel imports of Grundig products. Since, in the Commission's view, the object of the agreement was to restrain competition, an extensive market analysis of its actual competitive impact was not necessary.

The Court of Justice upheld the Commission's position on coverage of vertical restraints by Article 81(1) and on the absence of need for extensive market analysis in this case. However, it partially accepted the argument that, in ascertaining whether competition was restrained, the Commission ought to have considered the whole of the market for consumer electronics (where Grundig faced strong interbrand competition). Competition within the overall market, it was argued, was increased by the entry of Grundig into France through Consten's exclusive, territorially protected sales. This increase in interbrand competition, the argument continued, outweighed the restrictions on intrabrand competition in Grundig products.

The Court responded to these arguments by holding that only certain clauses of the Grundig–Consten agreement, the absolute territorial protection clause and the GINT assignment, infringed Article 81(1). Only these clauses were automatically void under Article 81(2). The remainder of the agreement, including the exclusive dealing provisions, was severable and legally binding. Thus, Grundig could enter the French market through an exclusive retailer, but that retailer could not be sheltered from other Grundig sellers in the Common Market. These principles were subsequently incorporated in Regulation 67/67 for which *Grundig* was an important test case. A modified Grundig selective distribution system was subsequently granted an individual exemption by the Commission.

MARKET DIVISION AND INTELLECTUAL PROPERTY RIGHTS

In *Grundig,* the Court of Justice affirmed the Commission's remedial order to the parties to refrain from any measure tending to obstruct or impede the acquisition of Grundig products. To reduce the negative impact of national industrial and intellectual property rights on regional trade and competition, the Commission and the Court of Justice have relied on a number of Treaty provisions. In the *Grundig* case, the Court held that Article 81 limitations may be imposed on the exercise or use of national trademark rights. In the Court's opinion, absolute territorial distribution rights are not essential to the protection or benefit sought to be conferred by trademarks. The net result was a Court order prohibiting Consten from exercising its rights under French trademark law to use GINT as a trade and competition barrier.

When used with the object or effect of preventing, restraining or distorting Common Market competition, national industrial and intellectual property rights have generally yielded to competition law. In *Deutsche Grammophon,* for example, results comparable to those in *Grundig* were achieved with copyright-based territorial restraints. When record imports into Germany from the French subsidiary of Deutsche Grammophon caused competition for the parent company, then enjoying lawful resale price maintenance in Germany, it sought infringement protection under German copyright law. Competition law restraints on the exercise (as opposed to the existence) of national copyright rights denied infringement protection. Deutsche Grammophon's German copyright rights were said to be "exhausted" by the sales to its French subsidiary. Dividing up the Common Market was not perceived to be essential to the financial reward and other purposes of German copyright. On the other hand, increased intrabrand Deutsche Grammophon sales and price competition was completely compatible with the Treaty of Rome.

Much of the litigation surrounding intellectual property rights in the Common Market has been undertaken in connection with Article 30 and the free movement of goods. As in the competition law area, such rights have generally given way to the Treaty of Rome. See Chapter 4.

ARTICLES 81 AND 82—TRADE IMPACT

De Minimis Trade Impact

To come within the prohibition of Article 81, an agreement, decision or concerted practice must raise a probability that it will affect trade between member states. Because of this requirement, it is insufficient to consider the object of restrictive agreements without also considering their potential trade effects. While in certain cases, such as *Grundig,* it is possible to avoid an extensive market analysis of the competitive impact of restrictive agreements because an intent to restrain competition is clear, analysis of an agreement's *trade* impact is always required. This is doubly true because agreements that affect trade or competition between member states in a *de minimis* fashion are not subject to Article 81(1).

In *Völk v. Vervaecke,* a German manufacturer of washing machines contracted with a Dutch exclusive dealer, Vervaecke. The contract was similar to that of Consten–Grundig and provided for absolute territorial protection. Völk's share of the German washing machine market ranged between 0.2 and 0.05 percent. This time the Court of Justice, on voluntary reference from the Oberlandesgericht in Munich, emphasized the overall product market effect of the restrictive agreement. From that interbrand perspective, the Court advised that the agreement "affect[ed] the market insignificantly" and therefore escaped Article 81(1). This *de minimis* doctrine has been developed more fully in subsequent decisions and the Commission's notices on agreements of minor importance.

Intrastate Trade

In theory, agreements, decisions and concerted practices of a purely national character not affecting trade between member states are outside the scope of Article 81. In practice, however, few national activities of any significance are likely to escape its reach. For example, in the *VCH* case, an entirely national cartel of cement merchants in Holland held a steadily declining two-thirds share of the Dutch retail cement market. The cartel maintained certain fixed and recommended prices and resale conditions as well as a variety of other restraints on competition among its members. Prior to 1967 the merchants' cartel had been exclusively allied with a German, Dutch and Belgian manufacturers' cartel for its supplies. The Commission noted that about one-third of the total sales of cement in Holland were of cheaper products imported from Belgium and West Germany. It held that the merchants' agreement therefore restricted competition within the Common Market and affected trade between member states. In the Commission's view, the agreement inhibited German and Belgian producers from increasing their share of the Dutch cement market.

On appeal, the Court of Justice upheld the Commission. It issued a broad opinion aimed at all restrictive national cartels even when imported products are not involved:

"A restrictive agreement extending to the whole territory of a member state by its very nature consolidates the national boundaries thus hindering the economic interpenetration desired by the Treaty and so protecting national production." *VCH v. Commission* (1972) Eur.Comm.Rep. 977.

The expansive approach of the Court of Justice to trade impact analysis under Article 81 is also relevant to Article 82 which contains the same language.

ARTICLE 82

Article 82 of the Treaty of Rome prohibits abuses by one or more undertakings of a dominant position within a substantial part of the Common Market insofar as the abuses may affect trade between member states. The existence of a dominant position is not prohibited by European law. Only its abuse is proscribed.

Article 82 proceeds to list certain examples of what constitute abuses by dominant enterprises:

(1) the imposition of unfair prices or other trading conditions;

(2) the limitation of production, markets or technical development which prejudices consumers;

(3) the application of dissimilar conditions to equivalent transactions thereby engendering competitive disadvantages; and

(4) the subjection of contracts to commercially unrelated supplementary obligations.

These examples are remarkably, although not exactly, similar to the examples of anticompetitive agreements, decisions and concerted practices provided in Article 81(1). Indeed, insofar as two or more enterprises are abusing their dominant market position under Article 82 they may well be simultaneously engaging in an Article 81(1) infringement. However, fines for the same conduct under both Articles 81 and 82 will not be permitted by the Court of Justice.

Article 82 differs fundamentally from Article 81. There are no provisions to declare abuses by dominant enterprise(s) automatically void, nor to permit any exemptions from its prohibitions. Thus, under the administrative framework of Regulation 17 and Regulation 1/ 2003, no individual or group exemptions can be granted for Article 82. The absence of exemptions means that there has been little incentive for dominant firms to notify their abuses to the Commission. Regulations 17 and 1 grant the Commission the same powers with reference to Article 82 as it possesses under Article 81 to obtain information, investigate corporate affairs, render infringement decisions, and fine or penalize offenders.

A few Commission decisions concerning Article 82 have their origins in complaints to the Commission from competitors or those abused. Generally, however, the Commission has acted *sua sponte* in Article 82 proceedings. Some of the Commission's decisions have been the subject of appeal to the Court of Justice and more recently to the Court of First Instance. A limited number of Article 82 cases have been resolved informally through Commission negotiations. To highlight the more important developments in the interpretation of the language and scope of Article 82, a selection of cases and issues follows.

ARTICLE 82—DOMINANT POSITIONS

Unless an enterprise or group of enterprises possesses a dominant position within a substantial part of the Common Market, no questions of abuse can arise. A dominant position may exist on either the supply or demand side of the market.

In establishing the existence of dominant positions, the Commission has tended to look at commercial realities, not technical legal distinctions. For example, the only two producers of sugar in Holland were legally and financially independent of each other. In practice they systematically cooperated in the joint purchase of raw materials, the adoption of production quotas, the use of by-products, the pooling of research, advertising and sales promotion, and the unification of prices and terms of sales. To other enterprises they appeared as if a single firm. They were involved in over 85 percent of the sales of sugar in Holland. The Commission and the Court of Justice held them to be a single enterprise for the purpose of assessing the existence of a dominant position under Article 82.

Continental Can Case

A celebrated mergers case involved Continental Can, a large United States corporation. It is a leading case on the existence of a dominant position under Article 82 law. Evidence of Continental Can's worldwide and German national market strength in the supply of certain metal containers and tops, a concentrated market characterized by ineffective consumers and competitors, and strong technical and financial barriers to entry were sufficient for the Commission to find the existence of a dominant position in certain areas of Germany. In so doing, the Commission stressed that enterprises are in a dominant position

"when they have the power to behave independently, which puts them in a position to act without taking into account their competitors, purchasers or suppliers ... This power does not necessarily have to derive from an absolute domination ... it is enough that they be strong enough as a whole to ensure to those enterprises an overall independence of behavior, even if there are differences in intensity in their influence on different partial markets." *Europemballage Corporation and Continental Can Co., Inc. v. Commission* (1972) Common Mkt.L.Rep. D11 (Commission).

Power to behave independently of competitors, purchasers or suppliers amounting to a dominant position must be exercisable with reference to the supply or acquisition of particular goods or services, i.e., a market. In *Continental Can* the Commission distinguished between that enterprise's powerful position around the world and in Europe with reference to the generic market for light metal containers, and its dominant position in Germany with reference to the particular markets for preserved meat and shellfish tins and metal caps for glass jars. Thus, initial Commission selection of the appropriate geographic and product market is the key to its analysis of whether a dominant position exists or not. It is also the key to the utility of its dominant position formula as set out in the *Continental Can* opinion. On such selection hinges the determination of the market power of the enterprise concerned. The broader the market for goods or services is defined (light metal cans versus cans for preserved meat, etc.) the less likely there will be overall independence of behavior from competitors, purchasers or suppliers. The same is true for broader geographic markets selected by the Commission (e.g., the Common Market versus Germany or parts thereof).

On appeal to the Court of Justice, the Commission's guiding principles for determining the existence of a dominant position under Article 86 were not seriously questioned. The Court did challenge the Commission's delineation of the relevant *product* market and its failure to explain in full how Continental Can had the power to behave independently in the preserved meat, shellfish, and metal top markets. Its German market shares were, by the Commission's calculation, 75, 85 and 55 percent respectively. Regarding the first criticism the Court said:

> "The products in question have a special market only if they can be individualized not only by the mere fact that they are used for packaging certain products but also by special production characteristics which give them a specific suitability for this purpose." (1973) Eur.Comm.Rep. 215.

In other words the Commission failed to make clear, for the purpose of assessing the existence of a dominant position, why the markets for preserved meat tins, preserved fish tins, and metal tops for glass jars should be treated separately and independently of the general market for light metal containers.

The Commission's failure here overlapped with the Court's second point:

> "A dominant position in the market for light metal containers for canned meat and fish cannot be decisive insofar as it is not proved that competitors in other fields but not in the market for light metal containers cannot, by mere adaptation, enter this market with sufficient strength to form a serious counterweight." *Id.*

The Court felt that the existence or lack of competition from substitute materials such as plastic or glass as well as potential competition from new entrants to the metal container industry or purchasers who might produce their own tins were also aspects of market power insufficiently explored by the Commission. Under the Commission's own formula for establishing a dominant position, the Court annulled the decision because it did not "sufficiently explain the facts and appraisals of which it [was] based."

The Court's emphasis in *Continental Can* on "special production characteristics," entry barriers and potential competition amounted to instructions to the Commission to do its homework a little better in future market power analyses under Article 82. Evaluating potential competition, of course, involves hypothetical calculations with which even an expert Commission would have difficulty. Yet these factors, as well as those considered by the Commission, made up the commercial realities of the German marketplace for canned meat and fish tins and metal tops for glass jars. What is clear from the Court's *Continental Can* opinion is that dominance can be found under Article 82 in sub-product markets such as these, provided the Commission is exhaustive in its research and analysis.

Market Analysis and Dominant Positions

Subsequent opinions of the Court have elaborated upon the product market analysis presented in *Con-*

tinental Can. The "interchangeability" of products for specific uses is a critical factor in determining the relevant product market under Article 82. Thus bananas were a proper product market since their interchangeability with other fresh fruits was limited. And the replacement market for tires (as distinct from original equipment) is another sub-market capable of sustaining a dominant position. In exceptional circumstances, even a brand name product may be the relevant sub-market.

Partial *geographic* markets can also be relevant to Article 82 market power analyses. A dominant position must exist within a "substantial" part of the Common Market. The Commission discussed geographic markets amounting to the whole of Germany in its opinion concerning tins and metal tops. Yet each of these products has different transport costs. The geographic commercial realities of competition in metal tops, given their relatively low level of transport costs, are likely to be much broader than that for tins. The same comparison can be made as between small and large tins.

The Court held that the Commission's geographic delineation of the markets for large and small tins in *Continental Can* was at odds with some of its own evidence on their relative transport costs. The commercial realities of potential competition in small tins appeared to go beyond the national boundaries of Germany. Thus the Commission's delineation of the particular geographic markets in *Continental Can* was insufficiently explained and appraised. Later decisions have deferred to the Commission's expertise and discretion in selecting relevant geographic markets. Belgium, Holland and Southern Germany, for example, have been held substantial parts of the Common Market for Article 82 purposes.

In 1997, the Commission issued a "Notice on the Definition of Relevant Market For Purposes of Community Competition Law." This Notice covers Article 81 and 82 cases, as well as mergers and acquisitions, and takes into account both supply and demand-side substitutability.

When exclusive intellectual property rights are conferred by national states, the question of the existence of a dominant position remains vital. A patent, copyright or trademark for an individual product does not necessarily give an enterprise independent market power. Other patented or non-patented products of a similar nature may provide effective market competition and thereby protect suppliers and purchasers from abuse. The full market power analysis required in *Continental Can* must be undertaken. Similarly, the absence of patent rights is no barrier to finding a dominant position where know-how and costly and complex technology give former patent holders complete market power.

Collective Dominance

In establishing the existence of a dominant position, the Commission has tended to look at commercial realities not technical legal distinctions. Thus, a dominant position may be collectively held by several otherwise independent undertakings even if these undertakings individually do not have a dominant position. In the *European Sugar Cartel* case, the Commission concluded that two producers of sugar responsible for 85 percent of all the sugar sales in Holland held a dominant position because of the contacts between them. In that case, the two producers had cooperated in the purchase of raw materials, the adoption of production quotas, the use of by-products, the pooling of research, advertising and sales promotion, and the unification of prices and terms of sale.

This theory of *collective dominance*, espoused by the Commission in subsequent cases, has been accepted by the Court of Justice. The basic requirement is that the undertakings "be linked in such a way that they adopt the same conduct on the market." For example, the Court of First Instance held that there is nothing to prevent two or more independent economic entities from being united by some economic links, and by virtue of that fact, together they hold a dominant position on the market. The Court noted that this could be the case, for example, where two or more independent undertakings jointly have, through agreements or licences, a technological lead affording them the power to behave to an appreciable extent independently of their competitors, their customers and ultimately of their consumers.

ARTICLE 82—ABUSE

If the existence of a dominant position in the supply or acquisition of certain goods or services within a substantial part of the Common Market has been established, the next issue under Article 82 is whether an abuse or exploitation of that position has occurred. In *Commercial Solvents,* the Commission and the Court of Justice found abuse in the activities of the only producer in the world of aminobutanol, a chemical used in the making of the drug ethambutol. Commercial Solvents, a U.S. corporation, sold the chemical in Italy to its subsidiary, Istituto Chemioterapico, which in turn sold it to Zoja, an Italian firm making the drug. After merger negotiations between Istituto and Zoja broke off, Zoja sought but failed to get supplies of the chemical from Istituto.

After receiving a complaint from Zoja, the Commission commenced Article 82 infringement proceedings. It eventually held that the *refusal to deal* of Commercial Solvents and Istituto (viewed as one enterprise) amounted to a leverage abuse. Commercial Solvents, through its Italian subsidiary, was ordered to promptly and in the future make supplies of aminobutanol available to Zoja at a price no higher than the maximum which it normally charged.

Many abuses do not fall under the examples provided by the Treaty terms of Article 82. Once a dominant position is established, the Commission feels free to roam the whole of the behavior of the dominant enterprise, including exploitative as well as anticompetitive abuses. Contractual and noncontractual relations, by-laws and general commercial practices can be reviewed and ordered stopped or altered by the Commission. Hoffmann–La Roche, the large multinational Swiss firm, was fined for abusing its dominant position in seven vitamin markets. It used a network of exclusive or *preferential supply contracts*, along with loyalty rebates, to reinforce its dominance by cornering retail markets.

United Brands, a U.S. multinational, abused its dominant position in bananas through *discriminatory*, predatory and excessive pricing in various countries. Its abuses also extended to refusals to deal with important past customers and prohibiting the resale of bananas. Abuse is also a legal concept that allows the Commission to review business profits. Taking into account the "high profits" involved, the Commission fined United Brands 1,000,000 ECUs. In the Commission's opinion, this was a "moderate" fine under the circumstances.

The Court of Justice has held that *predatory pricing* can constitute an abuse of a dominant position in violation of Article 82. Predatory pricing below average total cost (as well as below average variable cost) may be abusive if undertaken to eliminate a competitor. Regarding the former, pricing below average total cost is thought to be capable of driving out competitors as efficient as the dominant firm but lacking its extensive financial resources.

Other types of abuse have included refusal to supply, tying, and fidelity rebates, and using dominance to move into ancillary markets. It is important to note that abuse may exist without any fault of the dominant undertakings. For example, the British holding company of a group that controlled about half of the plasterboard production in the EU, abused its position by making promotional payments to its distributors even though the distributors themselves requested the payments. The Court of First Instance has held that abuse under Article 82 may occur independent of any fault.

ARTICLES 81 AND 82—MERGERS AND ACQUISITIONS

In 1965 the Commission announced in a memorandum to the member states that concentration ought to be encouraged to achieve efficiency and economies of scale, and to combat competition from large United States and Japanese multinational firms. These rationales have supported a long line of merger approvals by the Commission under its coal and steel concentration controls. It was not until a European merger boom was in progress and extensive studies revealed increasing trends toward industrial concentration that the Commission took action against a merger in *Continental Can*.

Continental Can

The Commission decided Continental Can abused its dominant positions in the manufacture of meat and fish tins and metal caps in Germany in only one fashion: By announcing an 80 percent control bid for the only Dutch meat and fish tin company. The Commission reasoned that Continental Can would strengthen its dominant German market position through this Dutch acquisition, to the detriment of consumers, and that this amounted to an abuse. The Commission emphasized that potential competition between companies located within the Common Market was to be eliminated. Acting quickly before the merger was a *fait accompli,* the Commission underscored its inability to block proposed mergers. Continental Can was given six months to submit proposals for remedying its Article 82 infringement.

On appeal to the Court of Justice, Continental Can argued that the Commission was acting beyond its powers in attempting to control mergers under Article 82. The Advocate General to the Court concurred. Nevertheless, the Court chose to go beyond the limits of the language of Articles 81 and 82 and interpret them in light of Articles 2 and 3 of the Treaty of Rome. These Articles set out basic tasks and activities. Article 3 calls for the erection of a system of nondistorted competition in the Common Market.

The Court reasoned teleologically that both Articles 81 and 82 were intended to assist in the maintenance of nondistorted competition. If businesses could freely merge and eliminate competition (whereas Article 81 agreements, decisions or concerted practices merely restrict competition), a "breach in the whole system of competition law that could jeopardize the proper functioning of the common market" would be opened.

> "There may therefore be abusive behavior if an enterprise in a dominant position strengthens that position so that the degree of control achieved substantially obstructs competition, i.e. so that the only enterprises left in the market are those which are dependent on the dominant enterprise with regard to their market behavior." (1973) Eur.Comm.Rep. 215.

One problem with relying on Article 82 for control of mergers and acquisitions was the need to prove a dominant position in the first place. Another was the absence of any pre-merger notification system. Once a merger is a *fait accompli,* it is always difficult to persuade a court or tribunal that dissolution is desirable or even possible. The key to effective mergers regulation, as the United States has learned under its Hart–Scott–Rodino pre-merger notification rules, is advance warning and sufficient time to block anticompetitive mergers before they are implemented.

The possibility of using Article 81 against selected mergers was surprisingly dismissed by the Commission in an early 1966 competition policy report. Article 81(3) notifications seeking individual exemptions could conceivably have been used for pre-merger regulatory purposes. One explanation for the Commission's early dismissal of this possibility is the contrast between the Treaty of Rome's complete absence of specific coverage of mergers and the Treaty of Paris' detailed grant of authority to the Commission of control over coal and steel concentrations.

By the 1980s, with industrial concentration continuing to increase, the Commission reversed its position on the applicability of Article 81 to mergers and acquisitions. It challenged a tobacco industry acquisition as an unlawful restraint under Article 81(1). The Court of Justice held that Article 81 could be applied to the acquisition by one firm of shares in a competitor if that acquisition could influence the behavior in the marketplace of the companies involved. Likewise, Article 82 could apply if the acquisition resulted in effective control of the target company.

After the ruling of the Court of Justice in *Continental Can,* the Commission submitted a comprehensive mergers' control regulation to the Council for its approval. Nearly twenty years later, a regulation on mergers was finally implemented.

COMMISSION REGULATION
OF CONCENTRATIONS
(MERGERS)

In December of 1989, the Council of Ministers unanimously adopted Regulation 4064/89 on the Control of Concentrations Between Undertakings ("Mergers Regulation"). This regulation became effective Sept. 21, 1990 and was expanded in scope by amendment in 1997, and significantly revised in 2004. It vests in the Commission the *exclusive* power to oppose large-scale "Community dimension" mergers and acquisitions of competitive consequence to the Common Market and the EEA. For these purposes, a "concentration" includes almost any means by which control over another firm is acquired. This could be by a merger agreement, stock or asset purchases, contractual relationships or other actions.

Advance Notice

The control process established by the Mergers Regulation ordinarily commences when a concentration must be notified to the Commission on Form CO in one of the official Community languages. This language becomes the language of the proceeding. Form CO is somewhat similar to second request Hart–Scott–Rodino pre-merger notification filings under U.S. antitrust law. However, the extensive need for detailed product and geographic market descriptions, competitive analyses, and information about the parties in Form CO suggests a more demanding submission.

Meeting in advance of notification with members of the Commission on an informal basis in order to ascertain whether the "concentration" has a regional dimension and is compatible with the Common Market has become widely accepted. Such meetings provide an opportunity to seek waivers from the various requests for information contained in Form CO. Since the Commission is bound by rules of professional secrecy, the substance of the discussions is confidential.

The duty to notify applies within one week of the signing of a Community dimension merger agreement, the acquisition of a controlling interest or the announcement of a takeover bid. The Commission can fine any company failing to notify it as required. The duty to notify is triggered only when the concentration involves enterprises with a combined worldwide turnover of at least 5 billion ECUs *and* two of them have an aggregate regional turnover of 250 million ECUs *unless* each enterprise achieves more than two-thirds of its aggregate Community-wide turnover within one and the same member state. Community-dimension concentrations subject to notification also occur if the enterprises have a combined aggregate world-wide turnover of at least 2.5 billion ECUs *and* they have a combined aggregate turnover of at least 100 million ECUs in at least three member states *and* at least two of the enterprises have at least 25 million ECUs turnover in the same three member states *and* at least two of them have at least 100 million ECUs turnover in the European Community *unless* each of the enterprises achieves more than two-thirds of its aggregate Community-wide turnover in the same member state.

As a general rule, concentrations meeting these criteria cannot be put into effect and fall exclusively into the Commission's domain. The effort here is to create a "one-stop" regulatory system. However, certain exceptions apply so as to allow national authorities to challenge some mergers. For example, this may occur under national law when two-thirds of the activities of each of the companies involved take place in the *same* member state. The member states can also oppose mergers when their public security is at stake, to preserve plurality in media ownership, when financial institutions are involved or other legitimate interests are at risk. If the threshold criteria of the Mergers Regulation are not met, member states can ask the Commission to investigate mergers that create or strengthen a dominant position in that state. This is known as the "Dutch clause." States that lack national mergers' controls seem likely to do this. Similarly, if the merger only affects a particular market sector or region in one member state, that state may request referral of the merger to it. This is known as the "German clause" reflecting Germany's insistence upon it. It has been sparingly used by the Commission.

Once a concentration is notified to the Commission, it has one month to decide to investigate the merger. If a formal investigation is commenced, the Commission ordinarily then has four months to challenge or approve the merger. During these months, in most cases, the concentration cannot be put into effect. It is on hold.

Evaluation

The Commission evaluates mergers in terms of their "compatibility" with the Common Market.

Prior to May 1, 2004, using language reminiscent of *Continental Can,* the Mergers Regulation stated that if the concentration creates or strengthens a dominant position such that competition is "significantly impeded," it was incompatible. The Commission is authorized to consider in its evaluation the interests of consumers and the "development of technical and economic progress." It is uncertain whether economic efficiency arguments fall within this language. A failing company defense has been recognized by the Court of Justice and a 25 percent market share is normally the minimum for purposes of ascertaining the existence of a "dominant position." However, "collective dominance" theories involving duopoly and oligopoly markets have been recognized by the ECJ as valid bases for challenging mergers that may facilitate tacit collusion among leading firms.

Effective May 1, 2004, this test was replaced by a prohibition against mergers that "significantly impede effective competition" by creating or strengthening dominant positions. Thus the new test focuses on effects not dominance. A set of Guidelines on Horizontal Mergers issued by the Commission in 2004 elaborate upon this approach. It is thought that this change will bring EU and U.S. mergers closer together (the U.S. test is "substantial lessening of competition").

During a mergers investigation, the Commission obtain information and records from the parties and request member states to help with the

cess in this case was widely perceived in the United States as pro-Airbus.

The Commission blocked the MC World-com/Sprint merger in 2001, as did the U.S. Dept. of Justice. Both authorities were worried about the merger's adverse effects on Internet access. For the Commission, this was the first block of a merger taking place outside the EU between two firms established outside the EU. Much more controversy arose when in 2001 the Commission blocked the GE/Honeywell merger after it had been approved by U.S. authorities. The Commission was particularly concerned about the potential for bundling engines with avionics and non-avionics to the disadvantage of rivals. Appeal of this decision is pending. The United States and the EU, in the wake of GE/Honeywell, have agreed to follow a set of "Best Practices" on coordinated timing, evidence gathering, communication and consistency of remedies.

The Court of First Instance overturned a 1999 decision of the European Commission blocking the $1.2 billion merger of Airtours and First Choice Holidays. The June, 2002 CFI decision was the first reversal of a merger prohibition since the 1990 inception of the review process. The CFI judgment confirmed that transactions can be blocked on collective dominance grounds, but found that the Commission had failed to meet the three conditions for proving collective dominance: (1) each member of the dominant group is able to determine readily how the others are behaving, (2) there is an effective mechanism to prevent group members from departing from the agreed-upon policy, and (3) smaller competitors are unable to undercut that policy.

In June of 2002 the European Court of Justice issued three decisions on the use by member states of so-called "golden shares." Such shares allow governments to retain veto rights with respect to acquisitions of or other significant accumulations in privatized businesses. The court outlawed a golden share decree allowing France to block a foreign takeover of a privatized oil company. The golden share decree created a barrier to the free movement of capital. The court also outlawed a law giving Portugal the ability to block the acquisition of controlling stakes in privatized state companies, but determined as a matter of public interest that Belgium could retain its golden share in recently privatized canal and gas distribution companies.

In October of 2002, acting under its new fast track review procedures, the Court of First Instance overturned two additional mergers decisions of the Commission. In both the Court found serious errors, omissions and inconsistencies. Credible evidence, not assumptions or "abstract and detached analysis," must be tendered to prove both the strengthening or creation of a dominant position, and the likelihood that the merger will significantly impede competition.

EMPLOYEE RIGHTS IN MERGERS AND ACQUISITIONS

Directive 77/187 is known as the "transfer of undertakings" or "acquired rights" directives. When European acquisitions, mergers or transfers occur, employees are entitled to keep their employment relationship and contractual rights (e.g., pensions), including those originating in collective bargaining. Substantial changes in working conditions (e.g., shifting employees to new locations) are deemed constructive dismissals. New employers can reduce the work force only if justified by "economic, technical or organizational reasons." Extensive pre- and post-merger employee consultation rights are provided, similar to those applicable in cases of mass lay-offs (known as "collective redundancies," see Directive 75/129 (1975)).

ARTICLES 81 AND 82—APPLICATION TO PUBLIC ENTERPRISES

It is important to keep in mind that the provisions of Articles 81 and 82 apply to both public and private business activities. Despite a noticeable trend toward privatization, many undertakings in Europe are still in the hands of the state. Although the Treaty does not prohibit such state ownership, because of the obvious advantages public undertakings have over private undertakings, it does prohibit the member states from enacting or maintaining in force any measure contrary to the competition rules concerning public undertakings or undertakings to which the member states have granted special or exclusive rights. It is noteworthy that Article 86(1) is directed at the member states and not at the undertakings themselves. These undertakings, even if public, remain subject to the direct application of the competition rules. Moreover, this principle is not limited to the competition rules but applies to all Rome Treaty provisions such as the right of establishment and the free movement of goods.

When Is An Enterprise Public?

The line between public and private undertakings is often the subject of dispute. In general, an undertaking is considered public whenever a member state exerts a controlling influence over it by virtue of their ownership, financial participation or the rules which govern it. The prohibition also applies to undertakings which have been granted special or exclusive rights by the state even if the state itself does not exercise direct control over the undertaking in the form of ownership. For example, Article 86(1) was held applicable to a corporation of navigational pilots exclusively authorized by the Italian state to provide compulsory piloting services in the port of Genoa. Additional examples of undertakings which would fall under that Article would be energy companies, public transport, telecommunication companies and postal services.

Thus the influence of government through subsidies, licensing or regulatory procedures can be important in determining the "public" versus "private" nature of an enterprise. The distinction has legal significance. An enterprise deemed private falls directly in the path of Article 82. An enterprise deemed public may also be subject to Article 86(1) or 86(2) which involve additional considerations. Article 86(2), for example, has its own exempting (and exception to the exemption) language and interpretive difficulties. The Court of Justice has indicated that companies with statutory monopolies that are unwilling or unable to fulfill market demands for their services engage in an unlawful abuse of a dominant position. Indeed, any state grant of exclusive rights that leads to an abuse of a dominant position is unlawful. Despite the uncertainties of the public versus private enterprise distinction drawn in the Treaty of Rome, the attempt at placing all businesses under the rule of competition is nothing less than fundamental.

Services of a General Economic Interest

According to Article 86(2), undertakings, regardless whether private or public, which are entrusted with the operation of services of general economic interest are also subject to the competition rules but only in so far as the application of such rules does not obstruct the performance of the tasks assigned to them. This provision can be seen as an exemption from both the prohibition placed on the member states in Article 86(1) and the competition rules of the Rome Treaty contained in Articles 81 and 82. The basic requirement is that the particular undertaking is entrusted with responsibilities of a general economic interest.

The essential issue in such cases is whether the application of the competition rules to the particular undertaking will undermine its ability to provide the services of a general economic interest with which it is entrusted. The Court has consistently held that such undertakings may be legitimately shielded from competition in one area so that they can achieve higher profits with which to subsidize other less profitable areas. In the *Corbeau* case, for example, the issue was whether a Belgian law granting the public postal services the exclusive right to collect, transport and deliver all mail in Belgium benefitted from Article 86(2) to the extent that it restricted other undertakings from competing in this market. In that case, the applicant was accused of infringing this law because he had established a service in a Belgian city consisting of collecting mail from the home of the sender and delivering it by the next day. The Court held that although the Belgian post office was an undertaking enjoying an exclusive right under Article 86(1), this provision of the Treaty must be read in connection with Article 86(2). Since the Belgian post office was an undertaking entrusted with the operation of a service of general economic interest, the question was whether the exclusive rights were necessary for it to adequately exercise this function. The Court held that if the post office were to perform its functions in a profitable manner, it must be able to offset its losses in one sector by its profits in another sector. Otherwise, undertakings would concentrate their business in the profitable sectors and offer lower prices there since they did not have to subsidize their loss making sectors like the undertaking entrusted with the operation of the service of a general economic interest (principle of equalization).

Another issue that has repeatedly arisen in Article 86(2) cases concerns the definition of an undertaking entrusted with the operation of services of a general economic interest. As an exception, this provision is to be interpreted narrowly. Nonetheless, the Commission and Court have held that the provision of energy, telephone and television services are services of a general economic interest. On the other hand, the Commission decided that the only German authors' rights society did not benefit from the exemption provided for in Article 86(2).

Commission Powers over Public Enterprises

A somewhat unique feature of Article 86(1) and (2) is that the Commission is authorized to adopt directives and decisions necessary to ensure its application. This has proven an effective instrument for the Commission in those sectors which it has decided to liberalize. In 1989, for example, the Commission issued a directive requiring member states to increase competition in the market for telecommunications terminal equipment, including telephones, modems, and telex terminals at a time when these services were primarily in the hands of public monopolies. The Court of Justice has re-

peatedly confirmed the Commission's broad authority to adopt such directives and decisions despite
protestations of certain member states to the contrary. A controversial feature of Article 86 directives is that they bypass the normal legislative
procedures, including Parliamentary prerogatives as
well as Council enactment.

NATIONAL LITIGATION AND REMEDIES FOR COMPETITION LAW VIOLATIONS

Direct Effect

Articles 81(1) and 82 are directly effective Treaty
provisions. All regulations, e.g., all of the group
exemption regulations, are directly applicable law in
member states. Directly effective Treaty provisions
and directly applicable regulations give individuals
within member states (including enterprises) the
immediate right to rely on regional law. This means
that they may raise competition law issues in private litigation before national courts and tribunals.
See Chapter 3. Indeed, under the supremacy doctrine, they may rely on such law to challenge contradictory national law. See Chapter 2. The directly
effective nature of Articles 81(1), and 82 helps to
explain the pervasive impact that competition law
has had in European business life.

Role of National Courts, Nullification, Damages

Article 81(2) renders offending agreements (or
parts thereof) null and void. Since this is a directly

effective Treaty provision, the national courts ordinarily enjoin such agreements. This assumes of course that the agreement is not group exempted by the Commission under Article 81(3), which under the 2004 modernization rules can also be applied individually by national authorities and courts. See above. National courts and tribunals may request advice from *the Commission.* Such requests may seek procedural as well as substantive advice. For example, the national courts may inquire whether a case or investigation into the same dispute is pending before the Commission, and how long the Commission will take before acting. They may also consult with the Commission on points of law, for example whether the necessary impact on regional trade is present and whether the contested agreement is eligible for an individual exemption under Article 81(3).

National courts can also obtain statistics, market studies and economic analyses from the Commission. All of this information and advice is intended to encourage national courts to efficiently and correctly apply Articles 81 and 82 to disputes coming before them. It is part of a broad policy of decentralized competition law enforcement designed to leave the Commission free to pursue cases of major importance. See Regulation 1/ 2003. National courts need not refer competition law questions to the Commission. They may simply rely upon their own analysis of the various block exemption regulations, guidelines and policy notices issued by the Commission under Article 81(3). They may also rely on existing ECJ, CFI and Commission case law.

If the agreement violates European competition law, it is up to the national courts to determine the consequences of the nullification of agreements by Article 81(2). This could possibly include an award of damages. Article 82 does not contain a provision that is comparable to Article 81(2). Thus the private legal remedies available when a dominant firm abuses its position must be determined strictly under national law. In Britain, for example, the House of Lords has suggested that Article 82 creates "statutory duties," the breach of which permits the recovery of damages under torts principles. As yet, no *Community* right to damages has been established or recognized for either Articles 81 or 82.

CONFLICTS OF COMPETITION LAW

Wilhelm Case

Conflicts between European and national laws governing business competition occur. National competition laws are not preempted by the Treaty of Rome. In *Wilhelm v. Bundeskartellamt,* a conflict of competition laws emerged succinctly before the Court of Justice. Four German producers of dyes were fined by the Bundeskartellamt authorities for price fixing activities under the German Law against Restraints of Competition. The dye producers appealed to the Kartellsenat of the Kammergericht in Berlin. The same 1967 price fixing activities of the four German firms were the subject of parallel competition law proceedings initiated by the Commission under Article 81. Before the Commission rendered its decision, defendants argued that in the light of the possibility of a conflict between regional and German competition law, the Kammergericht could not continue its proceedings. The Kammergericht stayed its proceedings and requested a preliminary ruling on that issue from the Court of Justice.

The European Court reviewed Article 83(2)(e) of the Treaty of Rome. This article authorizes the Council to define, by regulation or directive, the relationship between national and regional law on business competition. Such Council action has yet to take place, but it is worth noting that the Council could preempt national competition law entirely under this authority. The Court went on to read Article 83 in conjunction with Article 2, which enumerates certain fundamental tasks including the promotion of the harmonious development of economic activities within the Common Market. Reading Articles 83 and 2 together, while acknowledging that Europe has instituted its own legal order which is integrated into that of its member states, the Court came to the following conclusions:

"In principle the national authorities in competition matters may take proceedings also with regard to situations liable to be the object of the decision of the Commission ... conflicts between the Community rule and the national rules on competition should be resolved by the application of the principle of the primacy of the Community rule ... the application of national law may not prejudice the full and uniform application of the Community law or the effect of acts in implementation of it." (1969) Eur.Comm.Rep. 1

Multiple Liability

Insofar as regional and national laws are in harmony, their simultaneous application can result in multiple liability. In this particular case, the four German firms were fined by the Commission and ordered to cease and desist their price fixing activities. The Kammergericht in Berlin continued to hold its proceedings in abeyance and eventually, after the Commission's decision was rendered, annulled the violations and fines imposed under German competition law on constitutional and evidentiary grounds.

Supremacy

The *Wilhelm* decision reaffirms the supremacy of European law in the event of a conflict with national competition law. In such circumstances, litigants can ordinarily invoke regional competition law to nullify national proceedings and liability. Since European competition law is very extensive, the *Wilhelm* rule of supremacy in the event of conflicts of competition law has wide repercussions. Regulation 1/2003 requires national courts and authorities to avoid conflicts of competition law and reaffirms the principal of supremacy. Articles 81 and 82 must be applied concurrently with national law, which cannot bar agreements and practices not prohibited by European law.

International Liability

The *Wilhelm* principles extend to conflicts between United States antitrust and European competition law. For example, one European member of an international price fixing quinine cartel was fined under Article 81. Subsequently, that firm was fined for the same activities by U.S. authorities under federal antitrust law. The price fixer then requested a credit against the European fines in the amount of the U.S. fines. The Commission denied this request, noting that it had always been aware of the parallel United States proceedings.

THE EXTRATERRITORIAL REACH OF ARTICLES 81 AND 82

There is a question about the extent to which the competition rules of Europe extend to activity anywhere in the world, including activity occurring entirely or partly within the territorial limits of the United States or Canada. Decisions by the Commission and the Court of Justice suggest that the territorial reach of Articles 81 and 82 is expanding and may extend to almost any international business transaction.

For an agreement to be incompatible with the Common Market and prohibited under Article 81(1), it must be "likely to affect trade between

Member States" and have the object or effect of impairing "competition within the Common Market." Taken together, these requirements resemble an "effects test" for extraterritorial application of Article 81. This test is similar to that which operates under the Sherman Act of the United States.

Extraterritorial Application

The Court has repeatedly held that the fact that one of the parties to an agreement is domiciled in a third country does not preclude the applicability of Article 81(1). Swiss and British chemical companies, for example, argued that the Commission was not competent to impose competition law fines for acts committed in Switzerland and Britain (before joining) by their enterprises even if the acts had effects within the Common Market. Nevertheless, the Court held those companies in violation of Article 81 because they owned subsidiary companies within the Common Market and controlled their behavior. The parent and its subsidiaries were treated as a "single enterprise" for purposes of service of process, judgment and collection of fines and penalties. In doing so, the Court observed that the fact that a subsidiary company has its own legal personality does not rule out the possibility that its conduct is attributable to the parent company.

The Court has extended its reasoning to the extraterritorial application of Article 82. A United States parent company, for example, was held potentially liable for acquisitions by its European subsidiary which affected conditions within the Community. In another decision, the Court held that a Maryland company's refusal to sell its product to a competitor of its affiliate company within the Common Market was a result of united "single enterprise" action. It proceeded to state that extraterritorial conduct merely having "repercussions on competitive structures" in the Common Market fell within the parameters of Article 82. The Court ordered the company, through its Italian affiliate, to supply the competitor at reasonable prices.

Wood Pulp Case

In 1988, the Court of Justice widened the extraterritorial reach of Article 81 in a case where wood pulp producers from the U.S., Canada, Sweden and Finland were fined for price fixing activities affecting Common Market trade and competition. These firms did not have substantial operations within the Common Market. They were primarily exporters to it. This decision's utilization of a place of implementation "effects test" is quite similar to that used under the Sherman Act. And the reliance by the U.S. exporters upon a traditional Webb–Pomerene export cartel exemption from United States antitrust law carried no weight in Europe. The Court has also affirmed the extraterritorial reach of Articles 81 and 82 to airfares in and out of the Union, and the Mergers Regulation (supra) clearly applies to firms located outside the Common Market.

UNITED STATES–EUROPEAN UNION
ANTITRUST COOPERATION

In 1991 the European Union and the United States reached an Antitrust Cooperation Agreement. This accord commits the parties to notify each other of imminent enforcement action, to share relevant information and consult on potential policy changes. An innovative feature is the inclusion of "positive comity" principles, each side promising to take the other's interests and requests into account when considering antitrust prosecutions. Since the Commission has traditionally permitted U.S. lawyers to appear before it on competition law matters, the FTC announced on the same day as the signing of the agreement that European lawyers would be permitted to appear before it on a reciprocal basis. The agreement was prominently used to jointly negotiate a 1994 settlement on restrictive practices of the Microsoft Corporation, a settlement that is being revisited concerning Microsoft's web browser tactics. In the more recent round of public prosecutions of Microsoft focused on Windows as a monopoly, the United States settlement reached in 2001 is less demanding than the Commission judgment of 2004 which requires an unbundling of media playback capabilities. This example reaffirms that transatlantic antitrust "cooperation" need not necessarily result in similar outcomes.

Under the Agreement, each side must notify and consult with the other regarding antitrust matters, including mergers and acquisitions, that "may affect important interests." A large portion of these notifications concern international mergers and acquisitions. Since both Europe and the U.S. have premerger notification systems, the exchange of such information has increased rapidly. Such exchanges often, but not always, result in coordinated approaches to international mergers and acquisitions (see below).

CHAPTER 8

BEYOND ENLARGEMENT

The late President Mitterrand of France once said that European history is accelerating. Former Chancellor Kohl of Germany said that the deepening and simultaneous expansion of the European Union are decisive for securing peace and freedom . . . European integration is a question of war and peace in the new millennium. European Union law reflects these truths. This final chapter briefly and provocatively considers what lies beyond the year 2004.

FURTHER ENLARGEMENT

The European Union is like a magnet. The larger its size, the greater its force. With the campaign for a single market mostly realized, the attraction of the EU increased. With the creation of the common currency, and dramatic increase in its membership, the magnetic force of the Union is compelling.

The European Union will temporize less and less on new admissions, but still create interim arrangements like the European Economic Area and more Europe Agreements. It will enlarge out of self-interest, political pressure and moral imperatives.

As the costs of economic isolation mount, Switzerland and Norway will reconsider. Bulgaria and Romania in 2007 and (possibly) Turkey will follow. Albania, Bosnia, Croatia, Macedonia and Serbia/Montenegro are next in line. Another wave could bring in more countries of the former Soviet Union, notably Ukraine.

In time, the pressure to admit more European nations to the Union will prevail. An EU with as many as 40 member states is not inconceivable. This prospect makes study of the law of the European Union the study of much of the future of Europe.

THE CONVENTION ON THE FUTURE OF EUROPE AND ITS DRAFT CONSTITUTION

The growth in membership in the European Union raises fundamental issues of governance. The Nice Enlargement Protocol offers patchwork solutions, but will they measure up to the task? Less than a year after signing on to the Nice Treaty, the heads of state meeting at the Laeken Summit of the European Council established the 105–member Convention on the Future of Europe. Popularly referred to as a "constitutional convention," this body's very existence recognized that the traditional means of governance as revised by the Enlargement Protocol may not be up to the task.

Members of the Convention were drawn from national governments and parliaments, the European Parliament, and Commission. The 12 future member states had nonvoting observer status at the Convention. Chaired by former French President Valery Giscard d'Estaing and driven by an inner 12–member praesidium, the Convention became a focal point for change. Lobbying on all fronts was intense, running from strong federalists to states rights' advocates. In June of 2003, the Convention released its draft Treaty establishing a Constitution for Europe, some 260 pages of complex text merging the Rome, Maastricht TEU and EURATOM treaties. The draft went under review by the EU member states which unanimously signed off on a final version in June 2004. The Constitution will need individual ratification in all 25 member states, some of which (Ireland and Denmark, for example) will hold referendums. Optimists suggest that the Constitution will take effect by 2006. Pessimists believe it will (and should) end up in a waste bin.

Proposed Constitution for Europe

The proposed Constitution is already the subject of conflicting sometimes bizarre interpretations. The Union's Charter of Fundamental Rights ("declared" at Nice) becomes binding EU law, but may apply only to EU institutions, personnel and law. The principle of "subsidiarity" (Chapter 2) is retained, but subordinated to broad Union objectives. Most policy areas are to be "shared" with the member states, which nevertheless appear to retain vetoes over foreign policy, social security, taxation and defense. No doubt the proposed EU "Foreign

Minister,'' President of the European Council, and
EU Armaments Agency will have a tough time.
Qualified majority voting disappears as the triple
legislative majority system (Chapter 2) adopted under the Nice Treaty is reduced to a double majority
in the Council of Ministers to enact law: 55 percent
of the member states representing at least 65 percent of the Union's population, but not until 2009.
By 2014, the Commission is ''shrunk'' to two-thirds
the number of member states. Member states for
the first time can withdraw from Union, but they
can also be ''suspended'' by their fellow members. If
ratification of the final version of the Constitution
is not unanimous, but 20 member states have ratified it, the European Council will ''review the situation.'' Climb aboard, this promises to be an interesting ride.

POLITICAL UNION

Economic integration has clearly outstripped the
Union's political growth. Many suggest that the
European Union suffers a democratic deficit. How
long can governance of the Union postpone its
rendezvous with democracy? The predominance of
the Council will become increasingly embarrassing
and intolerable. But what will be the end result?
One vision of the future has the Council becoming
an ''upper house'' like the United States Senate to
the House of Representatives, though most probably with more power. In this scenario, the Commission becomes the Executive Branch of EU govern-

ment. It could have a directly elected President who then appoints a Cabinet with Parliamentary or Council approval. The variations on these themes are endless.

Another vision of the future was adopted, way before its time, in 1984 by the Parliament. In its "Draft Treaty establishing European Union" (Spinnelli Report), the Parliament showed strong federalist proclivities. This Treaty would have totally replaced the Treaty of Rome. The law-making powers of the Council would be shifted to the Parliament and Commission with limited member state ability to block new policy initiatives. There would also be serious sanctions on member states who persistently breach their EU duties. The Court of Justice would get the power to appeal decisions of national courts. A common monetary system, a common citizenship and effective protection of fundamental human rights were also part of Parliament's vision of European integration. In contrast, the Maastricht Treaty on European Union of 1993, the Amsterdam Treaty of 1999, the Nice Treaty of 2003 and the draft Constitution look timid.

FOREIGN AND SECURITY POLICY

The Foreign Ministers of the member states regularly meet and seek to coordinate EU foreign policy and security matters. Since the Amsterdam Treaty, the Secretary–General of the Council acts as the "High Representative for the Common and Foreign Security Policy" and the Union is authorized to negotiate treaties in this sphere. The Foreign Ministers have their own secretariat in Brussels to monitor and implement common foreign policy positions. Junior staff members supervise much of this work through what is called the European Political Committee. The Commission is represented at all meetings of this Committee and the Foreign Ministers. The Parliament, however, is merely briefed after the fact about these meetings and is for the most part limited to asking questions of the Foreign Ministers.

The heads of state and government also meet twice a year in what is called "The European Council," as distinct from the EU Council of ministers. The President of the Commission participates in meetings of the European Council. These meetings have increased the degree of foreign policy cooperation (known as "political cooperation") within the Union, but not without criticism. The European Council and the Foreign Ministers' meetings function outside the Treaty of Rome and its various policy making mandates and voting procedures, including consultation, cooperation or co-decision with Parliament. Hence, foreign policy coordination is intergovernmental in nature, and does not involve supranational mandates.

Foreign policy cooperation has been a part of Union affairs since 1970 and was formally recognized in the Single European Act of 1987. Under the Maastricht and Amsterdam Treaties, the Union's national foreign ministers decide which areas of foreign and security policy merit "joint action," a "common position," or a "common strategy." The details of such activities are now generally set by those ministers acting by qualified majority voting or with the "constructive abstention" of some members. This type of political cooperation remains outside the framework of the Treaty of Rome and is considered a separate "pillar" of the Union.

The net result is that the European Union increasingly but erratically speaks with a single voice on foreign affairs. This has been evident regarding political developments in Central Europe, the Middle East (much less so on the Iraq War), Cyprus, South Africa, Rwanda, Angola, Iran (especially to condemn the threats against Salman Rushdie), Burma, Cambodia, and Afghanistan. However, the remarkable disunity and dithering displayed by EU nations over the break-up and ethnic cleansings in Yugoslavia casts a long shadow over the political cooperation goals of the Union. The increasing involvement of the European Union in world politics also makes it more difficult for traditionally neutral nations like Austria, Sweden and Ireland. Already there are arguments over whether it is possible to segregate the Union's economic and political spheres for membership purposes.

DEFENSE

In the early years of the Coal and Steel Community, a European Defense Community (EDC) treaty was drafted and nearly adopted. It failed when the

French National Assembly refused to ratify it in 1954. Under this proposal, a European army would have been placed under the control of a European Ministry of Defense functioning within the North Atlantic Treaty Organization (NATO) alliance. The institutional structure of the EDC would have been similar to that employed in the Coal and Steel Community. The rejection by the French National Assembly was led by the Gaullists who quite simply did not want to surrender sovereignty over the French army, even if this meant that the West Germans could re-arm on their own. Following a British initiative, however, a looser confederation for military purposes was established, the Western European Union (WEU). It was under this Union that West Germany and Italy re-armed and were integrated into the NATO alliance. In 2000, the WEU transferred its principal activities to the European Union despite the fact that not all EU members belong to the WEU.

The vision of a common defense policy has started to become a reality. At the 1991 Maastricht Summit, agreement was achieved on language explicitly stating that defense cooperation is expected of member states. Moreover, the Western European Union is to serve as the bridge between the Union and NATO. The Maastricht Treaty on European Union referred to the "eventual framing" of a common defense policy to be implemented through the WEU as another separate "pillar" of the Union. The Amsterdam Treaty altered this language to "progressive framing," a subtle change in Euro-speak meant to convey progress. In 1992, the WEU defense and foreign ministers issued the "Petersburg Declaration." This Declaration affirms the ongoing efforts to develop a new Franco–German military brigade. By 2003, EU-led forces of 50,000–60,000 persons were ready for deployment in peace and rescue operations. A Military Committee and Staff have been created.

The integration of Europe's defense may be the ultimate in politically sensitive issues. Neutrality, the NATO alliance and a host of national interests stand in the way of a Common Defense Policy for the European Union. Transfers of sovereignty over war, peace, military forces, military weapons and military command are momentous issues not only for the member states, but the world.

INDEX

References are to Pages

A

B

D

E

F

I

J

L

M

N

O

P

Q

R

S

W

WORLD TRADE ORGANIZATION, see GATT/WTO

WORKERS' RIGHTS, See Free Movement of Workers and Social Charter

†